YOU CAN DO
FOR OUR
CHILDREN'S
FUTURE

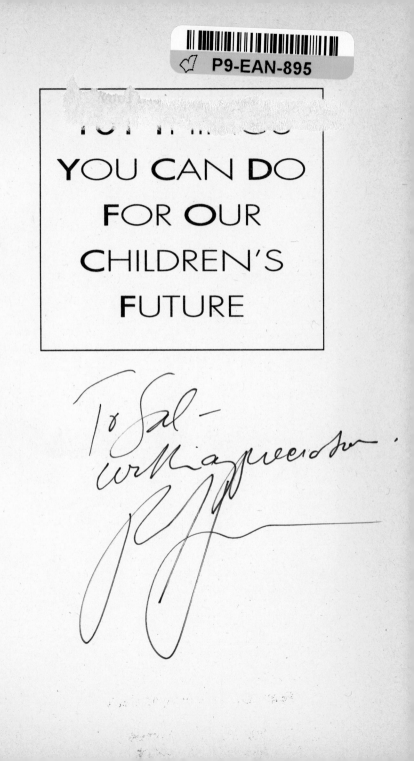

To Sal —
with appreciation.

Books by Richard Louv

101 THINGS YOU CAN DO FOR OUR CHILDREN'S FUTURE

Richard Louv

Anchor Books
Doubleday

New York   London   Toronto   Sydney   Auckland

AN ANCHOR BOOK
PUBLISHED BY DOUBLEDAY
a division of Bantam Doubleday Dell Publishing Group, Inc.
1540 Broadway, New York, New York 10036

ANCHOR BOOKS, DOUBLEDAY, and the portrayal of an anchor
are trademarks of Doubleday, a division of Bantam Doubleday
Dell Publishing Group, Inc.

Library of Congress Cataloging-in-Publication Data

Louv, Richard.
  101 things you can do for our children's future / Richard Louv.—
1st Anchor Books ed.
      p.   cm.
  Includes bibliographical references and index.
    1. Children—United States—Social conditions.   2. Children—
Government policy—United States.   3. Family policy—United
States.
I. Title.   II. Title: One hundred one things you can do for our
children's future.   III. Title: One hundred and one things you can
do for our children's future.
HQ792.U5L678   1994
305.23'0973—dc20   93-3774
                                                                 CIP

ISBN: 0-385-46878-4
Copyright © 1994 by Richard Louv

Book Design by Gretchen Achilles

TO MY WIFE, KATHY

ACKNOWLEDGMENTS

More than most, this book has been a collaborative work. Many parents, grandparents, children, teenagers, and a variety of organizations contributed ideas and inspiration. Its editor, Arabella Meyer, has been particularly supportive and helpful. Thanks, too, to Martha Levin for believing that life can be better for children and families. My wife and sons offer daily support and wisdom, as does my assistant, Marie Anderson. Maribeth Mellin helped collect many of these ideas and then helped shape them; she is a fine editor and friend. Karin Winner, Gerald Warren, Peter Kaye, Jane Clifford, Suzanne Choney, and John Muncie of the *San Diego Union-Tribune* offered invaluable support; some of the ideas here first appeared in my column for that newspaper. I am also grateful to Ann Pleshette Murphy and Alix Finkelstein of *Parents* magazine; a few of these ideas and stories also appeared in my column there. Thanks also to my agent, David Vigliano. Others who helped along the way: David Boe, Jon Funabiki, Bill Stothers, Ron Zappone, Richard Larimore, Jacquie Swabach, Dick and Suzanne Thompson (an idea scout), Ralph Keyes, Patricia Chryst, Treacy Lau, Viviane Warren, Scott Reed, Jackie Green, Barbara and Ralph Whitehead, Rosalie Streett and Parent Action, Susan Nall Bales and the Coalition for America's Children, and the *San Diego Union-Tribune* librarians, especially Anne Magill. I am also grateful to the academic internship program of the University of California, San Diego, and for the help provided by Corinne Grimm, Jim Gratiot and Dale Plumlee. I have probably missed 101 others who helped.

CONTENTS

"It takes a village to raise a child."
—*An African saying*

"Sometimes a mom can move a mountain."
—*Renee Edelman,*
a mother in Amherst, New York

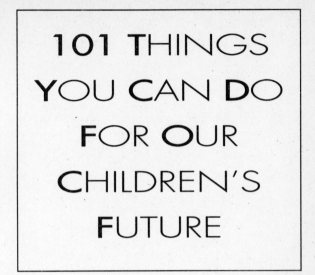

101 THINGS YOU CAN DO FOR OUR CHILDREN'S FUTURE

INTRODUCTION

No one raises a child alone, but too often that's how it feels for parents in America. During the past few years, in an effort to describe the new landscape of childhood, I interviewed nearly 3,000 children and parents across the country. In the course of this research I learned that, for many families, the invisible web of support that once helped parents raise children has all but disappeared. Here is our challenge: to weave a new web of support not just for our own children but for all children. It's time to roll up our sleeves and get specific.

101 Things You Can Do For Our Children's Future is a primer, an interactive workbook for parents—as well as seniors, non-parents, employers, teachers, all Americans—who want to create a better life for children *now*. Many of the ideas and suggestions in this book have been collected from kids and adults around the country. They are included because they are practical and do-able; they create connections to a wider community, directly or indirectly; and they are attainable now—or in the foreseeable future. This book has two primary objectives: to reduce the isolation of parents, and to increase positive contact between children and adults. A special emphasis is placed on creating *safe* environments for children since community enforcement is ultimately more powerful than law enforcement.

101 Things You Can Do For Our Children's Future offers practical tips for what you can do to weave a new web of support:

- in your home and family
- in your extended and super-extended families

- in your neighborhood
- in child-care settings
- in schools
- in your place of worship
- in your workplace
- in your town or city
- in your state or nation

These general areas are divided into 101 goals, along with numerous examples and suggestions. In addition, each section of this book includes stories of successful grass-roots actions and model programs around the country, and a resource list of organizations, experts, help-lines, publications—tools to help you weave the new web of support for children. Please note that each chapter ends with a page for you to jot down your own ideas.

Too often, parents and non-parents come up with creative solutions and programs without the rest of us knowing about them. So, at the end of this book, an address is listed for you to share your ideas with others working to reshape the environment of childhood and family life. Remember, this is a catalogue of ideas; it is not meant as the final word; hopefully, it will stimulate your thinking and creativity. Let me know what you think, and let your friends, relatives, employers, and policy-makers know, too.

101 Things You Can Do For Our Children's Future can be used as a cookbook of recipes or as a manual for wider change, a manifesto, if you will, of the burgeoning family movement.

To give context to what follows, consider this fantasy: What if we could bring together, in one room, organizational leaders of past and present social movements, including the antiwar movement, the civil rights movement, the environmental movement, the feminist movement, the men's movement? What if we then told them: "Here's the problem. Children and families in this country are in crisis. We need a family movement. How do we create one? What tools and strategies from the past would be appropriate for this movement? You'll find coffee and cold cuts in the corner. See you tomorrow."

Assuming no immediate bloodshed occurred, these leaders might find some common tactical ground. Here's a list of recommendations that might emerge from this unlikely, imaginary meeting of minds.

- DON'T WAIT FOR NATIONAL LEADERS.

A successful family movement will emerge mainly from the grass roots—from individuals, parents, churches, schools, and neighborhoods. National leaders will follow or get out of the way.

- DEFINE FAMILY AS BROADLY AS POSSIBLE.

Don't get hung up on Beaver Cleaver stereotypes. Studies show that children usually define families as related people who love each other. That's an inclusive and strategically smart definition. A family movement needs all the families it can get.

- IDENTIFY COMMON GROUND BETWEEN THE CULTURAL RIGHT AND LEFT.

Both sides, for example, might agree that encouraging more family time is a priority, or that tax breaks should be given to families with dependent children. This would relieve financial stress on single parents and also make it easier, in two-parent families, for one parent to stay home with the kids.

- TARGET THE MIDDLE CLASS.

Unless members of the middle class can express political compassion for their own children, no such compassion will be expressed for poor children.

- RECRUIT AND TRAIN MEN.

Women alone can't carry this movement on their shoulders. If a movement is to be successful, it must also identify male leaders. Convince them that real men fight for kids, that real men improve company policies toward families.

- RECRUIT SENIORS AS THE WINTER SOLDIERS OF THE MOVEMENT.

Older Americans often have more time, money, and energy than harried parents. Also, many are veteran parents.

- ENLIST NON-PARENTS IN THE CAUSE.

Not everyone is a parent, but everybody had one. Nearly everyone has some kind of family needs. In the workplace, for example, focus on solutions that work for all employees, whether they have children in day care, parents in nursing homes, or simply need to be involved.

- AVOID TACTICS OF DIRECT CONFRONTATION.

Marching in the streets doesn't seem appropriate for this movement, though public meetings—family town halls—would be useful for building solidarity among families.

- MOBILIZE THE CHURCHES.

Create more family-assistance programs within churches and mobilize interfaith family networks to support political change for children.

- USE ELECTRONIC ACTIVISM.

Employ computer bulletin boards, fax machines, and other electronic tools to network parents and others who care about kids.

- TARGET COMPANY CULTURES.

Launch a battle for the hearts and minds of the CEOs, but don't depend on good corporate intentions. Family leave bills create the new idea in law that parents have affirmative rights in the workplace. Just as the civil rights and feminist movements flexed their muscles in the courts, legal challenges could be used to decrease family discrimination in the workplace.

- LAUNCH PARENT VOTER-
  REGISTRATION DRIVES.

Set up voter-registration booths at schools, day-care centers, clinics, and hospitals. As long as election day remains a work-day, child-care centers could be encouraged to stay open an extra hour on election day so parents can vote without neglecting their children. Just as Jim Crow laws and literacy tests were racist, current voting laws are antifamily. Working parents facing the logistics of getting kids to school or day care and picking them up, find it difficult to vote between 7 A.M. and 7 P.M. on Tuesdays. Fight to change voting days to Saturday and Sunday.

- UTILIZE BALLOT INITIATIVES.

Survey after survey shows that Americans want to make children a national priority, but kids have few advocates in the legislative process. This calls for a dramatic expansion of direct, citizen-activated democracy.

- CREATE SELF-HELP AND
  CONSCIOUSNESS-RAISING GROUPS.

Parents are the best experts for parents to turn to; they may not always know the right answer, but they always know the right questions. It's easy to forget that feminism did not begin with a discussion of the Equal Rights Amendment; it began when women sat down at kitchen tables and began to talk about what it felt like to be a woman. Today, the same process, at kitchen tables and conference tables across the country, is necessary among parents and non-parents who care about children.

Our roomful of activists might finally conclude that a successful family movement will be more than political. Two slogans from the feminist and environmental movements would apply:

The personal will become the political.

Think globally; act locally.

A NOTE ABOUT FORMAT

101 Things You Can Do For Our Children's Future is divided into:

- 101 numbered goals and ideas, with bulleted sub-heads indicating specific actions;
- occasional check-lists for action;
- information boxes (shaded in gray) with material quoted directly or summarized from a variety of sources, which are indicated at the end of each box;
- sidebars (shaded in gray) with analysis or stories about successful efforts on behalf of children around the country. If not indicated otherwise, this material is by the author;
- resource lists of organizations, books, and publications;
- pages for your ideas.

WHAT YOU CAN DO IN YOUR HOME AND FAMILY

Let's start with the most important and personal family issue: time stress. The amount of time parents spend with their children has dropped forty percent during the last quarter century. In 1965, the average parent had roughly thirty hours of contact with his or her child each week. Today, according to the Family Research Council, the average parent has just seventeen hours of contact with children per week. When asked how they would improve their families, kids repeatedly say they wish there were more opportunities for fun time. But how do we do it?

1. Insist on Family Time.

- EAT MEALS AS A FAMILY.

Many families make eating together an important ritual: no books, newspapers, or TV allowed. Make eating in front of the TV a special event rather than a daily occurrence. One mom says her family has made a rule that they all eat one meal together each day. "The only meal we know we can eat together is breakfast, because that's the only time everyone is home." She jokes, "We eat at 4:30 A.M."

- CURE YOUR TELEPHONE HANG-UP.

Take the phone off the hook or refuse to answer it during

dinner time and family time. That's what answering machines are for.

- SHARE HOBBIES.

You may have trouble sitting down for a serious chat with your teenager, but you can explore all sorts of topics while fishing together. Help your child start a collection of baseball cards, seashells, bottle caps, stamps, or any other fascinating object. Work as a team organizing the collection, and create a special place where it can be displayed.

- COMPUTE TOGETHER.

Instead of isolating yourself at the home computer, put your child on your lap and play with a computer game. Tom Snyder, a well-known educational software designer, calls this parent-child activity "lapware."

- SCHEDULE DAYS WITH NO COMMITMENTS, EXCEPT TO YOUR FAMILY.

"I would give anything to do family things at least every other weekend," one junior-high student wrote. Another teenager suggested finding at least one day out of the month to be together without any promises to other people.

- RESPECT FAMILY COMMITMENTS.

Treat appointments with your kids or spouse as you would any other meetings. Apologize if you are late, and offer to make up the time in another way. Explain in advance if you know you won't be able to make it to your child's school play or soccer game, and reschedule your time together.

- GIVE KIDS, AND PARENTS, DREAMTIME.

Remember lying on your back in the grass as a child, watching the clouds move? Remember sitting on the carpet looking up at the dust fall in front of a sunny window? That was dreamtime, essential to the mental health and creativity of children—and adults. Emphasize dreamtime, not quality time.

2. Time Tricks.

Most children spend more time in front of the TV than they do with their parents, but there's hope. Here's a list of time tricks suggested by teachers who are also parents.

- MAXIMIZE CAR TIME.

"When my kids were tiny, I used our time in the car to talk or teach, and I'd sing the colors of the stop lights to them," wrote Brenda Canaris. "In the car, one's attention is almost guaranteed—at least we don't have a car phone! Over the years, the car has continued to be a place where important topics are questioned, analyzed, and discussed."

Canaris continued, "We've graduated to teen sex, marital infidelity, and living together before marriage. Teaching them colors by watching stop lights sure was easier on a mother's blood pressure. But I treasure the time we have in the car. I often hear what is most important to them there."

Pamela Andre wrote, "My twenty-one-year-old son has been carpooling with me for several weeks since his car died. In this brief period of time, we've probably talked to each other more than we have in the past year. He asked me if we could continue the practice as long as we could fit it into our schedules."

- CULINARY TIME TRICKS.

Corinne Towers follows this rule in her home: "Lower one standard so a higher priority item is saved. Example: a high priority—sitting down to dinner as a family; standard lowered—dinner may be a basic salad and a frozen pizza via the microwave."

- TIME TRICKS WITH CHORES.

Several teachers said their families considered chore time as talking time for the family—particularly grocery shopping.

Others suggested simply cutting back on housework to make more time. Louise Supnick advised: "Don't do a lot of housework until the mess gets overwhelming and then it's done as a family!"

Another teacher wrote: "Eliminate unnecessary jobs. Don't fold clean sheets—put them on the bed. Hang clean towels—don't fold. Do mindless chores (washing dishes, etc.) while spending time with children. Don't make the bed. Grocery shop only once a week—make a list. Live by the rule, 'Don't sweat the small stuff!' "

- RITUAL TIME TRICKS.

Sundays (remember Sundays?) are still official relaxation days for some families. "We walk around the lake or go out to brunch, without stress or pressure." "We go to church."

Some families regularly turn off the TV. Or, as a family, they regularly watch the same television show and then talk about the show. As alternatives to TV, board games and cards are popular rituals.

The evening before trash collection day is good family time, suggested one mother. "My younger son and I would go around the neighborhood with a wheelbarrow—which was also found in the trash—and collect treasures other people had discarded."

A kindergarten teacher reported that the parent of one of her pupils keeps her child out of school one day each month to visit the museums in the park on free admission day.

A single mother wrote: "When my daughter was young, I would invite her to 'spend the night' with me and spend the evening playing games, watching TV, or talking just as overnight friends would do."

"Doctor Spock may not agree," wrote another teacher, "but as a family with children ages three and six, we take a shower together in the morning."

• TIME-SHIFTING TRICKS.

Ann Wallace's prescription: "Shower at night. Get up before the kids to satisfy the need for alone time. Appreciate the simple things."

Similarly, Karen Fox wrote, "I get up at 4:30 A.M., an hour and a half before my husband and daughters. Don't get me wrong, I don't like getting up at 4:30, but it does resolve the 'me versus us' conflict."

"I arrive at school an hour and a half before starting time, to do my prep work," wrote Diane Johnson. "I leave right at

3 P.M., so I have quality family time every afternoon and evening."

Louise Supnick suggested staggered bedtimes.

Another teacher described how her retired husband, Tom, "is the mom at our house." She described her eight-year-old son, enrolled in a home study program, as a second-grade dropout. The reason was primarily time. Her son spends three hours a day doing schoolwork with his father. Then they, and sometimes the other siblings, are free for field trips.

"They go to the library," the mother wrote. "They go fishing, visit boatyards, cook, sail, drive to the mountains. Dishes don't get done and the laundry is still running at 12 A.M. because Tom and the troops don't like that group activity. Since my husband grew up in foster homes, he is raising his kids the way he thinks the Beaver lived. The Beaver never had it so good."

MAKING A LOVE LIST

"My family fell into the high-achievement trap," says Linda Hoover, a PTA officer in Shawnee Mission, Kansas. "We're having to re-evaluate our values. Our son was over stressed, we were over stressed. This realization came to us on one of those nights when all of our voices had raised an octave and all of our eyes were opened just a little wider than normal and we all were just . . . it was just too much. We all reached this level at the same time; we peaked out. And we said, 'This is not what we had in mind when we brought a child into the world.' We realized that we were giving our son the message that he had to achieve in order to be lovable. That sounds terrible for a parent to say, but it's true. My husband and I were doing it, too: He was working long hours to be lovable and I was doing all these extracurricular activities to be lovable in the community, and it was just crazy. We were getting less lovable."

So Hoover's family backed off, and made lists.

"Each of us took a piece of paper. We drew a line down the center, listed things we like, things we don't like, things we enjoy doing, things we don't enjoy doing. And then on the second column we listed things that we did that we really didn't want to do any more. It was very simple—because we didn't have much time." Hoover laughed. "I think we all saw where we were headed, and where we didn't really want to be. So we started deleting some of the activities we didn't need in our lives. I was working full-time but not for pay. I was a volunteer. Very dedicated, very committed, highly structured. It was easier when I worked for *money*. When I stopped to really think about it, I realized I didn't really enjoy much of it. It was just insane. I needed to learn to say, 'No.' "

Her son surprised them.

"Our son hated organized sports. We had never realized that. And we said, 'What would you like to replace sports with?' And he said, 'Playing with the neighborhood kids in the back yard.' It was an eye-opener for us. Soccer had more to do with social acceptability, and our expectations, than fun for my son. So he withdrew from soccer. He started working in the back yard vegetable garden. Both grandpas are farmers. He loves to do that, and we didn't know that."

Then there were the activities that the members of the Hoover family learned that they *all* wanted to do.

"Just to walk through the park. Or bike it or just to spend some time outside. That may not sound like a big deal, but that is what we found we wanted the most. And we didn't need to be talking to one another, either. It was just having that wonderful physical closeness. That was one thing we all put down. That we all wanted to be outside. We all like to camp. But we knew we couldn't just haul out the camper every time we all had some free time together, so now we walk.

"It's been almost a year. We still struggle with outside pressures. Every day, we have to consciously make the decisions, the small decisions. And I still find myself saying 'yes' too often and having to call back and say 'whoops, I changed my mind.' It's not easy, but it *is* worth it."

They made their separate peace: Her husband cut his overtime, Hoover cut her social activities, and their son quit soccer, and now they go on long, meandering walks together through the trees, listening to the Kansas wind.

—From *Childhood's Future*

3. Redistribute Stress.

• PUT ON THE BRAKES.

Review the family schedule with the whole family. See what you can eliminate. Listen closely to what your kids have to say. They may not want to go to all the activities you drive them to.

• ENLIST KIDS AS STRESS-BUSTERS.

Assign chores to the kids that relieve you during your busiest times. Make the chores part of the daily ritual. Kids need to be needed by their families.

• LOWER YOUR STANDARDS.

"If my kids were to lose their mom suddenly, would they be better off remembering that the laundry was always put away or that Mom always had time to read, to sing, to listen?" one mother wrote in the *Seattle Weekly*. "If my husband were to be lost to us, would we miss him most for his winning ways with a dust mop or hedge clippers?"

• HIRE TEENAGERS FOR MORE THAN BABY-SITTING.

Pay a high school or college student to help you around the house, while you are there. (In the process, you're a role model for a future parent.)

• ENCOURAGE KIDS TO SOLVE THEIR OWN PROBLEMS.

Resist going overboard when helping your kids with their homework—teach them to use reference books instead. Stand back from children's squabbles and quarrels and encourage them to work out a truce together.

4. Touch That Dial.

- CREATE A TV-FREE ZONE.

Believe it or not, some American households do manage to get by without a TV. Charlene Goldman and her husband have been without a TV for five years. Her husband recently decided to buy a video monitor (without channels) to watch movies at home. After finding, but before buying, a $600 monitor, he spent a Saturday evening staring at the fireplace with his son, who fell asleep in his arms. He decided even a channelless monitor was more TV than they needed in their home.

- LIMIT TV TIME.

Most families find it possible to decrease the number of television hours. Consider making one day each week a TV-free day, or allowing the set to be turned on only after dinner is over and all chores and homework are finished.

- ESTABLISH A NINTENDO-CONTAINMENT POLICY.

Julie Emerick, a mother I met at a video game store, limits Nintendo with a timer. When her twins get home from school, they do their homework, then eat a snack, then play Nintendo. "I have a timer, a baking timer," she told me. "On weekdays, they each get a half-hour of Nintendo. First, they flip a coin to see who gets to play first. That avoids fights. Then I put the timer on the TV and set it. When the timer rings, they're done, no matter how many men they have left on the screen. If they break the rules, they don't get to play Nintendo on the follow-ing day."

5. Manage the Media's Commercial Impact in Your Home.

• SHOP FOR QUALITY, NOT STATUS.

Ban logos from your clothing. Remove all those tags and labels that advertise the designer's name. Transfer grocery items (especially kids' cereal) from their brand-name containers to jars and canisters.

• MAKE A TOY SWAP.

One mother became fed up with violent toys, most of them connected to TV programs. "I told (my son) we could go to Toys-Я-Us and replace his violent toys with new toys—but they had to be creative. We came back with Play-Doh and games and art supplies and Legos and a giant box of new crayons. Later, I was listening to him sing as he played. Instead of singing cartoon superhero songs in that slightly mean-sounding, destructo-boy tone, he was singing something gentle: 'Put in the Play-Doh and out comes the fun.' He was still singing a TV-generated song, but it was about creation instead of destruction."

• TALK OVER TV.

When you see something that bothers you, say so. Let kids know they don't have to sit and absorb all that flashes before them. Teach them to be participant viewers, able to react to what they see.

Sesame Street's director of research, Valeria Lovelace, says, "I try to restrict television, but I let (my children) watch a lot of different types of programming, and I usually use a technique called *talking over television*. I intervene. I scream and holler. I say, 'This isn't right! . . . Look at this! Look at that! Now that man's not telling the truth there! Why is it that this cartoon doesn't have any females? Do you see how those people are laughing at this person? Do you think that this is right?' I'm like one of those irritating folks in the movie theaters who narrates everything. What I'm trying to do is to impose my own values on top of the medium. I talk *back* to the newscaster, but I'm talking *to* my children. So what if I'm loud and noisy and distracting at times? I'm getting my viewpoints across. If I wait, it's too late. I find out what topics my kids are interested in on TV, and then I take them to the library and get books and follow up in more depth.

"My smallest (child) watches the news. And we will talk—'those people died, those people lived, why do these people hate these people?' Even if I do not talk with them right away about what they have seen, I try to do it later, maybe riding in the car. The point is to talk."

6. Make Your Home Part of a Learning Network.

• CREATE A HOME LEARNING CENTER.

It needn't be a whole room—a corner of the living room or kitchen will suffice, and is better than the child's bedroom, where he or she is more isolated. Have shelves with lots of books and a user-friendly set of encyclopedias. Include standard reference books—a dictionary, thesaurus, atlas, almanac, nature guides, etc. Also include novels and magazines, changing subscriptions as children's interests change. Make a habit of looking up answers to questions and show your kids how to use research materials.

- HAVE ALL FAMILY MEMBERS READ AT LEAST ONE BOOK PER MONTH (ABOVE AND BEYOND SCHOOL AND WORK REQUIREMENTS).

Encourage children and adults to read by making reading time a part of your daily routine. Keep books and magazines in every room of the house.

Schedule a monthly family book group and have each person describe what he or she has read. Hold the meeting in a special place (around a fire at the beach, at a local park) and serve out-of-the-ordinary refreshments.

- DO YOUR HOMEWORK WHILE THE KIDS DO THEIRS.

Set a firm homework hour (or two) per evening and sit with the kids at the kitchen table, or wherever they work. Show them that adults have homework too; act as role models for developing responsible work habits. Pay bills; read the newspaper, magazines, or work materials; go over the work you've brought home; catch up with correspondence. Once the time is up, put your work away and play with your kids, read bedtime stories, watch TV (if you must).

• DO VOLUNTEER PROJECTS FOR YOUR
CHILDREN'S SCHOOLS AT HOME.

While many parents can still take time off to volunteer at their children's schools, some can't. But there are many helpful projects which can be done on evenings or weekends, at school or at home.

For example, some volunteer activities—reading and math tutoring, for example—can be conducted during the early evening hours.

"Even something as simple as sending in snacks a few times a year shows a child that you want to contribute to it," says kindergarten teacher Pat Cordery.

Here are some examples of projects suggested by the National Committee for Citizens in Education:

· Mount displays of children's work.
· Make additional copies of games and other classroom materials.
· Type children's stories, class lists, curriculum materials.
· Collect pictures from magazines.
· Collect recyclable items, such as egg crates, lids, spools, 35mm film cases, paper rolls, buttons, corks, coffee scoops, and fabric scraps.
· Buy small items such as pencil grips for the special ed program.
· Provide child care so another parent can volunteer in the classroom.
· Operate phone trees; recruit other parents to participate in special events.
· Arrange for field trips; contact local businesses and other places of interest.

7. Put Money in Its Place.

- CHOOSE TIME OVER MONEY.

Consider the cost of taking on extra projects at work versus time spent away from the family. The dollars you earn from overtime may seem beneficial in the short run, but may rob you of precious hours with your kids.

- LEARN TO GET BY WITH LESS MONEY.

Try bartering for the things you need, or trading skills with neighbors.

- MAKE DECISIONS ABOUT WHAT IS ESSENTIAL AND WHAT CAN BE DISCARDED.

Hold family meetings to discuss ways of cutting the family budget. Ask kids whether they'd like a new Nintendo game or more time with Mom and Dad. You might be surprised by their answers, and you may find you need less money than you thought.

8. Connect with Nature.

As a boy, I was not aware that my woods were ecologically connected with any other forests; nobody talked about acid rain or holes in the ozone or global warming. But I knew my woods and my fields; I knew every bend in the creek and dip in the beaten dirt paths. I pulled out survey sticks in advance of the slow-motion bulldozers that moved, ever closer, like an armored division. I wandered these woods even in my dreams.

But for many kids, maybe most, this relationship has reversed in the past fifteen or twenty years. Today kids express extraordinary awareness of the global threats to the environment. But at the same time, their physical contact, their intimacy with nature, is fading away.

One fourth-grader told me that he likes to play indoors better " 'cause that's where all the electrical outlets are."

If children's direct experience of nature is vanishing, where are future environmentalists going to come from? In 1978, Thomas Tanner, professor of environmental studies at Iowa State University, conducted a study of environmentalists' formative influences—what it was in their lives that had steered them to environmental activism. He polled staff members and chapter officers of major environmental organizations.

"Far and away the most frequently cited influence was childhood experience of natural, rural, or other relatively pristine habitats," according to Tanner. For most of these people, natural habitats were accessible nearly every day when they were kids, for unstructured play and discovery. "Several studies since mine have supported my findings," he says. "But for some reason, you don't hear many environmentalists expressing much concern about the intimacy factor between kids and nature."

Particularly in urban areas, exposure to nature doesn't come naturally. We need to bring nature to our kids.

• TAKE A NATURE BREAK.

Go for a walk outside instead of taking the kids to a movie or a shopping mall. Look for insects under leaves and birds in the trees. Get dirty. Play in the mud. Stand in the rain until your clothing is soaked. One of the most important benefits of intimacy with nature is its influence on mental health—lifting children and adults out of the lethargy and passivity of every-day videoized reality. Show your kids how good nature can feel.

- GO CAMPING, BOATING, ANYTHING OUTSIDE AND AWAY.

"When we go camping, I try to tap a vein of mystery I remember when I was a child," says John Johns, a Los Angeles businessman. "I get them up before dawn so we can see the coyotes. We hike under the moon, no flashlights. On camping trips, if the parents have a good time, the kids will have a good time. They'll connect with nature."

Gail Kempton writes: "We took the boys camping in a van with a seat built so they were close to us and we could talk. We were all trapped together."

Marlene Conway, now a grandmother, lists her outdoor time tricks: "Camping and the beach when we were poor." Later, her family bought a small boat, and made the kids go fishing, water skiing, and boating—sometimes under protest. "But today, they talk about how wonderful it was. We bought a mountain cabin for family togetherness. It's very noisy now—as the four have multiplied to fourteen."

- TAKE NATURE VACATIONS.

Those who don't enjoy camping can still vacation in natural settings by renting a mountain or beach cabin for a few days. Ski trips give kids a chance to roll in the snow. Dude ranches catering to families are popular right now, and give all family members a chance to ride horses, sleep under the stars, and pretend they are cowboys and cowgirls.

- ### BRING THE OUTDOORS INSIDE.

Collect leaves, rocks, seashells, and bugs. Grow plants from raw potatoes, avocado seeds, and pineapple tops. Hang nature photos on the walls. Listen to tapes of the ocean, rain showers, or wind.

- ### JOIN NATURE ORGANIZATIONS.

Become members of the National Audubon Society, the National Wildlife Federation, the Nature Conservancy, the Sierra Club, or other organizations. Most have monthly publications with spectacular natural photography; some have special memberships and magazines for kids. Buy a yearly membership at your local zoo, and stop by often to visit favorite animals or simply to take a walk.

- ### LIVE AS CLOSE TO NATURE AS YOU CAN.

Not all of us can afford to live in a rural setting. But some parents have decided that they are willing to forego the benefits of urban life for the potential enrichment nature can bring to their kids' lives.

One father describes how he moved his family a long distance to plug his daughters into nature. "I'm trying to communicate to them the wonder. I'm wrestling with how to do it," says Dave Greegor, who recently moved his family from Nebraska to Boise, Idaho, where he took a job as an ecologist for the Idaho department of water resources. "Maybe exposure to nature, to real wilderness, has a cumulative effect. You take your kids out and expose them and expose them and expose them. They're saying, 'Oh no, do we have to go on another hike?' But eventually it hits them, and then it's theirs forever."

9. Practice the Art of Storytelling.

"As I grew up, I loved listening to my grandparents' stories," a friend, Liz, told me recently. "I was drawn to their calm and intrigued by the scope of their lives. I remember my grandmother telling stories about my Great-Aunt Ag who once modeled camisoles and ladies' undergarments. . . ."

Today, Liz's family members rarely tell stories.

"One evening I was baby-sitting the nine-year-old daughter of a friend. This little girl loves to hear stories about her mother's life. So she asked me to tell her a story about my childhood, and I was stuck with panic. I couldn't think of a thing. I know I have stories. But here was a child asking me for something so simple as a story and I couldn't think of one.

"I learned two things that night. One was that I had lost touch with the stories I grew up with; and two, I'm not making many new stories."

Not everyone feels this way, but those who do wonder why.

"Maybe the lives we lead today are mind-numbing, and not the source of many good stories," Liz said. "A lot of the stuff of good stories has to do with family life, and we have precious little time for that now."

Somehow we assume that if a story isn't in the video store or on TV, it must not be worth much. But children are always entranced with the past, eager to hear about "the old days" when their parents were children. Interject pieces of your past into your children's lives whenever possible by relating anecdotes that fit their current predicaments or pleasures.

10. Carry on Family Traditions and Create New Ones.

Children and adults feel more secure and comfortable when they know what to expect, at least for a few moments a day. Mornings can begin with a predictable (if dreaded) wake-up call, be it a song or a rallying chant. Farewell hugs at the front door send family members into the world with a sense of security. Encourage kids to suggest new traditions, and follow old ones religiously.

- PLANT A TREE OR SHRUB WHEN NEW BABIES COME HOME.

If you have a yard, plant a tree when each child is born and watch it grow together as the child grows. If you don't have a yard, plant a flower in a pot.

- MAKE BIRTHDAYS A FAMILY EVENT.

Open gifts at breakfast, with everyone present, even if it means rising a bit earlier than usual. Let the birthday person choose the dinner menu (within reason, of course) and have a day free from chores.

- CARRY ON RITUALS FROM YOUR CHILDHOOD.

One man well into middle age talks about his craving for "sick man's eggs" whenever he's feeling down. His mother (now deceased) always fixed him soft boiled eggs stirred up with bite-sized bits of toast when he was sick; now he makes them for his own children.

- CHERISH HOLIDAY MEMORIES.

Unpack holiday decorations together, and talk about past holidays.

CHRISTMAS LOVE LETTERS

Linda Evangelist doesn't enjoy shopping. Like many people, she's offended by the holiday commercialism that seems to compound annually. A teacher in El Centro, California, Evangelist is the mother of two college-age sons. Last year, her son Todd announced that he was getting married in late December, and he wanted his mom to plan the wedding.

"But I had boys," she exclaimed, at the time. "I don't do weddings! And I don't do Christmas very well either, especially this close to a wedding."

Something had to give.

In the past, the Evangelists had been creative with Christmas. A few years ago, Linda and her family rented a mountain cabin for a week, dispensing with gifts entirely. "We spent the time together as a family exploring a new environment. Even the boys agreed that the week couldn't be beat."

But last year, faced with the wedding, they couldn't leave town.

So the Evangelist family came up with a new alternative Christmas celebration, which they plan to repeat this year.

First, rather than worrying about buying the perfect gifts for the other family members, they decided that each of them would buy a gift for himself or herself, keep it a secret from everyone else, wrap it, put it under the tree, and open it on Christmas morning.

Second, each person would write love letters to all the other family members, to be read aloud on Christmas morning. The family members would then give each other the letters.

Each member of the family would write three love letters listing at least 25 reasons why the person receiving the letter was loved or valued.

"Twenty-five?" said Todd, when his mother suggested the alternative celebration. "What if I can only think of ten?"

As Christmas Eve approached, Linda braced herself for the usual holiday tension—but it never came, even with the pressure of the approaching wedding. "Not one time did I become exhausted and out of sorts with anyone." She did worry about one thing. She didn't see Todd or her husband working on their letters. "That's their problem," she reminded herself, and continued to fashion construction-paper folders, decorated with holly leaves, for holding the letters.

On Christmas morning, the family wandered out to the tree, carrying their letters. Linda sat down expectantly. Nothing happened.

"I'll read my letters first," she said finally. She began to read her very earnest letter to her son, Brad.

"Are these all supposed to be serious?" he asked, after hearing his mother's first few reasons for loving him.

"That broke the ice," says Linda. "And the laughter began."

Among Brad's reasons for loving his dad: "You would let me stay up late and watch TV with you. . . . You would bribe me to go get ice cream late at night after Mom went to bed. . . . You are excited by your kids."

Among the reasons the sons gave for loving their mom, was that she comes up "with weird ideas like this one. . . . You came to all our games (even if you covered your eyes half the time). . . . You let your children be heard, not just seen. . . . You pick good back seats when buying cars. . . . You don't make scenes in public (usually). . . . You didn't put Mindy to sleep."

When Linda sent me these lists, she modestly left out the love list from her husband to herself, but she included hers to him.

"You let me do what I want to do with my life," she wrote to her husband. "You think I am cute. . . . You even like my nose. . . . You don't make fun of me, or tease me when I can't take it. . . . You are my best friend."

She says the letters that were the most fun were the ones that the boys wrote and read to each other. Here are some of the reasons they gave for loving each other: "You took me to lunch with you in high school. . . . You made me competitive 'cause I always wanted to beat you. . . . You broke me of my chewing with my mouth open habit. . . . You rode me on your handle bars to school when I was in Junior High. . . . You would let me hit you and not hit back when we would box. . . . You never hit me in the face when we fought. . . . You were considerate enough to put your banana peels under the couch. . . . You were born second."

Among the reasons the parents gave for loving their boys: "You go along with my unusual ideas. . . . You cleaned the sand out of the truck on your own. . . . You are so much like Dad. . . . You make me feel like my opinion counts. . . . You are so irreverent. . . . You are nice to animals (when I'm not looking.)"

Evangelist says, "There were moments when I was bent over crying because I was laughing so hard, and other moments when warmth and acceptance and love poured over me as the boys acknowledged thanks for helping them through some of their more difficult times."

When all the letters had been read and accepted, the family discovered that no one had bothered to buy a present for himself.

"Unwittingly, we gave the best presents we could have given each other," says Evangelist. "My sons felt this was the best Christmas we ever had."

HOME AND FAMILY RESOURCES

Children's Rights of New York, Inc.
Publishes a newsletter called *Hotline* with reports of status of children, reviews of books. 15 Arbutus Lane, Stonybrook, NY, 11790-1408; (516) 751-7840.

Family Research Council
A social policy research, lobbying, and education organization affiliated with Focus on the Family, publishes a newsletter called *Family Policy*. 700 13th Street NW, Suite 180, Washington, DC, 20005; (202) 293-2100.

Family Resource Coalition
Offers information on starting and finding parents' groups. 200 South Michigan Avenue, Suite 1520, Chicago, IL, 60604-2404; (312) 341-0900.

Formerly Employed Mothers at the Leading Edge (FEMALE)
A support and advocacy group for women taking time from paid employment to raise their children. Over seventy chapters nationally; $20 membership includes a monthly newsletter and ongoing assistance in starting and managing local chapters. PO Box 31, Elmhurst, IL, 60126; (708) 941-3553.

Institute for American Values
The institute publishes *Family Affairs*, a valuable and distinguished newsletter for people who care about family issues. Subscription is available free upon request. David Blankenhorn, president, 250 West 57th Street, Suite 2415, New York, NY, 10107; (212) 246-3942.

MOMS (Moms Offering Moms Support) Club
Over one hundred groups nationwide, provides information on starting and managing support networks for in-home mothers. 814 Moffat Circle, Simi Valley, CA, 93065; (805) 526-2725.

MOPs (Mothers of Preschoolers) International
Over 470 groups nationwide with the purpose of connecting mothers with each other. 1311 South Clarkson, Denver, CO, 80210; (303) 733-5353.

Mothers at Home
Dedicated to the support of mothers who choose or would like to choose to stay home to raise their children; serves as forum for exchange of information; publishes *Welcome Home* monthly magazine, with over 15,000 subscribers. 8310-A Old Courthouse Road, Vienna, VA, 22180; (703) 827-3903 or (800) 783-4MOM.

Mothers at Home More
Advocacy group to help mothers be home more. PO Box 74, Rowayton, CT, 06853; (703) 827-5903.

National Association of Mothers' Centers
Provides nationwide information on starting a Mothers' Center through the Mothers' Center Development Project. 336 Fulton Avenue, Hempstead, NY, 11550; (800) 645-3828.

The National Parenting Service
Operates a touch-tone phone service that provides recorded advice from noted parenting experts twenty-four hours a day. The number is 1-900-246-MOMS; calls cost $1.95 for the first

minute and 95 cents a minute thereafter. Phone service available to all; membership in NPS available to military parents and Department of Defense civilians for $14.95. PO Box 108748, Canoga Park, CA, 91309.

Single Mother
Magazine with reader forum, articles on health, family, finance for single parents ($11 per year, 6 issues). Just You and Me Kid Publishing, PO Box 68, Midland, NC, 28107.

Books
The Kid's Guide to Social Action, Barbara Lewis. Minneapolis: Free Spirit Publishing, 1991. 160 pp. Playground ethics teach kids how their actions affect others.

Mother's Club: Nurturing the Nurturers, Katie Williams Hoepke. Palo Alto, CA: Ark Press, 1989.

The Myth of the Bad Mother: The Emotional Realities of Mothering, Jane Swigart. New York: Doubleday, 1991. 260 pp.

Remaking Motherhood, Anita Shreve. New York: Viking, 1987. 227 pp.

School's Out: Now What? Afternoon, Weekends, Vacations, Creative Choices for Your Child, Joan M. Bergstrom. Berkeley: Ten Speed Press, 1990.

The Way Back Home: Essays on Life and Family, Peggy O'Mara. Seattle: Mothering Publications, 1989. Reprints of author's essays from *Mothering* magazine.

YOUR IDEAS FOR YOUR FAMILY

_____

_____

_____

_____

_____

_____

_____

_____

_____

_____

_____

_____

_____

_____

_____

_____

_____

_____

_____

_____

_____

_____

_____

_____

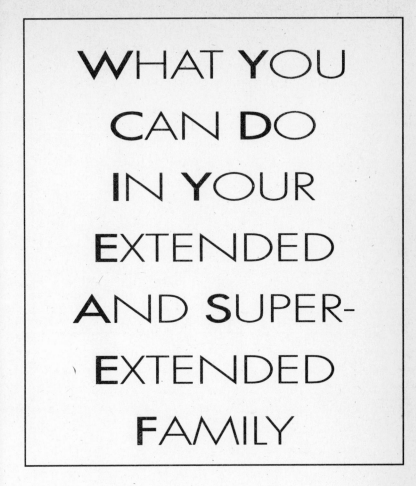

WHAT YOU CAN DO IN YOUR EXTENDED AND SUPER-EXTENDED FAMILY

In the past, an important part of the web of support for children was the extended family—grandparents, uncles and aunts, cousins. Most extended families today are overextended, spread all over the country. Some are separated by miles, others by stubborn grudges and resentments. In some ways we've romanticized the extended family's past and underestimated its future.

Take grandparents, for example. The television series "The Waltons" conjured up a wonderful image of the extended family with strong, loving grandparents. But in reality, fifty or seventy-five years ago, because life spans were shorter, it was rare for children to grow up with a close relationship to a grandparent. Today, for the first time in history, most people live long enough to get to know most of their grandchildren.

There's opportunity here, perhaps more opportunity for extended family relationships than in the past. For example, technology may make it easier than we might expect to strengthen these ties—to weave the strands across distance and time. Also, many families are redefining the extended family by creating *super-extended* families of friends, neighbors, non-parents, available seniors, and parenting support groups.

11. Reach Out and Touch a Relative.

- USE LETTERS, MODEMS, FAXES AS PHONES.

As recently as the end of World War II, only half the homes in the United States had telephones. Not only are telephones omnipresent today, but long-distance phoning is relatively inexpensive.

Kids and relatives can also communicate via computer bulletin boards.

If you own a fax machine, your kids can fax their latest drawing to their grandparents. They can create a fax newsletter; they can even broadcast-fax it to all the relatives. And they can probably operate the fax machine a lot better than you can.

Use video and tape recorders. Video cameras are commonplace for taping special occasions, but an even simpler method can be to tape a letter to grandparents on audio cassette. Encourage kids to become pen pals with distant cousins.

- TO BE UNITED, FLY.

Air tickets today are relatively cheap, and grandparents generally have a lot more money to spend on air travel than they did a generation ago. The cruise industry now encourages grandparents to bring their grandkids. Don't forget senior travel discounts.

- HANG LOOSE, KICK BACK, CHILL.

Encourage children to form their own relationships with relatives. Instead of trying to plan massive family gatherings, give kids the opportunity to get together with relatives one-on-one.

Emphasize informal connections. One father talks of the different relationships his young son has with his grandfathers:

"My father is American; my wife's father is Filipino. My father likes prearranged, complicated family get-togethers. We drive miles to them and everyone is often tense and formal. In comparison, my wife's father is informal about everything. He's visiting now. When I left for work, he and my son were building a fort out of pillows. What my son loves most about him is all the time they spend doing nothing."

12. Engage the History and Ritual of Your Extended Family.

- COLLECT FAMILY HISTORIES.

Ask grandparents to make tape recordings or videos of their memories and family histories. Include stories that took place when the grandparent was a child. Make photo albums of your childhood available to your kids; look through them together and tell stories from the past.

Incorporate traditions from your extended family's past. Incorporate your parents' and grandparents' family recipes in holiday meals, like the father who insists on making his grand-mother's Hungarian sauerkraut soup every Christmas eve. His kids hate the stuff, but love seeing their dad in the kitchen stirring his cauldron of memories. Ask your parents to pass on a few cherished holiday ornaments or special treasures you made as a child.

Such rituals give the context of time to relationships with relatives.

- HONOR THE DEAD.

Link your family to loved ones who have died by creating a living memorial, a chance to remember the dead and to be reassured that you will be remembered as well.

For example, Mexican families celebrate *Día de los Muertos* (Day of the Dead) on All Saints Day and All Souls Day, November 1 and 2. In the home, altars are set up honoring the dead with family portraits, candles, flowers, and favorite foods and drinks—a can of Coke or bottle of tequila, a loaf of bread, a pack of cigarettes.

You might wish to set up a similar altar in your home with your kids, talking about their ancestors, sharing memories of the people and the times in which they lived. Some of us might feel more comfortable skipping the altar.

But a true extended family reaches outward, and into the past, in order to reach the future.

THE NEW GUARDIANS

In a house filled with antiques, a circle of grandparents gathers. They tell their stories. Laura cares for two grandchildren, ages thirteen and nine, whose mother is a drug addict; her grandson was drug-damaged in the womb. Mary tells how her four-year-old granddaughter said everyone would have been better off if she had not been born. John describes how his grandson tried to jump out of a fourth-floor window. For the most part, removed from abusive parents and placed with their grandparents, the kids are doing fine now.

But for the kids and for the grandparents, the need for help never ends.

This particular support group, called Grandparents Raising Grandchildren, is sponsored by Mignon Scherer, a licensed family therapist and former school teacher. Scherer herself is raising a grandchild.

"If I talk enough, which I do, I hear my own answers," says Ellen, knitting, and peering through orange-framed glasses.

These Californians are part of a growing movement of grandparents, aunts, uncles, and older siblings around the country who become guardians of abused or neglected offspring of other family members. Some judges now believe this is better for the children than allowing them to be swept up in the bureaucratic nightmare of Child Protection Services or farming them out to non-family foster parents. The surprise is that this idea is considered novel.

"Ten years ago groups like ours and Mignon's didn't exist," says Margie Davis, founder of Southern California's GOLD (an acronym for Grandparents Offering Love and Direction). "Now they're springing up all over the country."

In the past year, more than 700 people seeking custody or trying to resolve problems with the system have been helped by GOLD.

As Davis points out, during the early part of this century, children were likely to lose a parent to death, and grandparents frequently stepped in. Then came better medical care, Social Security, welfare, and Americans came to believe that the nuclear family could survive on its own.

But now with the rise of single-parenting, drug problems and two-career households, the extended family is back—or at least returning.

This refocusing comes with a price.

First, there's the financial sacrifice of the new guardians. Grandparents can receive child support and Aid to Families with Dependent Children, but this money seldom covers the costs of raising a child. One grandfather spoke of spending $25,000, his life savings, on lawyers during the custody battle.

The psychological issues are more difficult. In the circle, the grandparents talk of the prejudice they encounter, sometimes from other seniors who don't understand why they prefer raising a child to playing golf.

They talk of the painful necessity to detach themselves from their own children.

One grandfather describes how his daughter-in-law arrives on visitation day and stays for hours, telling the child that the grandparents are old and may die soon. (Nothing is more frightening to a child than the threat that a guardian may disappear.) She says, "Mommy loves you, Mommy can't do without you," and she stays until 2 A.M. The child's psychiatrist has told the grandfather how hurtful that kind of visitation is for the child. "So now I have to set limits—'Visiting time is over. Out!'"

They speak of role reversal. The stereotypical role of grandparents is that they spoil their grandkids. But one man says, "My daughter comes like Santa Claus, with her gifts and her attention."

One woman describes how her grandchildren fear for their mother, a prostitute and drug dealer, how they blame themselves when she doesn't show up for a visit, and how they feel responsible for her.

One of the most attractive aspects of the guardianships, according to GOLD, is that they can be reversed if the parent proves he or she is capable of parenting again.

But this process can sometimes be painful.

One grandmother in the group gained custody of her granddaughter when the child was five years old. Today, the mother has regained her mental health and the custody of the little girl. At first, the court required the mother to allow the grandmother visitation rights—or at least implied the rights. Now the daughter has become, in the grandmother's words, "fanatically religious," and won't allow the grandmother to visit anymore. More court battles loom. "I planned my life around this child," says the grandmother. "I'm a big girl and I can handle this, but what about my granddaughter?"

A grandfather, holding a cane and wearing dark, wraparound glasses, asks, "What is our granddaughter missing—like camping, hiking—because we're not in the best of health?"

His wife, Ellen, says, "Well, I got my answer to that this week. My granddaughter is visiting her mother on the East Coast. She says she spends her days in her stepfather's law office, killing time. She wants to come home. That's my answer."

Slowly, these good people unload their fears and their haunts, and listen to each other's information (don't give advice, says Scherer, give information).

Scherer says that one of the issues of the last third of life is to "make everything right." What about those invasive in-laws who want to make everything too right for their relatives? The guardianship investigators of San Diego's Family Court Services believe that the legal hurdles are high enough to prevent frivolous guardianships.

The support system does have one gaping hole.

According to Family Court Services, family members

who are not grandparents—uncles, aunts, older sisters and brothers—constitute about 40 percent of guardianships. While there is increasing support for grandparents, virtually no support groups exist specifically for other family members who step in as legal guardians. That support should come. So should more government focus on the long-neglected extended family.

"Government must shift from its sole focus on the nuclear family to helping the extended family," says Margie Davis. "With budget cuts and the pain out there, we need to tap this wonderful resource. The guardianship movement isn't a division of the family but a coming together again." And that's good news.

13. Weave a Super-extended Family.

The family web grows far stronger when additional strands surround the core, sheltering it from harm while extending its boundaries. For the family, these protective strands are woven by relatives and friends—other parents, single adults, childless couples, neighbors, grandparents who join forces as a super-extended family. Children need and enjoy contact with adults other than their parents; when surrounded by caring adults, kids have both security and liberation, a broader base of operation, and the freedom to explore a variety of life-styles and beliefs. Grownups who are involved with children gain a sense of generational completion, an opportunity to influence, protect, and defend the young. We all long to belong in a family.

- SCHEDULE FREQUENT POTLUCK DINNERS WITH FRIENDS: PARENTS AND NON-PARENTS.

Keep it simple. Schedule them on weeknights as well as weekends so parents are freed from their nightly dinner chores.

- INVITE FRIENDS WHO ARE NOT PARENTS TO BE PART OF YOUR FAMILY.

Use friends as more than your escape from the kids; encourage them to visit when the whole family is home. Have them help kids with homework assignments, science projects, cookie sales.

- ENLIST CHILDLESS FRIENDS AS SURROGATE PARENTS.

When Eric and Nina Utne, publishers of the *Utne Reader*, became pregnant with what would be the fourth child in their combined families, they enlisted childless friends in a surrogate scheme, in which the baby, named Eli, became their allotted child—"sort of a timeshare baby. For this scheme to make any sense you have to view us not as a nuclear family but as designated breeders in a tribal or extended family," according to Eric Utne.

"One of the friends [my daughter] made in preschool is still one of her best friends. This little girl has a single parent as well, her father. He and I shared an unspoken cooperation. There was no need to ask for help, we just stepped in when we were needed. That little bit of trust and cooperation between two people made our lives not only easier but richer. I have the additional joy of loving and caring for another child like my own."

—Cynthia Fillmore, a mother in San Diego, California

- **HONOR YOUR FRIENDS BY MAKING THEM GODPARENTS TO YOUR KIDS.**

The concept of being a child's godparent needn't have religious trappings. One woman, a Catholic by upbringing, is a godmother to her Jewish friend's son. "We didn't have a ceremony," the godmother says. "I just agreed that Dylan would be a special child in my life. I keep his picture on my bulletin board, send him postcards from my travels and try to visit him whenever I can. Our relationship is a continuation of my friendship with his mother. When her life changed through marriage and parenthood, so did mine. She brought me along with her, and insured that I would be a part of her new family."

- **INFORMALLY ADOPT A FAMILY.**

Teach children civic and personal responsibility and compassion by adopting a family that's having problems, through divorce or death of a parent, homelessness, or other family disruption. Invite them to dinner, share toys and games, help with child care.

• SINGLE PARENTS: FORM SUPER-
EXTENDED FAMILIES OF SINGLE
PARENTS.

Single parents, among the most isolated and time-poor of families, can find relief and help by forming a network of other
parents (often, these are other single parents). Because of the
time and scheduling crunch, such a super-extended family can
be maintained over the phone line; some family phone nets
have survived for years.

A PHONE NETWORK OF SINGLE MOMS

A Los Angeles woman, a single mother for eighteen years,
tells how she formed a super-extended family of other
single mothers: "In the sixties, I connected with other
single parents through an alternative public school which
we helped start. We could just as easily have linked
through church or synagogue, but we didn't go. Rather,
we did politics together and what survived the politics
was friendship and connection. We were all single parents. We formed an informal extended family. With the
exception of Dr. Spock, I've never read a how-to-parent
book in my life; I have my friends. It's revealing, I think, that
most of us who made these kinds of connections can
truthfully say today that our kids are OK. The parents who
didn't make those connections tend to be the ones with
kids with severe problems. Those of us who connected

with each other shared resources; it's the people without human resources who are so terribly lost, in part because human resources often lead to other resources.

"The group was non-hierarchical, but I did consider some of the people in my group to be expert parents, because I saw them parenting. However, you don't turn to the same parent every time. Some parents are good at some kinds of advice; others are good at other kinds of advice. I was an expert on schools, so other mothers turned to me for advice on that. And I knew about how to collect child-support payments. Word spread. Other parents were experts on finding a baby-sitter or pediatricians. This was not a group that met formally. It was simply a group of women, and some men, too, who talked frequently on the telephone. I didn't know 'networking' was a word eighteen years ago. In a sense, networking is a spurious term. It simply means connecting with people."

—From *Childhood's Future*

• THE ELECTRONIC BACK FENCE.

On several computer bulletin boards around the country parents log on via modem and participate in parenting forums, seeking the kind of parenting advice they can't seem to get from the parents they encounter at work during the day.

• SEEK OUT OR BECOME A MENTORING PARENT.

Many parents have learned that they can find support by turning to parents with children slightly older than their own.

- ENCOURAGE YOUR CHILDREN
  TO ADOPT SURROGATE GRANDPARENTS.

When I was a boy, I adopted elderly couples in my neighborhood as surrogate grandparents (whether or not they wanted to be adopted). How they would listen to me, feed me cookies, and lend me books. They were, in the vernacular of therapy, my significant others.

Children today have a tough time finding such mentors. Older Americans continue to move into seniors-only communities, the ones with strict rules and walls and sometimes rolling razor wire surrounding them. But there's an intergenerational countertrend. The American Association for Retired Persons (AARP) has been working hard in recent years to show concern about the next generation. No organization has worked harder at achieving the connection between the old and the young than the Gray Panthers.

Seniors could become the winter soldiers of a national family movement; many of them have the time and the money to help the children of harried or impoverished parents.

Among the most effective programs in the schools, the classroom efforts most moving to observe are those that bring seniors into the classroom to touch and hold and read to children who are starved for any kind of positive adult contact.

The number of intergenerational programs is slowly increasing; the importance of surrogate grandparents is being rediscovered.

- CREATE A PARENT SUPPORT GROUP.

Parents around the country are beginning to fight their sense of isolation by forming support groups to help them regularly vent their feelings. Here are some tips for creating and sustaining a successful parent support group.

- Keep the group relatively small: ten to fifteen parents.
- Context counts: A parent support group can be established within a neighborhood, with parents taking turns offering their living rooms for discussions. But many parent support groups are associated with an institution—a school or day-care center, a church or synagogue, a public library, even a workplace. Such institutions can offer a meeting room and also serve as a social magnet; for example, when parents in the support group drop their children off at day care, they can spend a few moments catching up.
- If possible, provide child care during the meetings.
- Some groups ask a psychologist or other professional to lecture or serve as a facilitator. But the facilitator should not dominate the discussion. The most important goal is a free and open discussion among parents.
- Pick a topic of discussion in advance. In order to open the discussion, a parent can provide a prepared presentation on the subject. Among possible topics: feelings of deficiency as parents; sibling rivalry; convincing children to go to bed; discipline; conflicts between work and home; the generation gap between parents and grandparents; dealing with schools; parent exhaustion; safety.
- Participants should avoid giving direct advice, which can be perceived as subtle criticism. A better approach is to emphasize *options*. Rather than trying to solve a fellow parent's problem, the group can offer different ways of looking at the problem and an array of solutions.
- Establish clear ground rules for discussion. For example, some groups declare the topic of marital relationships,

how parenting strains marriages, off-limits. But such a discussion can be helpful, *if* the members of the group agree beforehand to enter that arena.

· While some parent support groups consist of moms only, or dads only, it's a good idea to bring the genders together. Emphasize diversity of family configurations; for example, include at-home parents as well as parents who work outside the home. A group might also consider inviting grandparents for intergenerational meetings.

· Consider inviting future parents; a parenting support group can offer invaluable help to first-time parents, easing them into the new world of raising children.

AN EVENING WITH A PARENT SUPPORT GROUP

The parents sit in a circle on the little chairs that their children use during the day. A six-year-old garter snake watches passively from a cage. The walls in this classroom are covered with the bold scrawls of children's drawings. Slowly at first, and a little nervously, the parents begin to talk about time-outs and burnout, about the joys of being parents and about the fears.

"I'm concerned that my daughter is so aggressive in preschool," says one mother, who is in her twenties. "Either she'll become a leader, and be strong and happy, or she's going to be a real *problem*."

"Your daughter is four years old, isn't she?" says Patty Eshelman, sitting across the circle. Patty, forty-four, has an eight-year-old and a sixteen-year-old. As often happens in groups like this, the older parent calms the younger one. She continues, gently, "It's easy to worry about how a four-year-old will turn out; they're incredible little people, filled with all that raw stuff. Sometimes, with a four-year-old, it's hard to see how that raw energy will ever come together to form a full, more integrated five-year-old, but it usually happens." The worried mother looks relieved.

Most parent groups do not spring up *ad hoc* but are associated with a school, church, or neighborhood. The group meeting tonight is made up of parents whose children attend the Unitarian Cooperative Pre-school in San Diego. Usually, when this group meets, a local psychologist facilitates the discussions; but sometimes the group gets together on its own, as they are doing tonight.

A visitor asks the parents to share some of the topics that they usually talk about when they get together. What are the hot buttons?

"Sibling rivalry drives me nuts. My kids are constantly at each other," says Karen Tisdale, the mother of two preschoolers. "We were discussing this at one of our parents' meetings, and I remember saying, 'It's not that one or the other of them is bad, it's that they're both bad.' I felt terrible that I had said that. They're not bad children. That's not what I meant."

"You meant they were equally troublesome," says her husband, Steve. But just talking about the problem with other parents helped Karen and Steve. "In the group, we discussed who our kids' fighting was bothering most. Our kids or us. We decided it was bothering us the most. They're not really hurting each other. Well, they're pinching each other."

Karen's sister, Barbara Tisdale, also a member of the group, says the problem she faced with her two-year-old was biting.

"I felt guilty about my child biting. I even thought about taking my daughter out of preschool. Talking with the group, I realized that I'm not the only one who faced that problem and that, within limits, biting is a natural behavior, just a phase that some kids go through."

Another hot button is the conflict between at-home parents and parents who work outside the home. The parents in this group say that, over time, such resentments fade; both types of mothers and fathers tend to feel isolated from other parents, and both tend to feel guilty that they are not living up to someone else's definition of politically correct parenting. Also, moms in this group have been surprised to hear how guilty some of the working dads feel about spending so much time at the office instead of at home.

The stereotype of fathers is that they're unlikely to open up about their feelings, but this group undermines the stereotype.

Tonight, the discussion touches on an especially sensitive and sometimes hurtful hot area: the feeling by some parents that *their* parents don't understand their pressures.

"I hear a lot from my mom how nice it would be if I could stay home with the kids," says one mother who works thirty hours a week as an accountant. She is smiling, but as she talks about her mother's remarks, her voice lowers.

How does that make her feel? someone asks.

"Bad . . ." She stops talking. Her eyes fill with tears.

"It's a different world today," says her husband,

reaching for her hand. "It's not *what* her mother says, it's the implication behind it, that my wife isn't a good mother because she works outside the home. It's a subtle thing, but it hurts."

The landscape of family life has changed so much in recent decades that parents and grandparents often have a difficult time understanding each others' world. Most of the parents in this group say they find it easier to seek support and understanding from peers than from their parents. And they suggest that grandparents might consider forming their own support groups. (Another possibility: intergenerational support groups for parents and grandparents.)

Parenting burnout is another hot button. "I remember opening the back door to my house when I had a two-year-old and just screaming out into the canyon because he was making me nuts," says one mother. "I figured that was a safe outlet for my frustration." Another mother says she and her husband give themselves "time-outs" when their parenting tensions boil over; she says she goes for walks around the block until she cools down. And Steve Tisdale, who works in construction, says he and his wife give each other frequent breaks. "My wife will hand our child to me and say, 'Here, he's yours,' " he says, laughing. "Even if the break is only five minutes, it can make a big difference."

This parenting support group has learned to avoid imposing direct advice on one another; rather, the parents offer options—they describe approaches that they, or people they have known, have tried.

"After one of these meetings, Steve and I usually drive home saying, 'You know, we're not such bad parents after all,' " says Karen.

Now the conversation moves on to the hottest of buttons: fear.

"At bedtime, I find myself reading a book to my daughter about how to deal with the dangers of strangers," says Steve Weber, with an edge to his voice, "and I realize how irritated I am that I feel compelled to read her a story about danger when I should be reading her *Winnie the Pooh.*"

In the room tonight, there is a sudden sense of helplessness. Someone wonders what this fear is doing to our families. Another parent suggests action.

"For example, some schools now have patrols . . ."

"Right. Parent patrols. In the neighborhoods, too. We're going to see more of that."

Another mother mentions the phone networks that some communities have created so that parents can keep track of their children. The conversation becomes animated; this talk may or may not lead to direct action, but as the parents explore their options, the sense of helplessness lifts.

These parents do not feel alone.

EXTENDED FAMILY RESOURCES

Step Family Foundation
333 West End Avenue, New York, NY, 10023; (212) 877-3244.

Generations United
% Child Welfare League of America, 440 First Street NW, Room 310, Washington, DC, 20001; (202) 638-2952.

Life Stories
A family game for all ages. 701 Decatur Avenue N #104, Golden Valley, MN, 55427; (612) 544-0438 or (800) 232-1873.

Life Story
A monthly newsletter about writing autobiography. Letter Rock Publications, 3591 Letter Rock Road, Manhattan, KS, 66502.

Retired Senior Volunteer Program
1100 Vermont Avenue, NW, Washington, DC, 20525; (202) 289-1510.

Books
Family Traditions, Elizabeth Berg. Pleasantville, NY: Reader's Digest Books, 1992. 288 pp. $22 hardcover.

YOUR IDEAS FOR YOUR EXTENDED AND SUPER-EXTENDED FAMILY

_____

_____

_____

_____

_____

_____

_____

_____

_____

_____

_____

_____

_____

_____

_____

_____

_____

_____

_____

_____

_____

_____

_____

_____

_____

WHAT YOU CAN DO IN YOUR NEIGHBOR-HOOD

James Comer, director of the Yale Child Study Center, believes that children are willing to accept parental influence until they're eight or nine years old. Then they begin to drift toward forces outside the home. "Between home and school, at least five close friends of my parents reported everything I did that was unacceptable," he says. "They're not there anymore for today's kids."

Today, we're more likely to socialize in what the academics like to call "communities of interest"—where we gather, sometimes electronically, with like-minded folk who share a keen interest in single issues, say computers, deep massage, or speed-walking.

In too many suburban neighborhoods, kids are chased away from the perfectly manicured lawns; instead they play in the street. Adults seldom talk informally with each other because there is no convenient place to talk. Inward-looking housing design discourages families from watching out for each other. All of this conspires to create isolation and loneliness for parents and children.

But many Americans are rediscovering the benefits to their children, and to themselves, of more cohesive neighborhoods. Indeed, some of the most exciting changes that a grass-roots family movement could make are on your block.

14. Make Your Neighborhood a Safe Refuge for Kids.

- PUT OUT THE WELCOME MAT
  TO PARENTS AND CHILDREN.

Our transient, mobile society causes children to change schools, neighborhoods, and friends frequently. Neighbors can help ease the strains of change by introducing themselves to the new kids on the block and their parents.

- SET UP AN ACTIVE NEIGHBORHOOD
  WATCH PROGRAM.

This is one of the best ways of forming instant community. But it isn't enough to simply have Neighborhood Watch stickers in your windows. Children, especially those who are new to the neighborhood, may not realize what the stickers mean. Hold regular meetings with local police officers, and explain how adults and kids can help keep the neighborhood safe.

- TAKE TURNS SERVING
  AS THE NEIGHBORHOOD SAFE HOUSE.

Licensed day-care providers in San Marcos place a smiling sunflower poster in a front window, designating themselves as safe havens where kids can go if they're scared or alone. Neighbors in any community could do likewise, by taking turns each month displaying a sign familiar to all the children and keeping an eye on activity on the street, particularly after school.

- MAKE STREETS SAFE FOR KIDS.

Children as young as two or three years of age need to explore beyond the boundaries of their front yard. They start learning about independence and safety by riding their big wheel to a neighbor's house, or pulling their wagon down the block. Here are some ways to make the neighborhood safer for kids:

- Post CHILDREN AT PLAY signs at frequent intervals throughout the neighborhood.
- Stop and talk with drivers who speed through the neighborhood.
- Write down license-plate numbers and report violators to the police.
- Lobby city hall for traffic lights and/or stop signs where needed.
- Mark off bike lanes.

- ESTABLISH A CHECK-IN SERVICE FOR AFTER-SCHOOL CARE.

A neighbor, such as an elderly person who is home during the day, can serve as the check-in person. Kids come home from school, call the neighbor, grab a snack, then go to the neighbor's house until parents get home. Others check in before going to friends' houses, or before attending after-school activities, such as soccer practice or piano lessons. Check-in caregivers can be paid a minimal amount, say a dollar per child per day.

- SPONSOR NEIGHBORHOOD OR PARK
CLEANUPS.

Children are bound to explore alleys, empty lots, abandoned houses, and other potentially dangerous places. Hold periodic Saturday patrols to clean up such areas, removing trash, broken glass, and other dangers.

"The changes that I would like to see in my community or simply at every community is the unity of family and friends. If there could be a special time or time for us to share some time together. So people can talk about how school was or how was work. Something we could remember when we are older. Like a fairy tale we can tell our kids."

—Vesenia Ojeda, Chula Vista High School, Chula Vista, California

15. Organize and Join in Neighborhood Social Activities.

- START A NEIGHBORHOOD MUSIC OR
ART GROUP.

In many parts of the world, every town has a community musical group that involves all ages. One mother says, "In our family, we have an on-again, off-again orchestra of friends, the Pepperoni Pizza orchestra (named for our post-rehearsal refreshment). Our players have ranged in age from four to seventy, and our record attendance so far is twenty-five. Needless to say, all ability and skills levels are accommodated."

Handle art in the same way, hosting arts and crafts parties with plenty of supplies.

- HOLD AN ANNUAL NEIGHBORHOOD BLOCK PARTY.

Block off a few neighborhood streets and set up booths, games, and activities for all ages. Bring your barbecue grills into the street and have a giant potluck picnic, featuring each family's favorite dish. In one San Diego neighborhood, neighbors have *carne asada* and *birria* parties. Suzanne Thompson of Poway, California, reports: "One of my neighbors, a police officer, says that these public social events are the best crime prevention there is." Community creates safety; people who know each other are more likely to watch out for each other. In Thompson's neighborhood, an annual Fourth of July block party now includes a parade and a children's talent show. (How about a talent show for parents, too?)

- ORGANIZE AN ANNUAL FOURTH OF JULY PARADE.

Tom and Alice Walker of Durham, North Carolina, began holding a neighborhood Fourth of July parade in 1950, when the neighborhood children expressed boredom at being stuck at home because their parents chose not to drive on the holiday. Alice Walker suggested the kids hold a parade, even though they lacked marching bands, flags, and floats. The six children marched ever so seriously to the end of the block and back, waving red and white crepe paper streamers. When they returned, they formed a circle with the adults, sang "My Country 'Tis of Thee," and recited the Pledge of Allegiance. Thus, a neighborhood tradition was formed.

Four decades later, the parade has remained much the same, though attendance has swollen to the hundreds. "March together, sing together, pledge together, drink colas and socialize together—in that order," Tom Walker wrote in *Parents* magazine. "Men growing bald and women growing gray now seek out Alice or me to say, 'I was in this parade when I was a child. Today I brought my children.' It warms the heart."

- ### SCHEDULE PERIODIC NEIGHBORHOOD YARD SALES OR OPEN-HOUSE BRUNCHES.

Clean out the garage, book shelves, and toy chests, and set up a sale in front of each house, with special tables for the kids. Reserve an hour at the beginning of the day for neighbors to trade their junk, then open the sale to outsiders.

- ### HOST A PHOTO ALBUM PARTY.

Have neighbors (adults and children) gather at one house to put their piles of snapshots into family photo albums. Encourage discussion about family memories—it's a great way to get to know one another while completing one of those tasks that never seem to get done. Include neighbors who don't have children.

- HOST A FAMILY GAME NIGHT.

Have neighbors bring over their favorite board games, and set up play areas around the house. Encourage family members to split up and play with members of other families.

- INVITE PEOPLE WITH TIES TO THE NEIGHBORHOOD TO JOIN IN PARTIES AND ACTIVITIES.

Service workers who visit the neighborhood as part of their jobs are part of an unseen community that keeps the neighborhood running smoothly. Invite those who contribute to your neighborhood—the mail carrier, trash collectors, police officers, meter readers—to join in block parties and other neighborhood social functions. The same goes for extended-family members, relatives, and friends who spend time in the neighborhood.

- INCLUDE SENIORS AND NON-PARENTS IN NEIGHBORHOOD FAMILY ACTIVITIES.

Seniors and other adults who don't have children of their own can be a valuable resource to you and your children. Be sure your neighborhood includes them in family-oriented parties and activities.

THE FAMILY ROOM

One long, cold winter day, feeling lonely at home with her one-year-old daughter, Meredith, Renee Edelman started thinking: "Where can I take her to play with other children? Where can *I* go to meet other parents?"

With a few phone calls, she discovered that her town of Amherst, New York, a sprawling Buffalo suburb of mainly new tract housing, offered virtually no structured recreation services for children under six years old. Neighborhood parks were run down; some were dangerous. Like many mothers, she considered taking her daughter to one of the commercial fast-food franchises that offer play areas. But she doubted that a commercial play area would offer much sense of community.

"What I wanted was a safe, bright room with a lot of toys and educational games," she says today. "I yearned for a place where parents could feel comfortable with each other, where we could get to know each other and become friends. There was no such place to go, so I decided to *make* a place, an indoor family center."

Before she became a full-time at-home mom in 1988, Edelman, now thirty-six, was a geriatric social worker. She had no professional training in child development or community organizing. Her financial resources were modest. "My husband is a scientist at the University of Buffalo, but it's been a struggle to live on one income." Nor was she aware of the burgeoning number of indoor playgrounds around the country.

Nonetheless, she began to research the possibilities. She learned that Amherst's town government had bought a beautiful abandoned school building for one dollar; the town planned to invest $2.5 million to turn the school into what would later be named the Harlem Road Community Center. Only one room was still available. At a town meeting in 1990, Edelman asked Amherst's town supervisor if she could turn the room into an indoor play center.

To her surprise, she was eventually granted permission to use the room for a new play and learning center that she called the Family Room.

First came the task of furnishing and equipping the room on no budget. She wrangled carpeting from the town, asked her in-laws for contributions (they gave $150), asked neighbors to donate toys, and brought in the toys that her daughter had outgrown. Then, concerned about liability, she personally bought $1 million in liability insurance for the Family Room, with $100 raised through a garage sale.

"On opening day, in January 1991, the only people who showed up were me, a friend, and our kids," she recalls. But after a television news spot about the Family Room, the mothers and children began to arrive. In a single year, attendance went from two families to two hundred. During the first year of operation, Edelman assumed most of the responsibility for the Family Room herself. With the help of a core group of two dozen parents, she raised money, cleaned, and staffed the center. "It was a labor of love," she says. "Moms who were nurses helped me with infection control. Teachers helped set up the room for learning. A mother with marketing skills helped with publicity."

In the beginning, Edelman thought the Family Room

(open three hours on weekday mornings) would attract mainly lower income families, but people of all incomes were attracted to it. As Edelman learned, most parents who work full-time outside the home use day-care centers or neighborhood child-care providers; ironically, such parents and their young children may be less isolated than at-home moms.

"There's so much isolation among at-home moms. My neighbors are either indoors or work full-time or part-time," she says. "They're not around. We live on a street with something like eighteen kids under the age of ten, but I don't see the mothers."

A few mothers who come to the Family Room work part-time outside the home. Nan Simpson, a mother of children ages two and three works a four-day week as a registered nurse. She brings her kids on her day off.

"It's wonderful being able to talk to other moms about such issues as toilet training or sibling rivalry. You can read about these challenges in magazines or books, but somehow it's different when another parent tells you you're going to survive." She laughs. "I also find that taking the kids to the Family Room helps keep the house clean on those days when I can't bear the idea of picking it up again."

Eleanor Pauly, seventy, brings her grandson, Blaine, to the Family Room. "Renee has only a couple of rules," she says. "A mom, dad, or grandparent must be there at all times. You're required to supervise your own child." She adds, "Blaine tends to think of himself as an adult. This little mite walks into a restaurant like a statesman. So he needs to be with other kids. At the Family Room, instead of hanging on so tightly to his toys, he'll go over to the toy box, get a rattle out, and put it gently into a baby's hand."

Interestingly, Pauly doesn't romanticize the "good old days" of neighborhood coffee klatches and park bench parenting discussions. "When I was raising my children, it was safer. But as a young mother, I wish I'd had a Family Room to go to. Kids found it easier to find someone to play with back then, but the parents weren't necessarily very sociable. You said good morning or good evening to your neighbor but you didn't get too chummy. And ethnic divisions often kept parents apart. A family center would have been good for us then; it would have brought us together."

What about fathers? "A few fathers bring their children to the Family Room," reports Edelman. "The dads tend to hang back a little bit, at least in the beginning. They need this kind of community, too." She hopes to extend the Family Room's hours to the early evening, to attract more fathers, and career moms as well.

Edelman offers these tips for how to start a family play center in your community:

- Contact your community's park, recreation, or youth department; tell them about your idea. They'll have more clout with local government than you will as a private citizen, but if they're not enthusiastic, don't worry. You can always try again once your play group gains numbers.
- Start your family center or play group wherever you can find donated space: a home, classroom, or library.
- Find out what your liability is if a child or parent is injured. Ask liability experts from your city or town to

review the room. If necessary, buy extra insurance.

- Establish a few clear rules. Remind parents repetitively, verbally, and in writing, not to bring sick kids to play and that they cannot leave their child at any time.
- Document your program: keep the names, addresses, and phone numbers of all involved parents and children.
- Raise money through garage sales or bake sales. Contact local charitable organizations in your area for donations. Send a press release to your local paper announcing that you're collecting used toys that are in good condition. Offer a thank you letter that can be used as a receipt by donors.
- Publicize, publicize, publicize.

Edelman also suggests that parents who want to create family and play centers find an ally in business or government. She found hers in Peggy Santillo, a new town council member. Santillo helped persuade the council to assume more responsibility for the Family Room. The center will now be run by a board of directors made up of representatives of Amherst's youth and recreation departments and participating parents, including Edelman. Membership, once free, will cost $20 a year.

As Edelman's experience illustrates, parents can help reshape the communities in which their children are growing up, and a single project can be a seed for wider change. As a result of her success, interest in family play areas has mushroomed in Amherst.

"We're now planning community cleanups for the parks and family concerts in the neighborhoods," says Santillo. "Creating and supporting public play areas is especially important during hard economic times because so many families can't afford vacations."

In September, the Amherst city council presented Edelman with a special award for creating the Family Room.

"Sometimes," says Edelman, "a mom can move a mountain."

16. Network with Neighbors to Reduce Parent Isolation.

- START A SUPPORT GROUP FOR PARENTS.

One San Diego mother, Michelle Powell, writes, "My biggest help has been finding the Las Madres support group for moms and babies. We get together at different homes once a week to talk, laugh, and let our infants and toddlers enjoy one another. We all look forward to sharing the latest story of our child's progress (or lack of it!)"

- ORGANIZE A PLAY GROUP FOR YOUNG CHILDREN.

Pat Girardi, an officer in the Parents League in New York, tells this story. "A mother in one of our toddler workshops signed up with a play group in her building, with other moms with children the same age. The group meets in the night time because all the parents are working parents. It was put together by the *doorman* in her building." She laughed with pleasure. "Each parent had asked him if he knew of other parents with young children, and he got everyone together."

- CREATE A NEIGHBORHOOD RESPITE-CARE CO-OP.

Parents can offer respite-care to neighbors, for their children, teens, or dependent elderly. Every family needs a break for an evening or a weekend.

- CREATE A NEIGHBORHOOD BARTERING CLUB.

Rely on neighbors for help with home-improvement projects, day care, transportation, and the like. Set up a system where individuals can trade services, such as one hour of gardening for one hour of baby-sitting.

SEVEN STEPS YOU CAN TAKE TO BUILD COMMUNITY CONNECTIONS

- explore existing groups.
- recognize that it's okay to start small.
- establish a regular time for getting together.
- occasionally plan something a little different.
- don't leave out non-parents and singles.
- be there for the people in your community or circle of friends.

> • work together on a project to benefit the community.
>
> —Source: "The Parent to Parent Connection" by Carol Copple, Ph.D. and Shanta Swezy. *Sesame Street Parent's Guide*, October 1992

17. Special Neighborhood Projects That Kids Can Do.

Kids in Action, a volunteer service program for elementary school children, was created in September 1990 at Mt. Washington Elementary in Baltimore City. As Silvia Golombek, director of the program, says, "Children are traditionally perceived as incomplete human beings (but) we know that children even younger than ten are aware through the media and through their personal experience of what needs to improve in their school and neighborhood and who needs help." Kids in Action's purpose is to turn their concerns into educational activities that allow them to overcome a sense of powerlessness, and to feel that they are valued members of their community, that they too can be "the givers" of care and not always passive recipients. Kids who participate in their community in this way show increased autonomy, motivation, and self-esteem. Examples of Kids in Action projects, appropriate for five to ten-year-olds, include:

- holding a story hour at a local bookstore or public library (eight to ten-year-olds read stories to preschoolers);
- making holiday decorations and baking cupcakes for a nursing home;

- organizing a school cleanup;
- working in a neighborhood park;
- food and clothing drives in their schools;
- decorating pots and planting seedlings as gifts for nursing home residents;
- making and sending get-well cards for sick children;
- brightening up a school wall with a mural;
- setting up a recycling program in the school;
- making peanut butter and jelly sandwiches for a soup kitchen;
- holding a sing-along, playing games or watching a movie together with nursing home residents or children in a hospital;
- making toys (puzzles, mobiles) for homeless children;
- writing their own stories and illustrating them to read to other children in a public library;
- assisting at a conference registration desk (checking off participants' names and giving out materials);
- assisting in parent-teacher association projects;
- caring for younger children at parent-teacher association meetings.

18. Encourage Learning in the Neighborhood.

- ### CREATE A NEIGHBORHOOD STUDY CENTER.

A local recreation center, YMCA, or library can serve as an area where kids can gather to do their homework, use resource materials, and have access to tutors. Parents can also take turns hosting the homework center in their homes for one or two hours in the evening. Neighbors can donate resource materials to be kept in a cart that moves from home to home.

- SWAP SKILLS AND TALENTS AMONG PARENTS AND KIDS.

Adults with woodshops can teach other adults and children old enough to handle tools how to build a bookshelf or make home repairs. Kids learning a language (Spanish) in school can teach phrases to neighbors. Someone who makes a great pie crust or bakes bread can offer a free cooking class.

- OFFER TO TEACH A REGULARLY SCHEDULED CLASS.

Lori Berger of Poway, California, teaches a weekly calligraphy class for ages eight to eighty-eight in her home. "Calligraphy is often easier for young people who haven't become as established and rigid in their handwriting, so there's a unique equality in the class, with older students taking tips from and admiring the work of the young."

19. Commemorate Major Neighborhood Events.

- HANG BALLOONS, BANNERS WHEN BABIES ARE BORN, ON BIRTHDAYS, AND SPECIAL DAYS.

Computer savvy kids can create and print out long signs to hang from the front of the house or garage, stating the new baby's name, weight, and length, or announcing the birthday person's age.

- RECOGNIZE DEATHS AND OTHER SAD OCCURRENCES AS WELL.

Rasa Gustaitis of the Pacific News Service wrote of a tragic accident in her neighborhood, when a ninety-one-year-old man died from a heart attack while driving his Cadillac, which struck two other cars, killing a woman and two children. The police quickly cleared the accident scene; by the following morning there was no sign that anything had occurred, except in the memories of the neighbors along the street. Gradually and spontaneously, neighbors began cutting flowers from their yards and tying bouquets to a stop sign where the accident had occurred. By afternoon, dozens of bouquets of asters, lilies, dahlias, and roses were piled by the sign. Someone tied a teddy bear to the pole with yellow police blockade tape. By evening, a whole row of candles had been lit at the foot of the sign.

Gustaitis wrote: "Looking out the front window, my daughter called out 'Look, it's a shrine!' The moon was almost full and the street was bathed in blue light. A woman in a long black skirt with a black shawl was standing, her hands folded, beside the flickering candles and the mound of flowers. A new picture had superimposed itself on the afterimage of the accident."

20. Make Your Neighborhood Teen-friendly.

- ACT AS A ROLE MODEL FOR FUTURE PARENTS.

Enlist the aid of neighborhood teenagers not just as baby-sitters, but also as helpers when you're home. As they help with the kids and do household chores they'll get invaluable exposure to the responsibilities of parents.

- HELP TEENS FORM A BABY-SITTERS CO-OP OR CLUB.

Neighborhood teens can compile a list of phone numbers for baby-sitters in your neighborhood. As a group they could standardize their rates, take classes in child care and safety, and rely on each other for advice and help.

The Baby-sitters Club series of young adult novels, published by Scholastic Books, has been an inspiration for over 1,000 baby-sitter groups nationwide. The series includes fifty paperback novels portraying real-life baby-sitting scenarios mixed in with other issues of importance to teens. Over sixty million books have been sold, and the author, Ann M. Martin, receives over 14,000 fan letters a year.

Though the baby-sitter clubs sprouting up all over the country follow no uniform program, most hold frequent meetings to talk about both books and baby-sitting. Some clubs hand out flyers and business cards to prospective parent-employers; some keep files on the families they work with so new sitters know what they're getting into. Often the sitters have taken baby-sitting classes offered by the Red Cross, local hospitals, or other agencies.

As a rule, parents are big fans of the clubs, since they know they have access to a reliable pool of sitters who have a built-in support system and extensive knowledge about caring for kids.

- CREATE A BAND PRACTICE ROOM.

Designate a soundproofed room at a neighborhood community center, or create one in a neighbor's garage, where budding musicians can play their guitars, keyboards, and drums without disturbing the neighbors. "And none of this closing up at 9 P.M. either," says Joan Bradley. "The room should be open at least until midnight. It should be available all night to kids over eighteen years who want to practice at night."

21. Establish a Neighborhood Association.

In the eighties, a majority of Americans believed that the best government was the least government; in the nineties, we may come to believe that the best government is the closest government—the one right around the corner. Political power is growing in the neighborhoods, often at the expense of larger-scale local governments. David Pijawka, Associate Professor of environmental geography at Arizona State University, studied neighborhood organizations in Phoenix. He found that over 90 percent have acted in some way to redress whatever it is that they consider their main problem. Half of the residents have made calls to their councilmen. While one study does not make a paradigm shift, a fundamental change in the way we live could be coming, a reversal of the trend toward regional or trans-regional living in which politically powerless families spend their days spread all over the place. "People are going to be taking the best of what we had in the sixties and forming new structures, a new system in which the neighborhoods become increasingly powerful," says Pijawka.

• HOLD PERIODIC NEIGHBORHOOD MEETINGS.

Condominiums and other private communities hold regular homeowner's association meetings; other neighborhoods can do the same. The regularity of these meetings will likely be determined by both the commitment of the neighbors and the number of problems the community faces. Use initial meetings as getting-to-know-you gatherings, allotting time for formal discussion of neighborhood issues. Even if there are no tangible problems, continue meeting to find ways to make your neighborhood even better. Choose one person, on a rotating basis, as the organizer and facilitator for neighborhood meetings. Use guest speakers only if they have specific skills to teach.

Topics for neighborhood meetings could include:

· How child-friendly is your neighborhood?
· Neighborhood Watch programs
· Mediation as a tool for solving problems between neighbors
· Empowerment and assertiveness techniques for dealing with outside authorities

- Q&A with city council members for your area
- Sharing information on services/programs available for kids

• ELECT A NEIGHBORHOOD COORDINATOR.

The Neighborhood Coordinator would act as a liaison with the larger community, including the school district, police department, planning department, health-care organizations.

• START A NEIGHBORHOOD NEWSLETTER.

In David Pijawka's survey of 105 Phoenix neighborhoods, 65 percent had newsletters. That's an astounding figure. Ten years ago, only a few of the neighborhoods would have had newsletters. The popularity of neighborhood newsletters suggests the power of desktop publishing and people's eagerness to create community. The newsletter could be just one page, announcing births, deaths, birthdays, and the like, or as involved as the volunteer putting it together wishes to make it. The newsletter should be as much of a community project as possible, with children submitting articles and receiving recognition for accomplishments. Include a bulletin board page with notices of items for sale or trade, upcoming classes and parties, services needed, tips on family discounts and specials run by local businesses. A neighborhood retiree could attend city council meetings and report on news affecting the neighborhood.

PHOENIX: RETURN OF THE FAMILY-FRIENDLY NEIGHBORHOOD

When David Pijawka set out to study Phoenix's neighborhoods, he believed the conventional academic wisdom that neighborhoods are dead—particularly in new, sprawling Phoenix, which until recently didn't really have many real neighborhoods. Over the past year, Pijawka and his students at Arizona State University asked Phoenicians to identify their neighborhoods and tell what they valued about them.

Here's what the Phoenix study revealed:

New neighborhoods are springing up right and left. The most common reason that new neighborhoods and neighborhood organizations emerge is to combat unwanted development. The second most important reason is to control crime.

The most surprising finding, according to Pijawka, was how highly people ranked the importance of neighborhoods to their social life. "We really believed that this would come out at the bottom of the list—but it came out surprisingly high," he says. "This wasn't true for all neighborhoods. For example, the residents in a strong old neighborhood didn't really consider a lot of socializing with their neighbors to be all that important. They took for granted the friendliness of their neighborhood."

The hunger for roots was highest in the new neighborhoods where everyone comes from somewhere else.

Over time, as new neighborhoods fight their battles against outside forces, people begin to remember that neighborhoods are also good places to get to know people.

"As we approach the twenty-first century, people are expressing real concern that the urban experience of the sixties and seventies has not worked out, that the cost of regional living on family life is too high, and that somehow we've got to move back to the neighborhood," says Pijawka. "One building block you can start with is the protection of children."

22. Share Housing with Other Families.

• EXPLORE THE COHOUSING OPTION.

This solution is especially workable in an apartment building or condominium. Each family has its own quarters, with common space for dining, day care, and other communal activities. Architects Kathryn McCamant and Charles Durrett, authors of *Cohousing: A Contemporary Approach To Housing Ourselves*, coined the term "cohousing," to describe resident-planned communities centered on a "common house" meeting area where all members can meet, share meals and build a neighborhood. The concept is based on a Danish model called *bofoellesskaber*, or "living communities," that became popular in Denmark in the early 1970s.

With cohousing, future residents are involved in all aspects of the project, from designing the project to working with developers on actual construction. Essentially residents govern the development without outside management. Since 1988, more than eighty cohousing groups have formed around the country. One site is a twenty-six-unit site known as Muir Commons, in the agricultural region in Davis, California, just outside Sacramento. Each adult resident cooks at least one common meal a month and participates on one of almost a dozen committees in the commons. At Muir Commons, children play along the gravel walking paths and use the special children's room in the common house. One of the primary reasons people enjoy cohousing is because of the added security for children.

- TEAM UP WITH OTHER SINGLE PARENTS.

The need to decrease parent isolation is especially crucial for single parents. Findings from Stanford studies indicate that the presence of an additional adult in the household brings adolescent control levels closer to those found in two-parent families. Single mothers who choose television's "Kate and Allie" model, in which two single parents join forces and share the burden, report that housing costs decrease (and the comfort and size of the house usually increases), baby-sitting headaches lessen, and emotional support increases. The Human Investment Project in San Mateo, California, assists people in finding shared housing possibilities; for example, older retired persons whose children have moved away can stay in their large houses by sharing space with single-parent families.

23. Create Community in Condominium and Apartment Complexes.

- IMAGINE NEW USES FOR OLD STRUCTURES.

Surprisingly, a KidsPlace study sponsored by Sacramento, California, showed a preference among sixth graders for apartment living. (Children may view apartment complexes as having a greater sense of community than the empty streets of many suburban neighborhoods.) As an increasing proportion of middle-income families with children can no longer afford to buy detached houses, more families are living in condominiums and townhouses. Many of these condominiums were originally designed for adult play, without children in mind.

Fortunately, it isn't all that difficult to adapt an adult complex for children. Common areas can be planted with hardy trees and furnished with child-size benches; tennis courts can be transformed into playgrounds, or divided into adult and child play spaces; jogging trails can also be used for nature hikes, biking, roller skating, and family walks.

Use the common-area party room for more than wedding receptions and football bashes. If possible, transform it into a recreation room or library/study center and keep it open day and night. If the homeowner's association, building manager, or insurance company protests, arrange to have neighborhood volunteers staff the room when open or use it during prearranged hours for at-home parents' coffee hours, after-school crafts classes, set study halls—make the party room your neighborhood living room.

(Refer to the family-friendly housing checklist on pages 93–94 for more ideas.)

- ORGANIZE CHILDREN AND ADULTS TO IMPROVE PUBLIC HOUSING.

Waiting for the landlord or housing authority to improve conditions seldom works. Instead of waiting, ask authorities to supply materials and the tenants can provide the labor. Let kids design a mural for a lobby wall, and give them a say in the colors and designs used throughout.

In St. Louis, Bertha Gilkey refitted her public housing project, Cochran Gardens, with flower-lined paths and a community center. Gilkey, as Harry C. Boyte reports in *Occasional Papers* (Community Renewal Society), grew up in Cochran Gardens when it was an ugly, fearsome place where shootings, junkies, gangs, graffiti, and tragedy were commonplace. When she was twenty years old, Gilkey was elected head of the tenants' association, and immediately began mobilizing the project's residents. She organized tenants to hold fund-raisers, formed work parties to revitalize vandalized laundry rooms, and eventually completely renovated the high-rise buildings.

"Everybody who lived on a floor was responsible for painting that floor," she told Boyte. "If you didn't paint that floor, it didn't happen. Kids who lived on a floor that hadn't been painted would come and look at the painted hallways and then go back and hassle their parents. The elderly who couldn't paint prepared lunch, so they could feel like they were a part of it too."

They built playgrounds and challenged the local housing authority to provide decent housing for low-income residents.

"Kenilworth-Parkside (public housing development in Washington, D.C.) was once considered a no-man's-land by city services and even the police. When residents were empowered to take over the management of the properties, they quickly set up neighborhood patrols to eliminate drug dealers and initiated numerous programs to address community problems. In an area where drug-related deaths had once averaged one every three weeks, not one has been reported in the past four years. Grass and picket fences have replaced rodent-ridden piles of garbage, and small businesses and a day-care center have been established. Teen pregnancies were reduced by 50 percent, welfare dependency by 60 percent, and crime by 75 percent. An independent audit by an accounting firm indicated that the residents' initiatives in this development would bring $5.2 million in savings to the city over a ten-year period."

—Robert L. Woodson, "Transform Inner Cities from the Grass Roots Up," *The Wall Street Journal*, June 3, 1992.

- HOLD FREQUENT PUBLIC CELEBRATIONS.

Plan a ribbon-cutting ceremony in the newly painted lobby. Schedule award ceremonies when report cards are handed out to encourage improvement in academic performance. Have a monthly potluck birthday party.

- ESTABLISH A CODE OF CONDUCT OR
  RULES OF BEHAVIOR FOR THE BUILDING.

Call a residents' meeting and discuss problems that make life unpleasant. Give children ample opportunity to air their concerns, and consider their need for places to play and to make noise. Keep the rules simple and direct: no fighting, no littering, no graffiti. Respect quiet hours. Post the rules in public spaces. Elect monitors for each floor to enforce the rules; change monitors monthly.

- CHANGE THE BUILDING'S NAME.

Hold a contest to choose a new name that reflects the residents' interests or ethnicity. Have kids design a sign for the front of the building. Hold a ribbon-cutting ceremony when the sign is hung.

- START A BUILDING NEWSLETTER.

Encourage kids to submit drawings, stories, and news reports. Use a letters column to air common concerns.

24. Become a Suburban Guerrilla.

- REFIT YOUR HOUSING TRACT WITH A
  SENSE OF NEIGHBORHOOD.

With the help of several neighbors, do an inventory of your

neighborhood: What physical changes can be made that will improve contact among adults and children?

- CREATE YOUR OWN FRONT PORCH.

Much of our outdoor living takes place in backyards, but front yards are where you see your neighbors and can watch your kids play. Put lawn chairs in the front yard, barbecue out front.

- TEAR DOWN THE FENCES.

In a Berkeley, California, neighborhood residents tore down the backyard fences separating their yards, creating a large open space where children could play and adults socialize.

- DESIGNATE A MESSY SPACE.

Kids need a place where they can dig in the dirt, make mud puddles, and generally get down and dirty. Someone in the neighborhood could offer a less-than-manicured place—a side yard, unused driveway, or even a garage—where kids can build forts and enjoy messy play.

- IF NECESSARY, CHALLENGE THE COVENANTS, CODES AND RESTRICTIONS (CC&Rs).

The theory of these strict CC&Rs—which control any physical changes in most new housing developments—is to protect property values. From whom? Too often these rules, established originally by developers, maintain sterility and prevent natural changes. With the help of a neighborhood lawyer, such rules can be bent in favor of children.

A SUBURBAN GUERRILLA IN THE STUCCO WASTELAND

As a distant thunderstorm looms over the Southern California hills and the sun begins to fade in the sky, neighbors wander up to Suzanne Thompson's front lawn and sit down in her family's new courtyard, furnished with several Adirondack chairs and surrounded by a low wall of river rock.

With no particular preamble, the neighbors just start talking, while their children sit on the wall listening to their parents tease each other.

What prompted Thompson to rip up her front lawn and put in a concrete patio? "I was sick and tired of the loneliness," she says. The Thompson family lives in Poway, California, a suburban enclave forty minutes outside San Diego. Stucco homes dot the landscape. "Some days, I'd come home and the only sign of life was when the automatic lawn sprinklers turned themselves on," says the thirty-nine-year-old mother.

Instead of surrendering to the loneliness, Thompson and her neighbors vowed to refit their block. "The most obvious reason that parents weren't getting to know each other was that there was no natural place for us to meet," she says. With her neighbors' approval, she hired a contractor and designed the fifteen-by-fifteen courtyard.

She built it, and the parents came.

Like Thompson, many of us grew up in neighborhoods where parents and kids got together naturally. Backyard barbecues, front-porch discussions, sharing garden tools, and "borrowing" eggs—these were some of the everyday encounters that brought neighbors together. In an era when so many grandparents and other members of the extended family live hundreds of miles away, the emotional and physical support that parents and children receive from neighbors is more important than ever.

Somehow, though, that easy sense of community has slipped away from many neighborhoods. This is particularly harmful to children; too many of them grow up not knowing many adults in their neighborhoods—or even, sometimes, any other children on their blocks.

If, however, you think you're powerless to create new social connections, consider what Suzanne Thompson's neighbors—now friends—say about her new courtyard.

"If someone's already here in the courtyard, you tend to come over and talk," says Jacky Jordan, a soft-spoken mom sitting in one of the Adirondack chairs.

"We don't get much exercise anymore," grins Betty Plunkett, thirty-six, mother of two. "Instead of walking the dog, we sit out here talking."

These easy, informal gatherings were exactly what Thompson, who sells playground equipment part-time, and her husband Dick, a Presbyterian minister, had in mind when they built the courtyard. Being a good neighbor, they believe, doesn't mean that you have to be a close friend. It just means being able to touch base, to get acquainted, to feel comfortable asking for the kind of help that only a neighbor can give.

The parents point out that it's not just the courtyard that's brought the neighborhood together. "Suzanne has inspired us," says Ione Guiffrida, the parent of a two-year-old. "We've started a play group." The neighbors also baby-sit for each other.

The impact of Thompson's efforts on behalf of her neighborhood runs deeper than play groups and baby-sitting networks. "One of my jobs as a police officer is to talk to neighborhoods about crime prevention," says Fred Wilson. "In so many neighborhoods I visit, I see the 'airlock' phenomenon. People come home, click the automatic garage door opener, and *whoosh*, they're gone until the next morning, when they leave to fight the traffic again.

"I tell other neighborhood groups what we've done. We're like the old neighborhoods where people sat out on their porches in the evening, watching their kids play, aware of any strangers coming through. There's no one way to build a safe community. You have to get to know your neighbors one house at a time."

"How can you trade this in?" asks Plunkett. "Our neighbors are there for us, even in an emergency. One day I was alone with my toddler and came down with a 104-degree fever. I was delirious. I'm not sure what would have happened if Jacky hadn't turned up at my door."

Sitting on the rock wall, two of the neighborhood boys offer their testimonials. Bugabug (also known here as the future President of the United States) describes how he and his friends sometimes help neighbors with their yard work, for free.

Why?

He shrugs. "I dunno. We like 'em?" And Scott Wilson, the policeman's thirteen-year-old son, says, "I figure by the time I get married my parents will move to a condo.

I wouldn't mind it to come back here and take over the old house and raise my kids in this neighborhood."

25. Demand Child-friendly Housing.

• INSIST THAT NEW DEVELOPMENTS BE
FAMILY-FRIENDLY.

Here are what most developers consider marketable amenities in new communities: a view of the eighteenth fairway, open space managed by someone else, security systems, trash compactors, ceramic tile entries, miniaturized fireplaces, cathedral ceilings, wet bars, and three-car garages. Recently, some developers have begun to build and market neighborhoods with front porches and sidewalks—they're returning to the nineteenth-century grid pattern and older theories of defensible space. As additions to a new housing tract, these are no more expensive than wet bars and three-car garages. But as families begin to realize the effect that neighborhood design can have on their children, the market may well change.

• FEATURES TO REQUEST
FROM DEVELOPERS.

· Wide sidewalks throughout the development, linking it with other nearby neighborhoods.
· Open spaces for play.

- Streets designed to keep traffic down by limiting straight stretches and creating speed barriers and bumps to discourage speeding; routing through traffic around periphery of the neighborhood; creating cul-de-sacs.

The new neighborhoods that we shape eventually shape our children; so, what if new development required a children's environmental impact report? Developers should evaluate the impact of the new development on children before construction begins.

- ENCOURAGE DEVELOPERS TO PROVIDE OPEN SPACE FOR KIDS TO PLAY AND EXPLORE.

Some places may have prefab play areas, but designating some corner with a sand box or a flat, green park area (often underused) as a play area is not enough.

Children need private spaces for themselves. They need to be able to build tree houses, forts, clubhouses in woods and fields away from public view according to Clare Cooper Marcus and Wendy Sarkissian, in *Housing As If People Mattered* (Berkeley: University of California Press, 1986). They need to be able to wander over to a friend's house without a formal invitation to play. To gain a sense of independence, they need to be able to travel safely farther and farther from home. Wild or leftover spaces, more attractive and useful to children than any play sculpture or swing, should be preserved, prior to development, and incorporated into new neighborhoods. Some housing developments in Denmark include "play woods" adjoining traditionally equipped play spaces; some Dutch landscape planners plant urban woods ahead of construction, so that the woods are ready for use when families move in.

> "We cannot buy off our children by merely providing playgrounds. Children are more deeply affected by the environment than any other age group. . . . Children learn from the environment what society values. . . . If a housing environment implies that kids are low-priority users, they will decode the message as 'we do not count.' . . . Three principal factors render an environment suitable for child rearing: (1) direct access to private open space for easily supervised outdoor play by small children, (2) direct, safe access to an area for communal outdoor play for school-age and older children, and (3) reasonable auditory and visual privacy so that children's daytime noise and prying eyes or infants' nighttime cries do not disturb the neighbors."
>
> —Clare Cooper Marcus and Wendy Sarkissian, *Housing As If People Mattered*

- WORK WITH DEVELOPERS TO PROVIDE FAMILY AMENITIES.

When asked, parents offer an array of suggestions, some banal, some fresh and creative, about how pro-family communities could be designed, and the services they could offer.

A Sacramento study asked parents who were members of homeowners' associations to list the housing service they would most want. The answers suggest some profitable marketing items to developers, as well as some possibilities for community associations and other neighborhood groups in existing communities.

Their preferences, in order, were:

- Security features.
- On-site manager who can give assistance to children.
- Recreation center for children and adults.
- On-site children's playground (supervised).
- Pay-as-used on-site day-care center.
- Pay-as-used dining room for prepared evening meals.
- Pay-as-used baby-sitting service for sick child care.

The flexible "pay-as-used" approach could relieve a great deal of stress on families now pushed by so many inflexible schedules—day care's, school's, the workplace's.

Use This Checklist When Choosing a Family-friendly Place to Live.

☐ Does the neighborhood or development allow pets?

☐ Is the assigned parking located near your front or back door?

☐ Are parking areas in courts with no through-traffic hazards?

☐ Is there a full playground with an adjacent grassy area?

☐ Are pool areas fenced safely?

☐ Is there a laundry facility?

☐ Are public grounds kept clean and hazard free?

☐ Are front doors and windows in plain view as a deterrent to burglary and other crimes?

☐ Is there access to open space for easily supervised play by small children?

☐ Is there access for children to natural fields or woods?

☐ Is there good insulation so kids playing and babies crying do not disturb neighbors?

☐ Are facilities for kids such as recreation centers, YMCAs, libraries, parks nearby?

☐ Are small neighborhood businesses accessible and amenable to kids—ice-cream parlors, five-and-dimes, office and school supply store, video parlor, fast-food or mom and pop restaurants?

☐ Is there a mixture of ages (older adults, childless couples, different-aged kids)?

☐ Is there something that passes for a village square—a place where kids and adults hang out and mingle?

☐ Is there a neighborhood association or group with a family-friendly focus?

☐ Are there informal parent groups, baby-sitting co-ops, etc.?

☐ And are there good schools that emphasize parent and community involvement?

MARKET YOUR FAMILY-FRIENDLY NEIGHBORHOOD

Gabriel Works, of Grand Rapids, Michigan, does not have children of her own, but like many non-parents, she is determined to make her neighborhood family-friendly.

She's a small, soft-spoken woman who wears granny glasses. When she speaks, however, you suddenly think of a description of Mikhail Gorbachev: nice smile, teeth of iron.

When drug dealers began to set up crack houses in Cherry Hill, a neighborhood of stately Victorian homes, Works and her neighbors decided not to run. Instead, they became, in effect, real estate agents, marketing abandoned or run-down houses, but more importantly, marketing themselves.

"We knew the neighborhood was marginal when we moved here," says Works, thirty-six, president of the Cherry Hill Revitalization Project. "But then one evening six of us were assaulted on the street by drugged-out men who didn't like our looks. We were surrounded by thirty youths and beaten." Her husband's cornea was badly scratched, and he had to get sixteen facial stitches. "The drug dealers were protecting their turf. It was time for us to protect ours."

A core group of twenty neighbors met to assess their assets and liabilities. The market value of these turn-of-the-century homes on wide, tree-lined streets averaged only $30,000; some houses were available for $2,000 in back taxes. Many houses were owned by absentee land-lords. "We decided that getting the city to enforce housing codes wasn't enough," says Works. "Often, the property owners who would evict drug dealers would turn around and rent to someone else in the drug business."

The key to the neighborhood's future wasn't code enforcement, but community—and owner-occupancy.

The neighborhood association's first step was to inform the landlords that they were expected to provide good neighbors as tenants. "We didn't threaten anyone," says Works, smiling pleasantly. "It was just an active campaign of polite harassment." When renters had a noisy fight at midnight, for example, members of the neighborhood association would call the landlord at home and inform him of the situation. "We tell the landlord that if we're awake because of his tenants, he should be awake because of his tenants. We believe it's our duty to keep landlords informed."

The Cherry Hill group collected police reports on the houses and sent copies to the absentee landlords and to city officials. If landlords failed to evict drug dealers, the association asked the police to employ a Grand Rapids ordinance that says, in effect, that a landlord doesn't have a right to profit from his tenants' illegal activities. The ordinance gives the police the right to padlock a known drug house for up to eighteen months.

Works and her Cherry Hill gang identified 40 houses (out of 120 homes in the neighborhood) that owners were willing to sell.

The association then staged home ownership and renovation workshops, open to the public. According to the promotional material, the Cherry Hill association was "looking for energetic, committed people, looking for a diverse neighborhood where they are not just the person next door; people who are willing to invest more sweat equity than money; dedicated people who will (work) with us to get problems to go away and stay away."

To prospective buyers, the group boasted of its neighborhood empowerment projects, including picnics, preservation workshops, neighborhood cleanup days and garden projects, a revived neighborhood store, and the neighborhood partnership with police. New owners were met by a welcoming committee, which, like barn raisers of the past, spent weekends helping rehabilitate the new neighbor's house. In addition, the Cherry Hill association helped prospective buyers arrange financing and wade through the paperwork of buying a home.

The group is determined to keep Cherry Hill's multicultural mix, which, says Works, "is one of the reasons we moved here."

"We've been honest about our neighborhood's problems," she says. "But we tell people that we're determined to stay, that this is a wonderful opportunity and that we want good people to join us."

The result: So far, fifteen of the forty homes have been sold to people willing to invest in the neighborhood, to bring it back from the brink.

NEIGHBORHOOD RESOURCES

American Red Cross
Consult the chapter in your area. Many offer baby-sitting classes covering child development, child care, child safety, accident prevention, and first-aid.

Boys and Girls Clubs of America
Offer after-school programs for latchkey-aged children. Consult clubs in your area or the national office, 771 First Avenue, New York, NY, 10017.

Maryland Student Service Alliance
Maryland is the first state in the country to require all high school students to do volunteer service, including mentoring, tutoring, working in nursing homes, cleaning up streets, and so forth. Offers a model curriculum to interested schools and states or organizations that wish to pursue similar legislation. Kathleen Kennedy Townsend, executive director. Maryland Student Service Alliance, c/o Maryland State Department of Education, 200 West Baltimore Street, Baltimore, MD, 21201; (410) 333-2427.

The Neighborhood Salon Association
A not-for-profit community service of the *Utne Reader*, designed to encourage the establishment and continuation of salons. c/o *Utne Reader*, 1624 Harmon Place, Minneapolis, MN, 55403.

The Neighborhood Works
Newsletter addresses urban problems, lists many resources

($25 year/6 issues). Center for Neighborhood Technology, 2125 W North Avenue, Chicago, IL, 60657.

Project Public Life

Publishes a quarterly newsletter *Public Life* ($15/year) and *The Citizen Politics Study Circle Guide* ($5), designed to help people of all ages learn the skills of citizen politics. Humphrey Institute, University of Minnesota, 301 19th Avenue S, Minneapolis, MN, 55455; (612) 625-0142.

Community Renewal Society

Publishes *Occasional Papers*, three issues a year (subscriptions $7.50/year). 332 S Michigan Avenue, Chicago, IL, 60604; (312) 427-4830.

Books

Babysitters Club, Ann M. Martin. Scholastic Books, 1987–92.
Backyard Adventure, Paula Brook. Old Saybrook, CT: Globe Pequot Press, 1990. 192 pp.
Cohousing: A Contemporary Approach to Housing Ourselves, Kathryn McCamant and Charles Durrett. Berkeley: Habitat Press, 1988. 208 pp. $19.95.
The Great Good Place: Cafes, coffee shops, community centers, beauty parlors, general stores, bars, hangouts, and how they get you through the day, Ray Oldenburg. New York: Paragon House, 1989. 338 pp. $14.95.
Housing As If People Mattered, Clare Cooper Marcus and Wendy Sarkissian. Berkeley: University of California Press, 1986. 324 pp. Site design guidelines for medium-density family housing.

YOUR IDEAS FOR YOUR
NEIGHBORHOOD

_____

_____

_____

_____

_____

_____

_____

_____

_____

_____

_____

_____

_____

_____

_____

_____

_____

_____

_____

_____

_____

_____

_____

_____

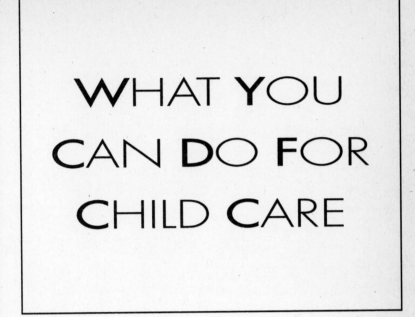

WHAT YOU CAN DO FOR CHILD CARE

Parents are often profoundly ambivalent about their child-care arrangements. The degree of parent anxiety is determined by several factors: how far the facility is from the home and workplace; the teacher-child ratio and general cleanliness of the provider; the parents' and child's relationship with the teacher; and the amount of parent involvement that the provider allows or encourages.

Professionals in this field still do not agree about what constitutes quality day care, but one factor does seem to stand out: parent involvement.

Some of the best child-care facilities are becoming family centers. These centers are sometimes co-operative facilities that require parents to volunteer a few hours each month. Minimally, they encourage parent interaction. "In the morning, when the parents come, some of them will be late to work because they're standing and touching base," one child-care worker says. "Or you get two or three moms that are all pregnant and they stand there and talk. We have parent orientation every year, and the parents discuss common problems—biting, whatever." The new family centers could also offer day-care services for elderly family members, while involving them, too, in the nurturing and loving of the newest generation. In these centers, the presence of parents and grandparents would improve the adult-to-child ratio and decrease parent and child isolation. The development of such centers could, indeed, fill part of the gap left by the disappearance of the old neighborhood structure.

In addition to more familiar kinds of child care, some

creative parents are developing such community-building approaches as the in-home neighborhood child-care co-operative.

(Note: Family day-care provides care for up to twelve children in a home setting. Child-care centers provide care by teachers and aides in a nonresidential setting; these centers require more licensing and permits than the smaller family based child-care homes. Most of the following suggestions are appropriate for child-care centers, but some can be useful for family day-care providers.)

FACTS ABOUT CHILD CARE

- American families' child-care costs rose sharply in the eighties, jumping an average of 35 percent from 1984 to 1988. The average child-care cost per U.S. family in 1984 was $40 a week; in 1988 it was $54 a week. Only about $5.50 of the $14 increase was due to inflation.
- Child-care costs in the Northeast are the highest in the nation. Costs in that region are $64 weekly, $10 more than the national average. The South is the lowest: $50 a week.
- Families with employed women spent $21 billion on child care in 1988.
- Poor women pay a higher portion of their income for child care than do other mothers.
- Fifty-seven percent of kids under fifteen have working mothers, up from 50 percent in 1984.
- Mothers with grade-school children work an average of nearly thirty-five hours a week.

- Fewer grandparents, aunts, and cousins are providing child care, possibly due to more female members of the extended families being in the workforce.
- Since 1977, care of children by relatives (excluding fathers) in the relatives' homes fell from 18 percent of all child-care arrangements to 13 percent in 1988. The proportion of children cared for by relatives in the child's home also dropped.
- Married mothers lose time from work five times as often as fathers do when child-care problems arise.

—Source: a 1992 study by the Bureau of the Census, reported by Murray Dubin, Knight-Ridder News Service

26. Involve Parents and Other Family Members in the Child-care Center.

Child-care centers can become family centers, where children spend time while parents are at work, but which include parents and other family members as much as possible in the daily operations, the events, the teaching. Family centers can offer classes for parents, meeting places for parent groups, social activities for families.

"I came here from England. My family is 3,000 miles away. Day care really did give us a sort of extended family. When we were trying to make a decision as to whether to enter our daughter into public school this year, it was the day-care teachers to whom I turned for advice, and they gave this advice to me in a way that was very loving and yet dispassionate."

—a mom in Swarthmore, Pennsylvania, quoted in *Childhood's Future*

- SCHEDULE MANDATORY OR VOLUNTARY PARENT PARTICIPATION DAYS.

Some co-operative child-care centers and preschools require parent involvement, such as one morning a month where a parent serves as a teacher's aide, and helps with other activities in support of the school. In exchange, parents are offered lower fees. As a traditional day-care center becomes co-operative, the transition can be uncomfortable for some caregivers worried about parent "meddling." In the long run, however, such a system is beneficial to children, parents and care providers— lessening the sense of isolation of each. This may also encourage parents to be similarly involved in their children's schools. If parents are unable to co-op directly, extend the requirement to include grandparents or other involved relatives.

Co-operative child care is also a good way to involve fathers in child care.

- PARENTS SHOULD DROP IN WHENEVER THEY CAN.

Unscheduled visits from parents can be disruptive, but are necessary for the parents' and children's sense of trust. Parents can't expect providers to be available for long, impromptu discussions. Visiting parents should also allow their children to continue with activities in which they are already involved. But when a parent visits, it can offer all parties more peace of mind. Some states, including California, require day-care centers to allow parents to drop in without advance notice and without discrimination or retaliation by the day-care center. But by one estimate, fewer than 1 percent of parents take advantage of this right. Even though state law requires parents to be informed of their visitation rights, parents aren't fully aware of them or of how important they are. Also, some day-care facilities subtly discourage parents from visiting. Considering the shortage of quality day care, many parents don't want to risk offending the providers. But the most important reason more parents don't police their children's day care is because they can't get time off work.

- ENCOURAGE GOVERNMENT OR WORKPLACES TO ADOPT A FAMILY TIES PROGRAM.

Businesses should give employees up to four hours off each month to visit child-care facilities, thereby releasing an army of day-care inspectors—called parents. (See "What You Can Do in Your Workplace.")

- SET ASIDE A CALM ROOM (OR CORNER) FOR PARENTS.

Some parents say that their primary contact with other parents is through their child's day care. "But it takes effort to make contact with the other parents," says one mother. "There needs to be a mechanism at the day care that encourages parents to stay a few moments and visit with other parents. Sometimes I think we should have our own time-out room to deaccelerate from work, drink a cup of tea, talk with other parents, before we rush our kids home to dinner and the bathtub."

Centers may not have extra space for parents, but can designate a corner of a playroom or a picnic table as the parents' meeting spot. Include some comfortable chairs and a bulletin board for networking information. Keep a coffee pot by the parents' corner so parents can have a cup of coffee with other parents before work. Encourage parents to visit with each other.

- INVITE PARENTS TO DROP BY
  FOR LUNCH.

Parents can brown-bag their lunches and visit with their children during lunch breaks from work.

- WRITE UP FREQUENT ACTIVITY
  REPORTS FOR PARENTS.

Both parents and children benefit from written reports prepared by caregivers. Such reports can simply be handwritten notes stating the activities the child was involved in, the kind of meals and snacks he or she ate, and how well they rested during nap time. Some centers use colored construction paper notebooks; others have mimeographed forms they fill out each day. By adding little individualized tidbits about each child, caregivers help parents stay in touch with their children's progress and activities.

- OFFER PERIODIC PARENTING WORKSHOPS.

Bring parents together on a formal basis to discuss a particular aspect of parenting, such as preparing for kindergarten. Use "expert" speakers only when they have practical, useful advice. Encourage parents to turn to each other for parenting support.

- SCHEDULE FREQUENT FAMILY POTLUCKS, PICNICS, AND PARTIES.

Family gatherings need not be complicated. Schedule one night a week or month when families are invited to bring their take-out dinner to the center, or pop their instant meals into the center's microwave. Potlucks can even occur on weeknights, with parents preparing their contribution the night before. Hold Family Fun nights at local ice skating rinks, pizza parlors, beaches, and parks.

- ASK FAMILIES TO HELP WITH BUILDING AND MAINTENANCE PROJECTS.

Child-care centers are typically short on space and in constant need of remodeling, painting, and refurbishing. If you have an idea for a new piece of playground equipment, or new organization for classrooms, talk with families—they may have the skills and materials you need.

- SCHEDULE PLAY GROUPS FOR PARENTS WITH INFANTS.

Parents who already have children in the center and are isolated at home with new infants can meet at the day-care center one day a week to visit and play. The center's staff members can become familiar with babies who will soon be in their care, and parents can network with other parents.

27. Provide Children with a Sense of Community Within the Center.

Many children spend more of their week days at day-care centers than at home. The center, in a sense, becomes their neighborhood. Parents, grandparents, and others can help expand that sense of neighborhood.

- MAKE T-SHIRTS WITH THE CENTER'S LOGO ON THEM.

Children can use fabric paints to color inside the lines of t-shirts printed with the center's name or logo. Wear the shirts on outings; this can be a great way to help keep track of wanderers, and can give kids a sense of belonging with the group. Make the logo an identifiable sight in the neighborhood; plaster it on decals, bumperstickers, and the like.

- TAKE KIDS TO THE LIBRARY.

They may be too young to check out books, but can attend story hours or look at picture books in the library. This is a particularly good idea if your library recruits seniors as reading partners.

- GIVE CHILDREN DREAMTIME: CREATE DREAM CORNERS.

Our drive to educate even our youngest children sometimes robs them of the most precious attributes of childhood, including opportunities to imagine, create, and dream. Set aside a corner of the room for dreaming: furnish it with big pillows, a book case, a blanket.

28. Link the Child-care Facility to the Neighborhood and the Larger Community.

- USE THE CENTER FOR VOTING.

Election day is a great time to welcome your neighbors into the center, though it may be a confusing and busy day. You'll make lots of new friends for the center, and may discover there is a ready and willing pool of volunteers in your neighborhood.

- ENLIST TEENAGERS TO WORK OR
  VOLUNTEER IN CHILD-CARE CENTERS.

Give teens the opportunity to work with younger kids, gain parenting skills, have something worthwhile to do after school. Boys in particular could gain from experience.

- TEAM UP WITH A NEIGHBORHOOD
  SENIOR CENTER.

Ask seniors to help at the center, giving the one-on-one attention kids always need. Take children to visit the seniors for lunch one day a month.

- INVOLVE CHILDREN IN A COMMUNITY
  OUTREACH PROJECT.

Even young children can begin learning about volunteering and good citizenship. Have them organize a play, skit, or musical performance and take their show on the road to nearby hospitals and senior centers. Older children can raise funds through recycling, bake sales, and car wash, and donate the money to a nearby program for the homeless. Have kids brainstorm about ways they can help others.

- START A PEN-PAL PROGRAM.

Widen the children's perspective of the outer world by assigning them pen pals from a day-care center in another part of town, preferably one with a different ethnic and cultural makeup than yours. Younger kids can send each other drawings with a common theme; older kids can write letters. Invite the pen pals to visit your center, and vice versa. Get together at a park or playground convenient to both groups and have a picnic, with families invited as well.

- SCHEDULE AN ANNUAL CHILD-CARE CARNIVAL OR FAIR.

The fair can be a fund-raiser or simply an opportunity to invite the larger neighborhood and community into the center. Have arts and crafts booths where children and adults can create artwork together.

- INVITE AT-HOME PARENTS TO YOUR NEIGHBORHOOD TO JOIN SOME ACTIVITIES.

Join parents who are staying home with their children at a neighborhood park, or invite them to spend part of a day at the center, letting their children play and helping with supervision.

29. Be as Flexible as Possible.

- PROVIDE EARLY AND LATE CARE.

Parents such as school bus drivers and shift workers often need care in the very early hours of the morning, at 5 or 6 A.M. Day-care centers can schedule their staff with staggered hours, having one worker come in early and another stay late.

- SAVE SOME DROP-IN SLOTS
FOR SIBLINGS.

Temporary slots may be reserved for siblings of children already using the center, parents must give twenty-four-hour notice that they need care for a child who has a day off school or will be without care for some reason.

- MAINSTREAM CHILDREN
WITH DISABILITIES.

At Best Friends, a day-care center run by the United Cerebral Palsy Association in Philadelphia, children with such disabilities as hearing impairments, spina bifida, head trauma, cerebral palsy, and Down's syndrome learn and play side by side with nondisabled children. Research shows that most children by age six already have preconceived notions about what it means to be disabled, but understanding between the groups can be achieved at an early age.

- FIND SPONSORS FOR CHILD-CARE
SCHOLARSHIPS.

Affordability is a key issue in child care, one that can make care unavailable to those who need it most. Ask local businesses and benefactors to donate funds for child-care scholarships. Establish an endowment fund to cover child-care costs for needy families.

30. Care for the Caregivers.

Caregivers in child-care centers are typically underpaid and overworked; day-care workers subsidize the nation's struggling child-care system far more than government does.

- IMPROVE PAY AND BENEFITS.

Child-care workers are typically paid less than kennel workers. Parents, companies, and government should support higher wages and benefits for our children's caregivers. The private sector is in a particularly good position to improve working conditions for child-care providers, through co-operative support and subsidy of existing child-care centers, offering employees child-care vouchers, and other techniques. (See "What You Can Do in Your Workplace.")

- VOLUNTEERS CAN HELP CAREGIVERS PREVENT BURNOUT.

Parent aides can offer respite for overworked child-care workers.

- PROVIDE FREQUENT SEMINARS AND REFRESHER COURSES FOR CAREGIVERS.

They deserve to be treated as professionals, and to be given opportunities to participate in workshops and educational programs offered through local hospitals, colleges, YMCAs, and other organizations that support child care. Ask parent volunteers to substitute for caregivers at the center a few hours a month.

• IF ALL ELSE FAILS . . .

In some states, child-care workers have contemplated going on strike to demand more support from the businesses that profit from their services.

31. Provide Health-care Services and Information.

A 1989 study by the Centers for Disease Control found that children in child-care centers are 4.5 times more likely to be hospitalized for illness than those cared for in other settings. While some experts recommend the establishment of national standards for infection control, others contend that such standards would burden child-care providers with more regulations and paper work. Here are ways that centers can protect children's health and become early detectors and preventers of serious childhood illness.

• ESTABLISH A CONSULTING RELATIONSHIP WITH A HEALTH-CARE PROVIDER.

Request the services of a nurse practitioner or other health-care worker to present talks on common diseases and health problems in children so caregivers can be alert to symptoms and help parents provide good health care for their kids. Caregivers may be the first to spot health problems and potential learning disabilities and, with proper education, they can advise parents of how they can help their kids.

- PRACTICE SOUND INFECTION CONTROL PROCEDURES.

Hire food handlers who are strictly in charge of preparing and serving meals and snacks, rather than using caregivers who handle infants and toddlers in diapers. Or, divide tasks between employees so that those who change diapers do not handle food. Also, food handlers should wear rubber or plastic gloves.

Post written reminders about hand-washing techniques. Caregivers who are constantly wiping runny noses and changing dirty diapers should wash their hands with antibacterial soaps frequently.

Clean toys, tables, chairs, blankets, and all items children often use with a disinfectant or diluted bleach water.

- KEEP A COMPLETE FIRST-AID KIT ON HAND.

Hold annual first-aid classes for staff—invite parents to participate as well.

- ESTABLISH CLEAR-CUT GUIDELINES REGARDING COMMUNICABLE DISEASES.

Inform parents that children will not be allowed to attend the center on days when they show symptoms of diseases such as chicken pox, pink eye, strep throat, and head lice. Be sure parents know of these restrictions in advance, and stick to them religiously.

- PROVIDE A QUARANTINE AREA
FOR SICK CHILDREN.

Parents should stay home from work with their children when their child is sick; often, however, parents afraid of losing their jobs do bring sick children to school. Child-care providers inevitably must deal with children who appear at the center with symptoms or develop them during the day. If possible, provide a separate, comfortable area where sick children can stay, even if it's only an office. Assign a volunteer or part-time worker to care for the child in order to minimize the chances of spreading disease to other children.

32. Act as a Link Between Home and School.

- OFFER INFORMATION.

Help parents prepare to send their children to school by providing information on nearby private and public schools.

- OFFER INVITATION.

Arrange for the invitation of child-care children to attend elementary school plays or other performances to expose them to the school setting.

- CREATE ACADEMIC LINKS WITH
  ELEMENTARY SCHOOLS.

Centers that offer before- and after-school care can work wonders in terms of keeping kids interested and involved in school. By communicating with teachers, caregivers can enhance the lessons being taught in school with additional, fun-oriented activities after school. Such centers can offer tutoring assistance to enhance what the schools provide, homework assistance, and exposure to libraries and educational field trips.

33. Encourage Developers to Subsidize Child Care.

In California's Contra Costa County, home builders as well as those constructing business and industrial property are required to provide an amount of child care appropriate to the size of their development. In the Contra Costa plan, child-care need is projected based on the number of homes or the size of other development. Developers then decide whether to build a child-care center themselves or contract with an existing center to provide for the estimated number of children, at a cost of $1,000 to $2,500 a child. Some developers like the flexibility of this plan, and the fact that fees go directly, immediately, into child care rather than disappearing into county coffers.

GOVERNMENT AGENCIES SHOULD SET THE EXAMPLE.

Government agencies, particularly those based in Washington, D.C., have an inside line to political influence. Such agencies could use that power to set a good example for the future.

For example, during the Bush administration, with the encouragement of Admiral James D. Watkins, Secretary of Energy, Sheila Watkins (his wife) created a privately funded, state-of-the-art child-care center in the Energy Department building in Washington D.C. When President George Bush named James Watkins to the post in 1989, Sheila Watkins toured the building and asked to see the day-care center. There wasn't one, but a site had been chosen down a dark and damp hallway. Sheila Watkins spotted the outdoor employee volleyball courts and declared a day-care center would be built there. The resulting Energy Child Development Center has 8,200 square feet of energy-efficient space, with solar power for hot water and lighting, toddler-height thermopane windows for conserving heat, and a roster of more than sixty students enrolled on a sliding-scale of fees. The model, a prototype for energy conservation as well as for child care, has been copied by the Park Service for use in remote park areas, and by the Atomic Energy Commission building in Maryland.

Of course, the U.S. Senate has enjoyed its own excellent day-care facility for several years. What about the rest of us?

34. Locate Child-care Centers Where They Can Best Benefit the Community.

Children and adults benefit from unlimited access to each other. Day-care centers have the power and ability to keep children in the forefront of the collective community consciousness. Jaquie Swaback, Child Care Coordinator, Sacramento, California, and other experts, suggest that child-care centers be located at the following sites:

- IN ELEMENTARY SCHOOLS.

Ease the adjustment for children graduating from child care into kindergarten and grade school through early exposure. Child-care centers located next to schools give children the advantage of playing and mingling with older kids. In addition, such centers can be used for before- and after-school care for latchkey-age children. Schools can also provide before- and after-school care.

- IN HIGH SCHOOLS.

Place day-care centers near high schools, so teenagers can work with younger kids, earning money, class credit, or a sense of civic spirit. In addition, the presence of young children can keep teens from acting in antisocial ways.

- **IN COMMUNITY RECREATION CENTERS.**

Putting day-care centers by recreation centers, libraries, neighborhood parks, and other facilities expands the resources available to children and caregivers, and allows various programs to work interdependently.

- **IN TRANSPORTATION CENTERS.**

Cities encouraging residents to ride-share or use public transportation can provide child-care facilities at park-and-ride parking lots and major public transportation hubs. Centers located by bus and trolley stops are particularly helpful to lower-income parents, helping them further reduce their expenses.

- **IN RETAIL CENTERS.**

By sponsoring and/or housing child-care facilities in shopping malls and smaller strip shopping centers, retailers are guaranteed a steady flow of consumers who will stop and shop on the way to and from the center.

- **IN SENIOR CENTERS.**

Place child-care centers near senior centers, and get the two groups involved with each other. For example, the Lil People's School in Sacramento is located in a complex that includes a market and deli, a hair salon, a travel agency, county offices, and most importantly, 120 senior apartments. Apartment residents are honorary grandparents at the child-care center, and help feed and diaper infants, fold laundry, tell stories or just listen to an individual child. On Halloween, the children are invited to the seniors' dining room to show off their costumes in a parade; the audience offers the children punch and cookies at the end. The seniors also keep the center well stocked with art supplies. Front row seats are reserved for the seniors at Christmas plays and other center performances.

The Lil People's School has another unique feature—a rooftop playground, complete with shade canopies and sixteen trees, planted by parent volunteers in large planters. The center is in the heart of downtown, close to transportation; children are taken on field trips using public transportation.

- IN THE NEIGHBORHOOD.

Too many neighborhoods are vacant and unused during the day, when parents are at work and children in day care or school. Allowing kids to stay in their neighborhoods, near their homes, provides a wonderful sense of security and belonging that's hard to duplicate elsewhere. Neighbors may protest that centers could create more traffic, parking problems, and noise, but such drawbacks can be dealt with if the centers are small. Current zoning regulations make it difficult to establish child-care centers in residential neighborhoods, but it is possible to bypass these regulations with special-use permits.

CHILD-CARE CENTERS IN DOWNTOWN

The Maria Hastings House, one of the oldest mansions in downtown Sacramento, was rescued from demolition through public outcry and creative planning. First built in 1860, the house had become a run-down, decrepit apartment building. After months of reconstruction, it became the Maria Hastings Child Development Center, a Montessori program serving sixty-six children age six weeks to six years old. The center is located just one block from a regional Light Rail station, near the State Capitol, and offices of the city, county, and private businesses, making it easy for parents to drop off and pick up their kids and stop by for lunch. The grounds include a large lawn, play equipment, and orange trees planted in 1898.

• IN THE WORKPLACE.

See "What You Can Do in Your Workplace."

Checklist: Tips on How to Choose a Child-care Center, or Rate Yours.

☐ Know the licensing requirements in your state and be sure the program's license is current.

☐ Ascertain that key caregivers are educated in child psychology and development and/or early childhood education.

☐ Determine that the ratio of children to staff is appropriate for each age group.

IDEAL CHILD-TO-STAFF RATIOS:

Infant to 18 months	4:1
18 months to 2 years	5:1
2–3 years	8:1
3–4 years	10:1
5–6 years	15:1
7 years or older	20:1

☐ Be sure there are thirty-five square feet of space per child indoors and seventy-five square feet per child in outside play areas.

☐ Determine that the facility and equipment are kept properly cleaned and disinfected.

☐ Determine that the caregivers are careful about personal hygiene.

☐ Ask whether there are appropriate facilities and procedures for taking care of sick children.

☐ Determine whether the activities program includes all of the elements necessary to foster child growth and development.

☐ Be sure that your involvement in your child's activities and progress is welcomed.

☐ Ascertain that corporal punishment, humiliation, or ridicule are never employed as disciplinary measures.

☐ Determine that safety precautions and security procedures are strictly observed.

—Source: "Parent's Guide to Choosing Quality Child Care," compiled by The National Association of Pediatric Nurse Associates and Practitioners.

35. Create a Neighborhood Child-care Co-operative.

Patricia McManus, who lives nine blocks north of the Liberty Bell in Philadelphia, figures that she's promoting an idea that the founding dads and moms—who believed in local self-sufficiency—would have approved: co-operative baby-sitting. The basic idea is that parents in a neighborhood organize to exchange baby-sitting on a barter system. McManus, a twenty-eight-year-old free-lance writer, community activist, and at-home mom, has assembled "The Babysitting Co-op Guide-book" to show parents how to do it.

"I had my first child when I was nineteen," she says. "I left college, got married and moved to the city, and knew no one. There was this little park and I saw all the moms there, but I never really connected with that network."

After the birth of her second son, in 1988, she was deter-mined to overcome her sense of isolation. "I asked one of the moms in the park if she was interested in trading baby-sitting. She told me about a baby-sitting co-op that she had just joined, one that had been functioning for seventeen years in the same neighborhood." McManus contacted the co-op's organizers. "They had this big old record book, this tome, which included the names of the members and when they took care of each others' kids." Over the years, the book had been passed like a community heirloom from family to family. Soon, though, McManus and her family moved, this time to a neighborhood with no park and no co-op.

"So I decided to start a co-op child-care network," she says. "When I would see someone with a toddler on the street, I would catch up with them with my stroller and ask them if they would be interested in forming a baby-sitting co-op."

Several parents were interested, but McManus didn't know how to start and maintain a co-op. So she did some research: She called members of the one in her old neighborhood; she went to the library and studied other co-ops (food co-ops, for example); and she decided that a good network demanded good organization—rules, regulations, and forms. "I found a mom who said she loved forms! She's a designer, and she designed our forms on her Macintosh computer." Now several years later, fifteen families belong to McManus's baby-sitting co-op.

Here are some of the essentials, as outlined in McManus's booklet:

- A family who needs a sitter calls another member of the co-op and asks for baby-sitting time.
- A baby-sitting co-op is built on points. The family who receives the help is charged points for each hour of sitting service; the family that baby-sits receives points. Points earned entitle a member to baby-sitting from another co-op member.
- All points are recorded by a co-op bookkeeper, a position that rotates monthly throughout the membership.
- The bookkeeper is paid in baby-sitting points.

In her guidebook she offers practical suggestions, among them: Name your co-op to give it a sense of identity; if possible, make the boundaries of the co-op within walking distance; make sure members know phone numbers, including the phone number of the child's doctor.

She emphasizes that baby-sitting co-ops are not a new idea, just an underutilized one. Some of the organizational methods that she suggests, however, are new; for example, using a home computer for record-keeping.

A co-operative baby-sitting network is useful mainly to parents who need a sitter for a night out or for an emergency. But, eventually, working parents might use such a network as an alternative to day-care centers. This would be more likely to happen as companies offer more flexible working hours, more part-time work, and four-day work weeks.

One of the benefits of the barter system is that it saves money. "My husband and I get to go out more," says McManus. "We go to art gallery openings, where they have free wine and cheese. So we go out on a date and come home with as much money in our pockets as when we left and it doesn't cost us six or seven dollars an hour for a baby-sitter!"

The system also saves time. One member of McManus's co-op, freed from anxiety of uncertain child care, was able to complete her doctorate in art history; another finished a novel. (Dads, as well as moms are involved in the co-op; several work at home and contribute baby-sitting time.) But most importantly, co-operatives build community.

"The familiarity and trust that develops among members allay the fears that many parents have about child care," says McManus. As she points out, community provides the best prevention of child abuse. "Co-op members can know and sit for each other for years. Paid sitters rarely last that long."

Children benefit from cooperative child-care networks as much as their parents. "The co-oping parents have become like aunts and uncles to my kids; and their kids have become like cousins to my children," says McManus. "Right now, we have a lot of two-and-a-half-year-olds in the co-op. You should see them in my home: They're all getting potty trained at the same time. They're very impressed when their peers sit on the potty; they want to be like their friends."

McManus's energized co-op members went on to create a neighborhood park on empty city-owned land. She says someone ought to form a national network of family co-ops. Certainly this is the kind of idea bound to spread as families realize that the best support they can get is from other families. "I spend a lot of time visiting the historical sites around Philadelphia," she says. "I feel a real kinship with people like Ben Franklin. Much of what they had to say about civic life can be updated and adapted to our current lives, even when it comes to something as ordinary as baby-sitting."

CHILD-CARE RESOURCES

Child Care Action Campaign
Publishes an information guide called *Care for Your Child: Making the Right Choice*. Available when you send a self-addressed stamped envelope. 330 Seventh Avenue, New York, NY, 10001; (212) 239-0138.

Child Care Information Exchange
PO Box 2890, Richmond, VA, 98073.

Child Care Operator's Guidelines
NAPNAP Child Care Guide, a sixteen-page booklet prepared by the National Association of Pediatric Nurse Associates and Practitioners through a grant from Lysol Products. Free. NAP-NAP Child Care Guide, % Lysol Brand Products, PO Box 4760, Westbury, NY, 11592.

Family Service America
A network of social service agencies in the United States and Canada. Publishes *The Family Guide to Child Care: Making the Right Choices*, costs $5.95. Available free as part of benefits package to employees of Equitable Financial Companies and Prudential Insurance Company of America, who commissioned the booklet. 11700 West Lake Park Drive, Milwaukee, WI, 53224; (414) 359-1040.

National Association of Child Care Resource and Referral Agencies
2116 Campus Drive SE, Rochester, MN, 55904.

*National Association for the Education of Young
Children*
1500 16th Street, NW, Washington, DC, 20036; (800) 424-2460.

National Association for Family Day Care
815 15th Street, NW, Suite 928, Washington, DC, 20005; (800)
359-3817.

*National Association of Pediatric Nurse Associates and
Practitioners*
1101 Kings Highway North, Suite 206, Cherry Hill, NJ, 08034;
(609) 667-1773.

Books
A Parent's Guide to Child Care and Baby-sitting. Warm Lines, 492
Waltham Street, West Newton, MA, 02165. A guide for estab-
lishing co-op day-care and baby-sitting clubs. Available for $8.
The Babysitting Co-op Guidebook, Patricia McManus, 915 N
Fourth Street, Philadelphia, PA, 19123, $12.50.

YOUR IDEAS FOR CHILD CARE

_____
_____
_____
_____
_____
_____
_____
_____
_____
_____
_____
_____
_____
_____
_____
_____
_____
_____
_____
_____
_____
_____
_____
_____
_____

WHAT YOU CAN DO IN THE SCHOOLS

The debate over school reform is too focused on the educational institutions themselves; our most pressing, and least understood, priority should be community reform, not just school reform. Cutting-edge thought on school reform suggests that the best schools are the ones that involve and serve parents by supporting families rather than replacing them.

Over the last decade, most educators have begun to recognize the importance of parent involvement. They realize that children learn more and schools function better when parents and schools work together. The tightening of school funds and the criticism of public schools have shown administrators and teachers that without parent assistance school budgets will not pass and other support will not be forthcoming. And educators have come to learn that parents are less likely to be active supporters if they have no role in the schools.

Parent involvement helps decrease the isolation felt by children, teachers, and parents.

Parent involvement helps make the school part of the community, rather than a fortress within it. The more that public schools can offer the kind of parental involvement often seen in many private schools, the better public schools will be able to compete.

Parent involvement convinces the child that parents really do care about school; communication is improved between the teacher and the parent, and between the parent and child. Many private schools figured this out long ago; some require parents to volunteer several hours a month in the classroom.

But adult involvement must go beyond parents. Some of

the most moving and effective programs in the schools involve seniors working, for example, as reading mentors.

FACTS ABOUT PARENT INVOLVEMENT IN THE SCHOOLS

- A Stanford study was designed to isolate those factors—independent of socioeconomic standing—that could improve a child's grades. The most surprising finding: *if a child's parent makes at least one visit to the school or a school function during the year, that child's grades are likely to improve.*

- In more than fifty schools around the country, a parent-involvement program pioneered by James Comer, director of the Yale Child Study Center, the results are dramatic. At one school, 92 percent of the parents visited the school more than ten times. In New Haven, Connecticut, the first city to apply Comer's ideas, the dropout rate has plummeted from 42 to 15.5 percent since 1980, and the number of kids going on to higher education has risen from 45 to 73 percent. Student suspensions virtually disappeared.

- Despite the known value of parent involvement, the "Imperiled Generation" report reveals "a startling 70 percent of teachers in urban schools say lack of parental support is a serious problem." At a New Orleans high school that required parents to pick up their children's report cards, 70 percent of the cards remained unclaimed two months after the marking period ended.

- A survey by the National Education Association found that more than 90 percent of teachers want more parent involvement. Parent indifference often rates above low teacher salaries as a cause of dissatisfaction for our nation's teachers.

36. Schools: Invite Parent Partnerships.

Despite almost universal approval of the idea of parent involvement, some teachers resist parent involvement in the schools, citing bad experiences with pushy parents. Some teachers feel that relying on parents may make them appear less professional. But when teachers do involve parents in their children's education, parents usually view the teacher as more professional. How can parents and teachers reduce the alienation and isolation that so many parents feel when they interact with their children's schools? Why is this, and how can parents, teachers, and principals communicate better?

- OFFER TEACHERS WORKSHOPS ON WORKING WITH PARENTS.

Hold parent involvement workshops at every school. Experts aren't necessary. Have a teacher who has a good track record with parents, or a parent who has worked successfully in the classroom, lead the workshops.

- HOLD A BACK TO SCHOOL FAIR.

Schedule a schoolwide Back to School Fair open to students, families, and the public (especially school neighbors) in the school playground, cafeteria, or auditorium on the first weekend after school starts. Students can make name tags for themselves and their families during class the week before the fair. Invite local organizations and nonprofit agencies to set up tables and distribute information. For-profit businesses and organizations (such as children's bookstores, educational toy companies, fast-food restaurants) can supply free materials for the fair or pay for booth space to participate. Encourage visitors to bring cameras; decorate a large bulletin board at school to display photos afterwards.

- MAKE SURE OFFICE PERSONNEL KNOW HOW TO RECEIVE PARENTS.

Office personnel should be trained to welcome parents into the school. Parents should be provided someplace comfortable to sit while they wait, and on days when parents wish to visit the classroom, office staff or assigned students should escort them to the classroom.

- INVITE PARENTS TO LUNCH.

Establish an open-door policy in the cafeteria. Let parents know when their children's lunch hours are, and make it clear that parents are welcome to drop in for lunch.

- INVITE PARENTS TO DINNER.

So parents don't have to make dinner between getting home from work and going to an after-work school function, offer pizza or other fast-food on Open House nights at school, or encourage parents to brown-bag it.

- INVITE PARENTS TO ATTEND
TEACHER-TRAINING SESSIONS.

Let parents know when the teachers will be attending seminars or previewing new materials. Invite parents to join the teachers as silent observers (not interfering with the teachers' need to learn and interact).

- GIVE TEACHERS TIME OFF
TO VOLUNTEER IN OTHER AREAS
OF THE COMMUNITY.

This helps teachers link to the wider community, building support for the school, and also helps them welcome volunteers in their classrooms.

THE PARENT EFFECTIVENESS PROGRAM (PET)

In 1981, the Missouri State Department of Education hired child psychologist Burton White (author of *The First*

Three Years of Life), whose work in the late sixties, which led to Head Start, showed that many children were already educationally disadvantaged by the time they entered kindergarten. In Missouri, White set up a model parent-education program in four school districts representing a wide range of social and economic backgrounds—urban, suburban, small town, and rural settings. The pilot program continued for three years. Among its elements: monthly home visits by a parent-educator for the first three years of the child's life; group get-togethers for parents; a battery of monitoring procedures; and a referral service for parents to obtain help if any signs of educational difficulty appeared.

The verbal, videotaped, and written assistance given to parents in the private and group sessions was simple. The teachers outlined child development stages, but did not advocate high-pressure procedures designed to produce superbabies. Instead of setting aside structured teaching times, parents were encouraged to set up interesting *environments*, to allow the children to indulge their natural curiosity, and then to follow the children's leads. Parents were also taught how to set limits, and alternatives to spanking.

An independent organization in Overland Park, Kansas, evaluated the Missouri program's effectiveness and found that the children scored significantly higher than average in intellectual and linguistic development. Surprisingly, the program worked about the same with children of parents with doctoral degrees and parents who were high school dropouts. The approach also worked about the same with black families and white families, teen-age parents and parents in their thirties, married parents and single parents, with families with an annual income of more than $40,000, and those below the poverty line. Though not all of the advice was followed by the parents, most of them were eager to get the help and the contact.

The idea has spread, successfully, to several school districts around the country.

—From *Childhood's Future*

37. Schools and Parents: Create a Community Volunteer and Visitation Program.

In a parent survey at De Portola Middle School in San Diego, 60 percent of parents said they could visit the school, 40 percent said they could not, primarily because of work pressures. Seventy percent of parents wanted to participate in classroom visitations. Ninety-five percent of parents felt that teachers would welcome them into the classroom.

- HIRE A PAID OR VOLUNTEER COMMUNITY VOLUNTEER COORDINATOR.

The parent-teacher partnership is unlikely to be a positive experience, or to happen at all, without organization. If, as in most school districts, money is tight, funds to pay a parent volunteer coordinator can be raised by local service clubs. As one teacher says, "Good teachers do want parents in the classroom, but they want the visits to be organized."

- CREATE VOLUNTEER CENTERS AT
EVERY SCHOOL.

Give parents a headquarters within the school, staffed by parent workers, some of whom might be paid. The center staff would coordinate all parent volunteer activities on a daily basis, including supervision, class visitations, phone calls to other parents, and support for teachers and staff.

- RECRUIT PARENTS WHEREVER YOU CAN
FIND THEM.

Brenda Lee, the principal of Edison Elementary School in Dayton, Ohio, approached parents at bus stops, parks, and playgrounds to encourage, beg, and beseech them to come in to their children's school and lend a hand. Every weekday morning, five hundred students, twenty-five teachers, and fifty parents now wait for the bell to signal the start of a new school day.

- ASK PARENTS TO TEACH PARENTS.

Parents are each other's best source of information, support, and advice, but often have trouble connecting. Give parents plenty of opportunity within the school framework to meet and network with each other. The PTA can hold parenting workshops led by parents, or open forums where parents can learn from each other.

- CREATE BUSINESS/VOLUNTEER ACTION
TEAMS.

De Portola Middle School in San Diego is identifying key

businesses that employ parents of De Portola students. The
school is sending action teams of parents and teachers into the
community to encourage these businesses to allow their employees paid time off to visit and volunteer at the school.

- ASK STUDENTS TO MAKE NAME TAGS
  FOR ADULT VOLUNTEERS.

This involves students in the process and underscores that
volunteers are there to help the students, not only the teachers.

- ASSIGN STUDENTS TO OFFER PARENT
  VOLUNTEERS AND VISITORS A SCHOOL
  TOUR ON THEIR FIRST DAY.

This is another way of involving students and honoring (and
educating) volunteers.

- EMPHASIZE THAT PARENTS CAN VISIT
  WITHOUT VOLUNTEERING.

The De Portola survey results suggested that most parents
believe if the school invites them to come to school that means
they have to volunteer to do some work. Schools need to
emphasize that parents are welcome to simply visit and observe.

- RECOGNIZE AND HONOR ADULTS WHO
  HELP THE SCHOOLS.

Include adult volunteers in Good Citizenship assemblies and
other school functions where students (and parents) receive
awards and recognition. Create a wall of honor. Prominently

display parent badges, with photos, on the hall wall. Honor a volunteer-of-the-month.

> "Ideally, a parent would be present in every classroom every day, observing the educational process. Too often I have heard my colleagues protest the presence of 'too many' parents; apparently, many of us feel intimidated by the thought of them observing our teaching on a daily basis. Yet excellence has nothing to fear from observation."
>
> —George J. McKenna III, "Heartware, Not Hardware," Los Angeles *Times* March 27, 1992. McKenna is superintendent of the Inglewood Unified School District and the former principal of George Washington Preparatory High School in Los Angeles.

38. Parents and Other Adults: Don't Wait for an Invitation.

- GET ORGANIZED! HELP YOUR FELLOW PARENTS ASSIST YOUR CHILD'S SCHOOL.

Don't wait for your child's already over-stressed teachers to organize volunteers. Do it yourself. Some parent groups organize day-long workshops once a week for parents to do all the duplicating, all the stenos, cutting. In Houston, the Volunteers in Public Schools program coordinates 20,000 citizens as special classroom speakers, tutors, and screeners for new kindergartners. At Memorial Primary and Elementary School in New

Braunfels, Texas, parents have established a PTA office right in the building. On a typical day, at least ten parents are at the office or in the school filing, preparing bulletin boards, or working on teacher requests from a teacher's "wish box." Up to 400 adults in the community pitch in during the school year. And the school encourages parents to join their children for lunch.

- PRESENT A WORKSHOP TO TEACHERS ON HOW TO WORK WITH PARENTS.

Who better to explain how parents feel in the school and classroom? Skip lectures from education professionals on such lofty subjects as "the educational impact of parent involvement in the learning environment." Instead, get a small group of parent volunteers together and create a teacher-training program on working with volunteers. Emphasize the uncertainty and intimidation parents feel when they first enter a classroom; ask teachers how volunteers can be most helpful.

- COMPILE A TIPS FOR VOLUNTEERS HANDOUT.

Keep it personal. Solicit tips from teachers and seasoned volunteers. Emphasize the teacher's roll as boss in the classroom and the importance of not usurping the teacher's power/control/ rapport with students. Offer suggestions on handling disruptions and discipline problems.

SCHOOL HERO

Norman Manasa established the Washington Education project in 1969. The project gives college credit to students who volunteer to tutor public school students in reading. Manasa raises the money through corporate gifts and sponsorships.

39. Volunteer in the Classroom.

- START IN THE CLASSROOM—AND START SMALL.

Traditional classroom volunteering works. Spell words for children's personal dictionaries. Read to a small group of children or listen to them read individually. Play math games. Practice word-recognition flash cards. Tutor slow readers in one-to-one reading programs. Give emotional support to children. For teachers, simply having another person in the room can be invaluable. "When there is another adult I can get twice as much done!" says one first-and-second-grade teacher.

GIVE CHILDREN THE
ATTENTION THEY CRAVE

At Van Asselt Elementary School in Seattle, one mother says she started volunteering because she needed to decide soon between public and private education for her son, then in preschool. "My fear of public schools came from friends and the media," she says. "I decided to find out for myself, to go into the school and get involved. I expected the fault to fall on classes that were too large, and curriculum that was too hard. Instead, the fault falls on parents who are not involved in their children's lives."

Indeed, the most important role for an adult volunteer is surrogate parent. "More than anything else, I've been overwhelmed by the emotional needs of so many of these children," this volunteer adds. "One little girl I'm working with is unwilling to learn anything right now. She just wants me to hold her, to be hugged, and to lay her head on my lap. I find myself—more than teaching these children—I find myself trying to love them. To love away the hurt."

—From *Childhood's Future*

- DECREASE THE WORKLOAD
OF OVERBURDENED TEACHERS.

While the parents are teaching, the teachers can work with a small group of students, observe students interacting with other adults, work on paperwork, confer with other parents, or simply take a break.

- COLLEGE STUDENTS VOLUNTEER.

Ask college students to talk with junior and senior high school students, describing their experiences in college.

PARENTS AS CLASSROOM STRESS BUSTERS

Sometimes merely the presence of parent volunteers in the classrooms can decrease the level of friction and disruption in the classroom. Tina Kafka, a mother who volunteers in her child's second-grade classroom noticed this phenomenon.

"I was observing a reading group being run by a warm, and obviously competent, teacher," she says. "The teacher's regular aide was absent that day. While the teacher was engaged with her group, two other tables of students were supposed to be working on some worksheets which required them to interpret some directions in their book. The teacher was frequently interrupted by the goofing-off behavior from these other tables. Finally one boy beckoned me over. 'I don't understand this work-sheet,' he said to me, 'can you explain it?' Once I explained it, the whole group seemed to settle down. It was clear how difficult it is for one lone adult to run a large classroom of children."

- EXPAND CHILDREN'S EXPERIENCE OF THE WORLD.

"In the typical school setting, you have one classroom teacher, and perhaps an aide or a support teacher. But essentially children are being educated by a small number of people with little range in background," says Christiann Dean, author of the Cornell Cooperative Extension pamphlet, "Becoming Part of Your Child's School." "Parents can bring a tremendous cultural and experimental diversity. Classroom studies spring to life when family members share travel, job, and other experiences."

Some examples: With less than an hour's preparation, one father, a bird enthusiast, creates a matching game using his collection of bird's wings and photocopied pages from a field guide. Another parent shows slides of her trip to the Soviet Union. Another brings in foods traditional to his Greek homeland. A parent with an interest in entomology brings in part of a university insect collection and a microscope. A parent who plays a stringed instrument performs for the children and demonstrates how the instrument works.

• VOLUNTEER TO TEACH MUSIC, ART,
DRAMA, CRAFTS, ETC.

Most adults have a hobby they could share with kids. Assemble a team of volunteers to teach one hour a week. Solicit donations of materials from local stores. Schedule a hobby day when kids can display their creations and perform for other students and friends.

40. Volunteer After Hours.

Not everyone can volunteer during class hours, but consider the other possibilities:

• VOLUNTEER A FEW AFTER-WORK
HOURS AT SCHOOL.

Volunteers can work for one or two hours a week in the evening to help teachers prepare materials for future lessons, decorate classrooms, inventory supplies, complete paperwork, and whatever else the teachers might need.

• HELP TEACHERS BY REVIEWING
SCHOOL WORK AND HOMEWORK.

Volunteers can take work home: They can review tests or homework assignments for their child's class one night a week. Parents can work on the papers at the school or at home and return them to school with their child. The emphasis should not be on grading the papers, but rather on reviewing the type of work the children are doing and whether they seem to be learning.

- HELP AT HOME WITH OTHER CHORES TO HELP THE TEACHER.

Some examples: mount displays of children's work; collect recyclable items, such as egg crates, lids, spools, 35-mm film cases, fabric scraps; buy small needed items such as pencil grips for the special ed program; provide child care so another parent can volunteer in the classroom; operate phone trees (recruit other parents to participate in special events); provide child care so that another parent can volunteer in the classroom. (See "What You Can Do in Your Home and Family.")

"The one line you hear from parents all the time is 'I can't, I work.' That was going to be my logo. 'I can't, I work.' Draw a big circle around it with a line through it, just like the traffic signs: 'I can't, I work.' Well, I work too. I don't get paid for what I do. But that's not a good enough excuse. It's showing up in the kids. I can see what's happened to the high school children. I remember in grade school, their parents weren't involved then and they still aren't involved, and those kids are in trouble today. They're not following through."

—PTA president in Shawnee Mission, Kansas, quoted in *Childhood's Future*

41. Help Give the School a Face Lift.

Increasingly, parents find themselves participating in the upkeep of the school, spending their evenings or weekends helping with physical maintenance, etc. Faced with limited resources and a growing education crisis, more and more schools are seeking support from parents, businesses, and civic groups, who help refurbish playgrounds, assemble new equipment, clean classrooms, paint. For many schools, the parent cavalry is arriving just in time.

THE PARENT CAVALRY

Principal Dennis Doyle had a problem.

Each day, at Torrey Pines Elementary in La Jolla, California, Doyle watched his students eat in the lunch court under the San Diego sun. The court had no covering to shelter students from ultraviolet rays, and parents and teachers were worried about the threat of skin cancer.

"On days when the Santa Ana winds blew, the kids fried. We asked students to bring hats to school, but that wasn't enough," says Doyle.

"So we went to the San Diego school system and asked them to build a screen over the lunch area."

School district officials responded with an estimate of $40,000 to cover the area and that money, Doyle was informed, would have to come out of Torrey Pines Elementary's budget, "which was laughable," says Doyle. "Our capital outlay is almost zero."

So Doyle took the problem to the parents.

Over the next few weeks, parents raised the money among themselves, contributed materials, and built a shelter over the lunch court, complete with vinyl netting that screens out 60 percent of the ultraviolet rays.

The total cost: $2,000.

That's $38,000 less than the estimate given by the school district. So far, Doyle hasn't let the school district know about the screen.

Torrey Pines is one of many schools nationwide where parents are coming to the rescue. Often, this is done quietly—the stealth school-improvement program—circumventing bureaucratic radar.

42. Create Hands-on Learning Activity Centers.

At one San Diego school a sixth-grade class failed the hands-on science test given nationwide by the National Teachers Association. So the school enlisted the parent posse. This year, parents—coordinated by teachers—set up weekly hands-on science learning centers which explain everything from magnetism (using a compass demonstration) to weather (with a miniature weather station). Parents, staff, and students also work together on weekends to create the ultimate hands-on science lab, restoring a canyon behind the school to its natural state. Half of the parents were from a wealthy part of town, the other half were from a low-income neighborhood. Such an experience binds people together more than any formal integration program.

43. Seniors: Become the Winter Soldiers.

By the year 2000, about thirty-five million Americans will be sixty-five years or older. This is a vast resource waiting to be tapped by schools.

• START A SENIOR READER MENTOR PROGRAM.

In 1978, the city of Seattle decided to use some of its extra school buildings—the "temporary" structures set up on playgrounds during the height of the baby boom—as senior citizen centers.

Every afternoon at Whittier Elementary, the septuagenarians and octogenarians would walk the thirty feet from the senior center to the school, then down a hallway to the cafeteria for a hot lunch. The old people and the kids seldom interacted; they might as well have moved in parallel universes. For ten years this went on. No one, during all that time, tried to create a formal relationship between the old and the young.

Not until the summer of 1987, when Monica Roberts, school librarian, watching seniors moving like ghosts down the hall, thought to herself, "What a waste. We could *use* those people."

As a result, the Whittier Senior Reading Partners program, possibly the first of its kind and financed with private money, was begun. Now the seniors arrive at the school library in the morning and sit with children—many of them homeless or abused children from emergency shelters. These children have the lowest reading scores in the school. "They're desperate for some kind of adult contact," said Roberts. "At first we weren't sure how the kids would respond to the seniors, but now we have kids—good readers—on a waiting list to get a senior reading partner. It's the contact they're after. That's what they're missing most of all; ironically, that's what the seniors, too, are missing. I look at these elderly folks and the kids sitting at the same tables, holding the same books. I see these kids' reading abilities and attendance improving dramatically."

HOW SENIORS RESCUED THE SCHOOLS OF DADE COUNTY, FLORIDA

In March 1988, Dade County voters passed the largest school-bond issue in the history of the United States— nearly a billion dollars. In the close election, the bond was supported by 72 percent of the senior vote.

"The condo congregation—the seniors—they were the ones who turned the tide," according to Freeman Wyche, former Dade County PTA president. The bond issue was crucial because Dade County, the fourth-largest school district in the nation, is overflowing with a new generation of immigrants and children. Ironically, other groups which one might have expected to be more supportive of school spending voted against the referendum. "We were amazed," said Wyche. "The seniors came through."

How and why did this happen? In part, the shift may reflect a change in attitude among the old toward the young. More specifically, proponents of the school bond organized an effective person-to-person, young-to-old sales campaign that employed a guerrilla tactic: PTA and school officials infiltrated the senior condos with *kids*.

"The PTA and other groups went to the retirement condos and sold the bond issue directly," said Wyche. "One of our appeals was that if you don't pay now, you pay later—if you fail to educate our citizens, they'll be illiterate, they'll be on welfare, they'll be stealing, they'll be breaking into your homes. But if you educate them, they can become productive citizens, and that's going to lower your taxes later."

"We took kids into the condos and the *convals* (convalescent homes)," explained Ramona Frischman, Dade County's coordinator of senior volunteers in the schools. "We brought music groups in. We thought, well, the seniors will enjoy the music, and they'll see that the children are adorable; we'll get in and make our pitch. And it worked."

The foundation for the Miami campaign was laid several years ago when the Dade County school district created six aggressive senior volunteer programs—which now enlist the help of 2,500 senior citizens. These volunteers help children learn basic skills.

—From *Childhood's Future*

44. Match Adults with Students.

Solicit neighborhood and community volunteers to pair up with individual students for the full school year (and more). Though mentor programs might initially be geared toward high-risk students in danger of dropping out, the program should include all students. Mentors matched through common interests or experiences can help students:

- develop and achieve a set of personal goals;
- build self-esteem;
- make wise decisions;
- increase interpersonal skills;
- increase literacy;
- stay in school;
- become a valuable member of society.

Some schools offer monthly workshops that bring parents into the schools to work with their children on such problems as organizing work, not procrastinating, writing essays, note-taking. Parents and kids talk together about school in a structure that encourages them to communicate.

IT'S THE LAW

In California, a law allows parents to request paid time off from work, of up to four hours per year per child, to visit school during school hours. This law, sponsored by Assemblyman Curtis Tucker, Jr. (D-Inglewood) has been in effect since 1991, but most parents are not aware of their right to visit their child's school. Few schools promote it.

45. Calling All Dads: Create a Fathers' Volunteer Corps.

The presence of males is needed now more than ever.

At Arlington High School in Indianapolis, a third of the 1,650 students are being raised by single parents, mostly mothers. But the Security Dads, a group of volunteer fathers, has arrived on the scene. Originally there to provide security, their duties have widened considerably, as *Parade* reports.

"The kids respect us, and we respect them," says Carl Black, Sr., forty-seven, one of two-dozen dads on call to appear at ballgames, dances, and other events attracting crowds of students. "When kids see their parents involved, they're more willing to participate in school activities. And parents become willing to let them attend, knowing there won't be a lot of trouble."

"What works is that father image," says Ron Cheney, thirty-five, "so we don't need to say very much. Just being there is what counts . . ." —Source: "Dads Who Shaped Up a School" by Hank Whittemore, *Parade Magazine*, September 27, 1992

46. Let Kids Help the Kids.

- ### USE PEER COUNSELORS.

George McKenna suggests that schools incorporate peer counseling and community service: "This should be mandatory,
particularly for grades seven through twelve. Teams of peer
counselors trained in conflict resolution, nurturing, and peer
support activities would be as active as athletic teams and as
aggressive as middle linebackers in rescuing potential dropouts
and other at-risk students. The celebration of saved lives is
more significant than any athletic awards banquet. Community
service projects should be required of all student clubs and
athletic teams."

- ### ENCOURAGE OLDER STUDENTS
  ### TO MENTOR YOUNGER ONES.

High school freshmen might have an easier time adapting,
especially in large schools, if they had a senior student mentor.
Older students can give younger ones the lowdown on
teachers, homework, organized activities, and other kid issues.

- ### ALL KIDS CAN TUTOR.

Stay away from the concept of having the "advanced" or
"gifted students" as the only peer tutors. Instead, find a way for
all kids to act as tutors at some time. Those in higher grades can
tutor those in lower grades; the kid who struggled through
fourth-grade reading and is now at a sixth-grade level may be

more empathic and understanding toward a struggling fourth-grader than one who seemingly has learned effortlessly.

47. Use Volunteers to Combat Illiteracy.

- BEGIN A FAMILY LITERACY PROGRAM
IN YOUR SCHOOL.

In Louisville, Kentucky, parents are encouraged to enroll in a family literacy program called PACT—Parent and Child Together. The adults must commit to one year of classes toward taking and passing the GED exams for a high school equivalency certificate. Adults also take classes in parenting and in finding employment and spend time daily in their children's classrooms. Child care is provided.

Sharon Darling, who began Louisville's family literacy program, says, "All of these parents dropped out of school for one reason or another. Many of them were afraid of school and afraid of teachers. That translated to one generation after another of parents not having the confidence to go into schools and take part in their child's education."

- PROVIDE ONE-ON-ONE TUTORING
TO ENSURE THAT CHILDREN LEARN
TO READ.

Use volunteers, older students, seniors, parents, anyone who will commit to ongoing sessions with students.

- GIVE COLLEGE STUDENTS ACADEMIC
  CREDIT FOR TUTORING NON-READERS.

The Washington Education Project, begun in 1969, provides a $25,000 start-up grant to college and universities. College undergraduate students take the semester-long course and agree to tutor public school underachieving students a minimum of six hours per week, attend weekly seminars with faculty supervisors, submit written reports every three weeks, keep private journals, and submit final reports at the end of the semester. Teachers get assistance for students who need help, the students get a chance to reenter the academic mainstreams, and tutors get practical experience in the classroom.

THE LITERACY
OF THOUGHTFULNESS

While pursuing the goal of literacy for youngsters and adults, make sure your definition of literacy is wide and deep.

Years ago, Americans were considered literate if they could sign their names, says Rexford Brown. Then came a series of redefinitions of literacy.

During the 1970s, critics charged that too many Americans, while not totally illiterate, weren't literate enough to balance a checkbook or read the poison label on household canisters. The concern about functional illiteracy created near panic at the administrative levels of school districts.

Now the ante has been upped again. Get ready for the new "literacy of thoughtfulness." This new literacy, according to Brown, "includes capacities once demanded only of a privileged college-bound elite: to think critically and creatively, solve problems, exercise judgment and learn new skills and knowledge throughout a lifetime." In other words, to think and converse clearly, and to grow.

Brown, the author of *Schools of Thought: How the Politics of Literacy Shape Thinking in the Classroom*, is a former high school and college teacher, and senior policy analyst for the Education Commission of the States, a nonprofit education policy and research organization with headquarters in Denver. "What we've done is offer thoughtful literacy to a few select students," he says, "and to many of the rest who we consider disadvantaged we have offered a hand-me-down literacy."

Most recent educational reform, he says, has centered on the need to bring students up to some minimal reading and writing standard. In the process, many schools, perhaps most, have virtually destroyed the joy of reading for children, sterilizing it with an elaborate reading technology. In many reading classes, students don't even read much. During course work in reading, about 70 percent of the time is spent doing skill sheets in workbooks. The rest is spent reading isolated words and sentences. Millions of students—particularly minority students, were tracked (as educational jargon puts it) into remedial course work that would, theoretically, bring their basic skills up to par. Books were "dumbed down" for these students.

The teacher seeks factual answers rather than challenge. The classes tend to move fast; the teacher tends to ask questions to which students already know the answers, and the students answer quickly, tending not to show any tentativeness or doubt. Though there is ample research that seating students in a circle so that they face each other encourages inquiry and discussion, the students usually sit in standard rows, making thoughtful discussion next to impossible.

The result: deadened kids who don't see any relationship between the real stories of their lives and the lifeless jargon they hear in the classroom.

Brown insists that most students can do far more than they are being asked to do, "but few teachers know how to ask them to do more."

Meanwhile, a few lucky students do get exposed to the literacy of thoughtfulness. In every school district, exceptional teachers still challenge their students. But too often, thoughtfulness and discussion are considered luxuries to be enjoyed mainly by the most gifted of students, tracked into intellectually segregated classrooms.

But there's hope. School districts in Pittsburgh and Toronto are leading the way toward the new (or is it old?) literacy of thoughtfulness.

Toronto's multicultural school district aims to create classrooms where the clock does not rule, where standardized testing is taboo, where discussions about controversial issues are open and ongoing. "The bottom line is, we don't have graffiti on our walls," Brown quotes one Toronto school administrator as saying. "The bottom line is that we have an increasing number of students who are graduating out of our high schools with higher and higher skills."

Brown praises Pittsburgh's school district for establishing two teaching centers to train teachers to conduct real discussion groups, and to be better writers themselves. After one Pittsburgh teacher-training discussion group, an instructor told Brown, "A lot of these teachers have never talked about ideas the way they did today. Not when they were in school, not in their education course, not in their schools. It's a whole new thing. And it excites them, once they get over the initial risk of it all. Our studies show that they talk to each other more after they have been in these seminars."

48. Parents and Schools: Increase Parent Involvement with Children's School Work.

The conventional wisdom is that student success is tied to income, family education, and culture. But research at the University of Wisconsin which compared high-achieving and low-achieving students from poor, black families found that the parents of the better students monitored their children's progress and consistently set high goals. One of the best ways you can help your child's school is to closely monitor your own child's progress.

- **ASSIGN HOMEWORK THAT REQUIRES FAMILY PARTICIPATION.**

Have students interview family members and report what they've learned to the class. Topics can reflect the skills being taught in class: Math students might ask to see and copy the family budget (or create the budget their parents have long dreamed of); beginning readers could make a list of their older siblings' favorite first books. Allow at least two days for the assignment to be completed so busy families can adjust their schedules. Benefits of such assignments are: They encourage family interaction and discussion; give children insights into parents as human beings; give students a chance to find out how their peers live; translate school work into meaningful experience.

- ASK STUDENTS AND PARENTS
TO WATCH TV TOGETHER.

Instruct students to observe the family members as they watch the program, looking for signs of boredom (yawning, talking, leaving the room), and interest (rapt attention, hushing the talkers). When the program is over, have the student interview each family member and discuss reactions.

SUCCESS STORY

The Farrell School District in Pennsylvania has 1,000 students in an urbanized, racially mixed district; of the 502 school districts in Pennsylvania, Farrell ranks among the 10 poorest. As Richard Kordesh, an assistant professor at Pennsylvania State University, reports, Farrell has only a one percent dropout rate; sends a disproportionate number of graduates to college; runs the most comprehensive array of early childhood programs of any district in the state; has minimum discipline and security problems; almost no graffiti; and has received national recognition for programs. Experts say the district is a living vision of community for children. Schools build trust, which leads to hope and sense of common mission. The district makes a promise to each student: to offer a high quality of education and make sure he or she graduates. Younger students see older ones succeed. Farrell's schools, used for community activities after hours, weekends, and summer, are the centers of the community.

—Source: Richard Kordesh, "Community for Children," *National Civic Review*, Fall 1991

49. Schools: Recognize Parent Pressures.

- LIGHTEN THE WEEKEND AND HOLIDAY HOMEWORK LOAD.

Particularly in junior high and high school, teachers tend to pile on lengthy projects for weekends and holidays, decreasing the time students can spend with their families.

- SEND NOTES HOME PRAISING STUDENTS' ACCOMPLISHMENTS.

A note from the teacher is usually seen as bad news. Communicate with parents when there is good news as well.

- ENABLE TEACHERS TO VISIT
STUDENTS' HOMES.

Home visits increase parent involvement in the schools, increase student self-esteem, help alleviate communication problems between home and school (especially in bilingual families), provide follow-through in curriculum, and offer many more intangible results that benefit children and families. Though home visits are a part of Head Start and other early-childhood programs, they are virtually nonexistent in the older grades.

The logistics of providing teachers with the time and resources to make home visits may seem prohibitive, especially in classrooms with large numbers of students. Teachers can limit their visits to one hour a year per student, on evenings, weekends, and holidays. Teachers' aides can make home visits as well. Teachers could accumulate compensatory time by taking time away from the classroom while reliable volunteers take over.

- START A PLAY GROUP AT THE SCHOOL
FOR YOUNGER SIBLINGS.

Some schools offer play groups or child care for a few hours each day, so parents needn't find child care in order to work at the school. The play group has the added advantage of introducing preschoolers to the school setting and their future classmates.

"No one sees the daily pain of these children, and the daily struggle of teachers, unless they're *here*. I'll tell you what it's going to take to create better schools. It's going to take parents coming into the school. Their attitudes change very quickly once they're here. Everybody thinks they know exactly what we should be doing in the classroom, but somehow you never see those people in the classroom. My own relatives sit there at family gatherings and put teachers down. But nobody comes in and finds out what we're doing. We're asking you to come in, but not just to watch. Come in and put your hand to the plow and *help* us."

—Seattle teacher, *Childhood's Future*

50. Set Up a College Scholarship Program.

Our generation may have been born to run, but young people today were born to pay. Because of the skyrocketing cost of higher education, T. C. Williams High School in Alexandria, Virginia, has set up a special endowment fund, through the Scholarship Fund of Alexandria. "We ask parents to contribute," says Jim McClure, director of guidance at T. C. Williams. The approach is similar to what some schools have taken for decades for their top athletes, but these endowments will be for mainline students. "We've decided that tenth grade is not soon enough to approach the parents," says McClure. "We're going to go into the junior high schools this year, and eventually we're going to get into our elementary schools, to show people they're going to have to plan ahead. That's what it's going to take."

51. Parents and Other Adults: Help Make Schools Safe.

High school campuses that once were open now have locked gates and security guards all about, making them look more like prisons than schools. But parents and other adults can create more safety with their presence than gates and bars can with their steel.

• ORGANIZE PARENT PATROLS.

Some schools sponsor parent patrols that guard hallways and school grounds, and watch out for children dropped off early or picked up late at school. Parents walking the halls of schools daily are more effective than police officers in creating a nurturing and "student-friendly" environment. At San Diego's Sherman Elementary School, a crew of parents cut back bushes in a nearby vacant lot that drug abusers used as a shooting gallery. Sherman teachers and parents also established a school Neighborhood Watch. Signs were placed all around the school; homes that face Sherman now sport School Watch signs, and the school employees and students keep an eye on the surrounding homes.

- ENCOURAGE THE SCHOOL TO OFFER A NONVIOLENCE CURRICULUM.

In response to a shooting at a public high school, George J. McKenna III, superintendent of the Inglewood Unified School District, wrote, "Students can be taught to recognize the systemic and personal behaviors that create conflict, hatred, oppression, racism, sexism, classism, poverty, and other conditions that generate violent responses. Conflict resolution should be taught at all grade levels. . . . Programs in this aspect of nonviolence, particularly designed to meet the needs of young men, must be implemented no later than grade four. Male mentors must be actively recruited to serve as role models for male students."

ONE-STOP SCHOOLS FOR THE WHOLE CHILD

It's not uncommon for children and families to be receiving assistance from multiple agencies with little or no contact with each other. The State of Kentucky has attempted to facilitate more efficient distribution of services through the Kentucky Integrated Delivery System (KIDS), established in 1988. Under a mandate from then Governor Wallace Wilkinson, the state departments of education, social services, health, mental health, mental retardation, and employment signed an agreement committing their local affiliates to work closely together and provide services at school sites.

In 1990 the Kentucky Education Reform Act was passed, requiring Family Resource Centers to be created in schools in which at least 20 percent of the students are disadvantaged. The KIDS project was transformed into the Resource Centers, enabling multiple agencies to serve the entire family at one location.

—Marion Pines, "Family Investment Strategies: Improving the Lives of Children and Communities," published by Partners for Livable Places

52. Help Create True Community Schools.

In any true education revolution, public schools must be identified—clearly and forcefully—as the most important community hubs for families: complete with large counseling centers, day-care facilities, and in-house and outreach parenting programs. These new schools should augment the family, rather than replace it.

• SCHOOLS SHOULD SERVE ADULT AS WELL AS CHILD NEEDS.

Some high schools are attempting to become community centers, for their students as well as the elementary schools that feed into them. In San Diego, Hoover High's administration hopes to make the school the hub for weekend sports and weekend classes for adults and children in foreign languages, computers, karate, and a variety of other subjects taught by volunteer instructors. To reduce neighborhood violence and relieve the courts, schools could also be the sites of legal mediation centers for adults in the surrounding neighborhoods.

- INCREASE PARENT INVOLVEMENT.

Giving parents a choice of schools within the public school system is one step toward ensuring parental involvement. The more that public schools can offer the kind of parental involvement often seen in many private schools, the better public schools will be able to compete. Some private schools, in fact, require parents to volunteer a certain number of hours per month in the classroom. Under my suggested Family Ties legislation, employers would be required to give every employee (not only parents) two to four hours per month to volunteer in schools, visit their child at day care, or visit a parent in elder care. In San Diego, the Southland Corporation, which owns 7-Eleven stores, has adopted such a plan as part of its benefits package. Foodmaker Corporation now offers its employees one paid day a year for volunteer work. That's a start.

- SCHOOLS SHOULD OFFER MORE MENTAL HEALTH, SOCIAL, AND MEDICAL SERVICES.

Traditional guidance-counseling is crisis-oriented, concentrating on the most troublesome or talented 10 to 15 percent of students. Nationally, counselor-to-student ratios are abysmal; elementary schools have been virtually ignored. Yet, more cuts in these services are coming, even as Governor Wilson promotes preventive government and the creation of hub schools connected to government social and health services.

- SCHOOLS SHOULD BECOME PARENT
FITNESS CENTERS.

The public school should be the primary place where parents go to get help in parenting and where they meet with other parents. Schools should be, in short, family support centers. Programs such as Head Start have already proven successful in helping children overcome many social, nutritional, and learning difficulties in the early years. Such full-service schools could offer guidance and support for first-time parents, both within the school and in outreach programs for families with children not yet school age. This should be available for any family, not only those that have crossed the line into abuse.

- SCHOOLS SHOULD OFFER CHILD CARE.

The best place for day care is the public school. The brick and mortar already exist; the public school has a long tradition; we know where to find it; and, underutilized during much of the day, it needs the business.

- BIG SCHOOLS SHOULD BE DIVIDED
INTO CLUSTERED "NEIGHBORHOODS."

Schools of 1,500 to 2,000 students have torn apart the idea of community; no one teacher is responsible for following an individual child's development over time. One goal should be that students spend a longer period of time, preferably spanning several school years, with mentor teachers who follow their development.

- SATELLITE SCHOOLS SHOULD BE
ESTABLISHED NEAR MAJOR WORK
CENTERS.

In a commuter society, it may be more appropriate for many parents that their children's school be on the way to work or at work. As old, unsafe schools are closed, smaller facilities should be leased or built. These new facilities could easily be located in commercial buildings close to where students live or parents work. The revival of true neighborhood schools may gradually take place as the pressure to bus children recedes (because of either successful residential integration or political fatigue) and as more parents begin to work at home, thereby giving life to the neighborhoods.

- SCHOOLS SHOULD BE LINKED
TO THE COMMUNITY.

Intergenerational programs in the schools, by increasing the contact between seniors and children, could reduce teacher and child isolation.

- SCHOOL SCHEDULES SHOULD MATCH
WORKING FAMILY NEEDS.

Schools could meet the needs of working parents by offering teacher-parent conferences on Saturdays or during the evening. To high school students, schools could offer work-study and weekend programs, five- and six-year diploma options, independent study, early college entry. Some young people drop out of school not because they are failing, but because they have so many other obligations to fulfill. Just as we need workplace flextime for parents, we need school flextime for children. Helping kids match work and school time is one reason to move toward school flextime; but a more important reason is to match the parents' schedules with the child's—to give the family more time together.

Family life and community, not academic curriculum, should be the most important goals of school reform. Better grades will follow.

CREATE A COMMUNITY CURRICULUM IN PARENTING

"Every high school student in America should be required to take a course in parenting and child development.

"Here's what the schools should say to students:

"You're required to take (5, 10, 50?) hours of instruction in parenting. As a last resort, this school will offer you a course. But here's what we prefer: Go out into the community and find a course. Go to your church, your synagogue. Go to the YMCA. Go to Planned Parenthood. Within reason, we don't care where you go to discuss family issues; we just require you to go do it.

"Such an approach would not only solve the 'whose values' problem, but would help weave the community web of support for children and schools."

Source: *FatherLove* (Pocket Books)

SCHOOL RESOURCES

Magic Me

A program that works with at-risk kids in middle schools, taking them in groups to nursing homes or other places where they volunteer and then reflect on their experience. Offers a national curriculum and training to such institutions as schools, community groups, churches, and PTAs. Kathy Metcalf, program director. Magic Me, 2521 North Charles Street, Baltimore, MD, 21218; (410) 243-9066.

Maryland Student Service Alliance

Maryland is the first state in the country to require all high school students to do volunteer service, including mentoring, tutoring, working in nursing homes, cleaning up streets, and so forth. Offers a model curriculum to interested schools and states or organizations that wish to pursue similar legislation. Kathleen Kennedy Townsend, executive director. Maryland Student Service Alliance, c/o Maryland State Department of Education, 200 West Baltimore Street, Baltimore, MD, 21201; (410) 333-2427.

National Association of Partners in Education

School superintendents, teachers, principals, parents, and community groups devoted to promoting the value of school volunteers and partnership services. Assists school systems in starting or improving volunteer programs and business partnerships. 209 Madison Street, Suite 401, Alexandria, VA, 22314; (703) 836-4880.

National Center for Family Literacy
401 S Fourth Avenue, Suite 610, Louisville, KY, 40202-3449; (502) 584-1133.

National Coalition of Chapter I Parents
Parents, teachers, administrators, and concerned citizens in support of total community participation in the development of educational programs for disadvantaged children. Five thousand members. Has established National Parent Center, which seeks to help parent groups become actively involved in all aspects of their children's education. Edmonds School Building, 9th & D Streets, NW, Room 201, Washington, DC, 20002; (202) 547-9286.

National PTA–National Congress of Parents and Teachers
Parents, teachers, students, principals, administrators, and others interested in uniting the forces of home, school, and community on behalf of kids. Works for legislation benefiting children and youth. 700 North Rush Street, Chicago, IL, 60611-2571; (312) 787-0977.

Books
Schools of Thought: How the Politics of Literacy Shape Thinking in the Classroom, Rexford Brown. San Francisco: Jossey-Bass, 1991. 290 pp.

YOUR IDEAS FOR WHAT YOU CAN DO IN THE SCHOOLS

_____

_____

_____

_____

_____

_____

_____

_____

_____

_____

_____

_____

_____

_____

_____

_____

_____

_____

_____

_____

_____

_____

_____

_____

_____

_____

WHAT YOU CAN DO IN YOUR WORKPLACE

In recent years, modest progress for families and children has been made in the workplace. But progress is slow.

In 1991, *The Corporate Reference Guide to Work-Family Programs* was compiled by the non-profit Families and Work Institute in New York. The study, one of the first efforts to measure what U.S. companies are doing for families, reviewed the personnel policies and benefits of 188 of the largest Fortune 500 industrial and service companies in 30 industries.

The survey identified thirty family-friendly programs offering everything from part-time work to child care. None of the companies surveyed offered all thirty. The maximum number reported by any company was nineteen; the median was eight. Only 2 percent of 188 companies surveyed had implemented major family-friendly policies.

In the current recession, workers are finding they can't be choosy; many companies have tightened or eliminated whatever flexibility they might once have offered their employees. Also, the quality of jobs, measured in pay, health-care benefits, pensions, and other benefits, has declined. In May 1979, 23 percent of job openings offered health insurance, compared with only 15 percent in 1988, the latest year measured. Given the economic context, one might be discouraged from any expectation that companies will become more family-friendly. However, family-friendly policies in the workplace, along with a priority on education, are essential if the country is to achieve any kind of long-term economic health. Our European and Asian competitors understand this well.

Some American companies *are* making enormous contributions to the lives of children and family, particularly in the 1990s. Hal Morgan and Kerry Tucker, authors of *Companies That Care*, published by Simon & Schuster in 1991, visited small and large companies throughout the United States, researching employer and employee attitudes and progress toward enacting family-friendly policies.

"We found companies of every size, in every region of the country, in almost every industry moving forward to meet the challenges posed by the work force of the 1990s," Morgan and Tucker report. "We also found that these businesses are a part of a growing trend." The authors included 124 family-friendly companies in their book and say that at least 30 of those companies would not have been included if their research had been compiled three years earlier. "Had we written the book five years ago, we would have been hard-pressed to come up with fifty names," they write. "The fact is that the American workplace is in the early stages of a fundamental revolution. . . ."

53. The First Step to Making Your Company Family-friendly: Establish a Checklist of Goals.

Is your company, or the company you work for, family-friendly? That's the office question of the nineties. But somehow we haven't defined what a family-friendly workplace is. By one definition, a family-friendly company provides a job to a parent who would otherwise be without employment. That definition is simply too limited. So, here's a list of twenty features and benefits a family-friendly company might offer.

A Family-friendly Company Checklist

How does your company measure up? (Take the quiz yourself, or make a copy for your boss.)

COMPENSATION

☐ Equal pay for equal work. If your company is paying women less than men for comparable work, it's hurting children—particularly the children of single mothers.

☐ A fair wage for office and clerical workers, one which reflects the actual cost of living.

In Southern California, for example, typical take-home pay for lower-level office workers (often single parents) is $8.50 an hour, or about $1,100 a month. Once single parents pay the bills for rent, food and supplies, gas, car insurance, car payment, clothes for work, clothes for a child, telephone, and child care—never mind incidentals like car repair, birthdays, or health insurance—they're likely to come up about $400 short each month. If the worker is a single mother—lucky enough to be receiving a child-support payment of, say, $250 a month—she'll still run in the red about $150 a month. Not exactly a family-friendly budget.

☐ Overtime regulations that prevent the company from abusing salaried workers.

SCHEDULING FLEXIBILITY

Parents today are less concerned with the number of hours worked than with flexibility in the workplace, including:

☐ Job sharing: Two employees, working half-time, to meet the demands of a full-time position.

☐ Flexible working hours: The ability to adjust work schedules to school or child-care schedules.

☐ A provision for employees to work at home, when appropriate. (Organized labor often opposes this, because of fear that at-home workers could be easily exploited and are hard to organize.)

☐ Satellite offices close to residential neighborhoods, to help employees cut down on commuting time and increase family time.

☐ Two weeks or more of paid vacation. (In the United States, the average yearly vacation is ten days. In Denmark, Austria, Sweden, and Brazil, the average is thirty days.)

☐ Family Ties time: A few hours available each month, preferably paid, to volunteer in or visit schools, day-care, or elder-care facilities.

☐ Time off for family emergencies.

☐ Temporary emergency care for those days when an employee's regular arrangements fail.

OTHER BENEFITS

☐ Health insurance for all family members. (Health insurance should cover preventive health measures including well-child care, with children's immunizations and physicals. According to the child advocacy organization "Children Now," as many as half of all private insurance policies do not cover immunizations.)

☐ A cafeteria approach to benefits so that an employee can choose among child-care reimbursement, more vacation days, and health insurance. For example, if one spouse's company offers a health-care plan, the other spouse can choose a child-care or elder-care benefit rather than a redundant health plan.

☐ Pre-tax accounts for dependent care. For example, Hewlett Packard's employees can estimate the cost of child-care or elder-care expenses and set that amount aside in an untaxed account.

☐ On-site day care.

☐ Company voucher payments for child-care or company sponsorship, sometimes in partnership with other firms, of off-site day-care facilities.

☐ Company help in finding quality child-care, through networks that identify good child-care providers in the community.

☐ A career break plan. This benefit should be imported from Great Britain, where, at Lombard North Central, a London finance house, parents who have worked two years can apply for an extended leave to care for babies or toddlers. A typical leave lasts five years. Firms require unsalaried participants to complete two week's paid work each year to maintain contacts and update skills.

☐ College-tuition assistance. Beginning in the 1992–93 academic year, R. J. R. Nabisco will offer scholarships and loan subsidies under a tax-deferred savings plan. The company will match annual contributions of up to $1,000 for each of an employee's child's four years of high school. The company will offer the plan to 35,000 employees.

☐ Family leave. Today, three in five working women are employed by companies with no form of maternity leave. Few fathers now take paternity leave, even when it's offered. But times change. (On October 1, 1991, California Governor Pete Wilson signed the Family Rights Act, which offers most California employees up to sixteen weeks of unpaid leave to care for a sick family member, give birth, or adopt a child.)

Like many family-friendly benefits, this one helps the company as well as the employee. Merck and Company, one of the nation's larger pharmaceutical firms, estimates the cost of losing an employee, in lost productivity and training, to be $50,000. By permitting a worker to take a six-month child-care leave (cost: $38,000), the company achieves a net savings of $12,000.

SCORING YOUR COMPANY

These twenty options aren't the only ways that companies can be family-friendly. Some are duplicates, and not all are appropriate for smaller companies or firms with special scheduling requirements.

But here's a rough test:

- If your company offers ten or more of these items, it's family-friendly.
- If it offers between five and ten, it's family-ambivalent.
- And if it offers fewer than five, it's family-unfriendly.

In my newspaper column, I offered the above list of twenty benefits and policies that companies should consider adopting if they want to be family-friendly. Readers were asked to rate the companies they own or work for. A handful returned surveys, most anonymously, all scoring their companies poorly.

"All twenty points were valid and needed to be put into writing," wrote one reader who has been looking for part-time work since her daughter was born two years ago. "I have not found any companies willing to accommodate."

She has worked part-time in the past and wants to do so again so that she can spend as much time as possible with her daughter during the early years of her life.

Despite her productivity as a part-time worker, she found that "the attitude toward me from my fellow employees and management was that I was not dedicated to my position or the company. Time goes by so fast, and my daughter is growing up every day," she writes. "If I sound bitter, I am. Society's attitudes need to change toward children in order for more companies to provide the benefits that you outlined in your article. Children are not objects, but the future of our country."

SHORTCHANGING THE FAMILY: THE PENDULUM WILL SWING

Priority Management Systems, an international management consulting firm, surveyed attitudes of workers toward their jobs. In this study of 1,000 upper and middle managers, personal values and corporate demands were found to be out of kilter. Only 2 percent of the managers surveyed indicated that they lead a balanced lifestyle. The survey revealed that workers are increasingly resentful that they are being asked to devote more and more of their lives to their jobs. According to the survey, nearly 70 percent of the waking day is now consumed by working and commuting. The managers surveyed said they think it should be about 55 percent.

"We need to be looking for ways that companies are more receptive to the needs of their workers," said Peter Dickens of Priority Management Systems. "If we don't do that, once the recession lifts, workers will find those places on their own. The companies that don't change are going to be left with the workers that nobody else wants. That's all they will have left."

—Source: "Leaner and Meaner Companies Frustrate, Alienate Employees," Michael Kinsman, *San Diego Union–Tribune*, June 12, 1992.

54. Employees: Get Organized!

Simply installing family-friendly policies into your overall personnel policies isn't enough. Employees must know that they will not be penalized for taking advantage of these policies. According to the Families and Work Institute, many employees avoid using such policies for fear it will hurt their careers and their chances for advancement. To make sure your policies are employee-friendly:

- WORK TO CHANGE YOUR COMPANY CULTURE.

Research and solicit information on organizations that offer workplace support to families; compile the results in a clearly written, brief memo to department heads, personnel and human resource departments, and upper management. Word this memo as a request rather than a demand, with options for employers to choose from. Enclose a copy of the family-friendly company checklist, above.

- CREATE A FAMILY CAUCUS.

In some workplaces, parents have joined forces to affect company policy, or to provide a forum, sometimes a brown-bag lunch, for parents to simply meet and talk.

- EDUCATE EMPLOYERS.

Just a few years ago, many of the companies that now have the most progressive family policies in the nation were oblivious to their employees' needs. A 1987 study at Corning showed that women and minorities were leaving the company at twice the rate of white men. A 1988 survey at DuPont showed that 25 percent of male employees and 50 percent of females had considered leaving the firm for a company that offered more considered leaving the firm for a company that offered more flexibility. Today, both companies are leaders in family-friendly policies. The same story is repeated in businesses small and large.

Employers who haven't begun offering policies should survey their employees' needs. Employees who are frustrated by their bosses' ignorance should conduct a survey themselves and present the results to the company president. Once the issues are out in the open, the dialogue and change can begin.

"When managers in General Electric's aerospace division met with 550 employees in 1990, they were startled to learn that many would consider changing jobs for better family benefits. "We had heard of people moving for money or location, but not" for family policies, says Warren Clinnick, a GE human-resources manager. Moreover, workers were well acquainted with the family-leave and flexible-hours policies of competitors that also employed electrical and computer engineers.

"When the GE unit responded by embracing family leave, part-time work and flexible schedules, 1,500 of the division's 40,000 employees used the new options in the first year. All 203 people who switched to part-time work were still with GE a year later.

" 'In an industry in which it is difficult to recruit, I found that absolutely remarkable,' " Mr. Clinnick says.

—Sue Shellenbarger, "Work and Family," *The Wall Street Journal*, February 12, 1992

• EDUCATE YOUR UNION.

Too often, company policies affecting families are the first bargaining chips to be given away during negotiations. As salary increases become more difficult to obtain, family-friendly policies and benefits should become more important during labor negotiations.

WHAT'S IN IT FOR THE FAMILY —AND THE COMPANY?

In 1991, Johnson & Johnson was rated as having the most family-friendly programs and policies among Fortune 1,000 companies by the Families and Work Institute in its publication, *The Corporate Reference Guide to Work Family Programs.*

Among the impressive benefits offered by its Balancing Work and Family Program: child care resource and referral, on-site child development centers, dependent care assistance plans, family care leave, time off for short-term emergency care for family members, flexible work schedules, adoption benefits, SchoolMatch (a resource and referral service that assists parents in choosing public or private schools), elder care resource and referral, relocation planning. In addition, the company has also provided work-family training for managers and supervisors.

Did the program work? That was the question asked by the study "An Evaluation of Johnson & Johnson's Balancing Work and Family Program," billed as the first of its kind—an attempt to weigh the claims made for work-family programs against the actual effects.

The results, released in April 1993, were encouraging. Among the findings of the study:

• Johnson & Johnson employees reported that from 1990 to 1992 their immediate supervisors became more responsive to their personal and family needs. The proportion of employees increased significantly of those who agreed strongly that their immediate supervisors were helpful with routine family or personal matters. "Since supervisors are less likely to be supportive of routine, everyday problems than major emergencies, this is a real test of family responsiveness," according to the report.

• Employees have become much more open to telling the truth about family issues.

• The proportion of employees who felt they paid a price for using flexible time and leave policies decreased significantly.

• Johnson & Johnson has become a better place to work; fully 53 percent of employees surveyed felt that their work environment had improved because of the work-family initiative.

• Two years after the introduction of the program, employees report that their jobs interfere less with their family lives. This has occurred despite the fact that the average employee worked longer hours and harder in 1992 than in 1990.

• Flexible time and leave policies did not open the door to abuse. Absenteeism and tardiness did not change following the introduction of the program.

• Among employees with children under thirteen, those who have used flexible work schedules and family leave policies place more importance on Johnson & Johnson's family-supportive policies in their decision to stay at the company than those who have not made use of the policies.

• Employees in the program are less stressed; experience less negative spillover from their jobs to their family lives; feel more successful in balancing work and family responsibilities; are more loyal to the company; are more satisfied with their jobs; are more likely to recommend Johnson & Johnson as a place to work.

Source: "An Evaluation of Johnson & Johnson's Balancing Work and Family Program," Families and Work Institute, April 1993

55. Employers: Get Ahead of the Curve.

- BE AN EQUAL-OPPORTUNITY EMPLOYER.

According to a study by the Families and Work institute, high-paid professionals are far more likely than the rank and file to have benefits such as flexible scheduling, child-care assistance, and other family-related benefits. Employers with a large percentage of highly educated professional employees are more likely to offer such benefits, and large corporations tend to offer greater access to family benefits to employees working at corporate headquarters.

- STRESS PRODUCTIVITY AND RESULTS RATHER THAN HOURS ON THE JOB.

Look at the employee's overall performance record. Just because he or she does not work a sixty-hour week does not mean the job isn't getting done.

- OFFER PRENATAL WORKSHOPS AND PROGRAMS TO EMPLOYEES.

According to the latest evidence, many workplaces are offering prenatal programs, seminars, and support groups for pregnant women at their places of employment. These programs are aimed at reducing the number of problem pregnancies in order to reduce insurance costs. For example, Burlington Industries started a Handle with Care Program after three premature babies were born to Burlington workers in one year. Each baby's medical costs amounted to half a million dollars. The company estimates that the program saves them ten dollars for every dollar it costs.

These programs include information on nutrition, breast feeding, the hazards of smoking and drinking before and after the baby arrives, and other vital health information that young parents should be familiar with.

—Source: Amanda Smith, Scripps Howard News Service, 1993

56. Change the Rules of the Road.

- REEXAMINE POLICIES REGARDING RELOCATION.

In the past, corporations have expected upper-management workers to relocate their families; some now transfer managers within the same location. When relocation is necessary, companies are more inclined to offer services that aid the entire family, such as spousal relocation assistance. Many companies look for positions for spouses within their company, or within the larger work options at the new location. Some offer referral services for finding schools for children. Companies that require some overseas relocation are occasionally allowing employees to perform shorter stints such as six months rather than the traditional two or three years. The family has the option of not moving abroad, and the parent who is overseas receives paid time off and paid transportation costs to visit home.

• TAKE FAMILIES ON THE ROAD.

Travel is often an inevitable part of business, and it has become relatively common to take along spouses or older children when traveling to conventions or business meetings. Less common is the practice of bringing babies on the road, but some parents, particularly nursing mothers, are breaking new ground. Calls to NannyCare USA, a San Francisco nanny service, from women planning business trips to the West Coast have tripled since 1989. With both parents working and traveling, overnight care has become a problem, which some find easiest to solve by bringing the kids along and hiring a babysitter at their hotel.

• TAKE CARE OF THOSE LEFT AT HOME.

Lincoln National, a Fort Wayne, Indiana, insurance company offers a referral service of house sitters and overnight child-care providers for employees planning business trips. Wells Fargo Bank reimburses employees for extra child-care costs incurred because of travel and overtime work.

57. Formalize Employee Support.

• PROVIDE AN EMPLOYEE ASSISTANCE PROGRAM.

Offer information and referral services within your personnel or human resources department. Provide information on child and elder care services within the community, counsel employees on the options, and offer referrals. These services can be provided directly by the employer or contracted through an outside service. Some companies even hire professionals to counsel parents over the phone on how to rate local schools or help their children with homework.

- OFFER CLASSES ON FAMILY AND PARENTING ISSUES FOR FATHERS.

In recent years, Hewlett-Packard has drawn a larger-than-expected attendance at its Fatherhood in the Nineties seminars. Aetna Life and Casualty also sponsors a father's support group. The Los Angeles Department of Water and Power offers seminars for fathers on tax planning for child-care expenses, concerns about pregnancy and childbirth. As *The Wall Street Journal* reports, men in hard hats and work boots now attend programs on contemporary men's issues. Father support groups meet regularly, including a 6 A.M. gathering of ditch diggers and repairmen.

Fact: Single fathers are one of the fastest-growing groups in the work force. Among U.S. households with working parents and children, those headed by single fathers have grown 34 percent in the past five years to more than one million, according to the Bureau of Labor Statistics. Single working mothers outnumber single fathers by 4 to 1, but their numbers only rose 7 percent in the same period.

- SCHEDULE WORKSHOPS AND DRAMATIC PRESENTATIONS ON FAMILY/WORK STRESS.

Exxon commissioned a play called *Cross Currents* that shows how home tensions affect the workplace. Comdisco, Union Carbide, Bell Atlantic, and other corporations have hosted professional performances of *Cross Currents*. Plays for Living, a nonprofit New York theater group with forty-eight affiliates around the country, performs *Cross Currents* and other plays on racism, drug abuse, teen pregnancy, and other social issues. At Comdisco, calls requesting help from the company's employee-assistance program surged after the play was performed.

- EMPHASIZE THE ROLE THAT MEN PLAY IN CHANGING COMPANY CULTURE.

Too often, the job of creating a family-friendly company culture is assumed (by management and employees) to be solely women's work. Unless men are recruited and trained as leaders in the effort to create family-friendly companies, change will happen far too slowly.

Real Men change company cultures.

HOW PARENTS AT HEWLETT PACKARD CREATED THE ELECTRONIC WORKING PARENTS NETWORK

When Channah and Bill Horst's child died of SIDS (Sudden Infant Death Syndrome), they needed support from other parents, and they needed information about SIDS and about the grieving process.

Years ago, they might have turned to their neighbors, or to their extended family, but today it's tough to find that kind of community. So they sat down at the computer and asked for help from others on the Working Parents Network, part of Hewlett Packard's in-house electronic-mail network.

Like many companies, Hewlett Packard's Cupertino branch office has an E-mail system. Employees send messages back and forth to each other's work stations about a variety of topics, from computer designs to billing procedures to meeting notifications. If parents wish to communicate with other parents, they send their message to Kathy Mirtallo, in the communications department.

Mirtallo, herself a mother, collects the messages and every few days sends them out in a kind of electronic newsletter to six hundred parents who have joined the network. (The list also includes a few grandparents and parents-to-be.) They can then read the messages on their computer screens and respond.

When the Horsts sent out their call for help, they

received a string of messages from other parents who knew about SIDS.

"One man sent us information about SIDS research in France," says Bill, who works in technology licensing. "In true engineering fashion, he had methodically researched the subject and passed all this information on to us about the statistical likelihood that a sibling might also die of SIDS."

Armed with this information, as well as a lot of research of their own, the Horsts felt safe having a second child. Today, they still marvel at the emotional support they received from other parents on the network. The Horsts did not know most of the people who reached out to them electronically.

"What mattered was that we knew there were people out there who cared, and who shared useful information with us," says Channah.

Indeed, it might seem odd that parents would find so much comfort talking across this electronic back fence. But the Horsts and other Hewlett Packard employees find that an electronic parent support group is better than no support group at all. And an E-mail support group has some advantages over a real-time meeting.

As Channah explains, parents who communicate via E-mail aren't time-bound; they can send and receive messages anytime they want. They don't have to find a babysitter and commute to a sit-down discussion. These are important considerations for overstressed, time-poor working parents.

Not only does Hewlett Packard, one of the nation's most family-friendly companies, encourage the Parent Support Network, but its operation is part of Kathy Mirtallo's job description. Mirtallo started the network three years ago. "It was a grass-roots thing. I was meeting with several parents to talk about the stresses of raising children, and we started communicating over E-mail as well," she says.

Today, child care is the main issue people on the network want to discuss. "Who's good, who's not," says Mirtallo. "We've had parents send us a panicked message saying that their day care had shut down that day without notice. What are they going to do?"

The word goes out on the network, and almost immediately these parents get suggestions for available child-care slots or for temporary assistance.

Many other topics cross the wires.

One woman's child needed surgery in San Francisco and could not afford to pay for a hotel for an extended stay; she described her problem on the network, and someone offered her a place to stay.

Through the electronic network, parents locate other employees who want to job-share, something Hewlett Packard encourages. Other messages include notices about children's fairs, parenting classes and books.

In addition to communicating within the Cupertino plant, Hewlett Packard parents can also send and receive messages to parents at several other HP sites around the world. (San Diego's HP plant does not participate in the parenting network.)

Hewlett Packard hasn't measured the effectiveness of the Parents Support Network, says Mirtallo. But she believes that parents who participate must be more productive. It's easy to imagine all the hours saved by employees who must find child care and don't have to take days off from work to find it.

"In my case, I know the network makes us more

productive," says Bill Horst. "We used the network to find child care for our second child. I can't tell you how relieving it is to get the help of other parents in finding child care we can trust. As SIDS parents, we're especially worried about our new daughter. Who's going to hold my baby? The network has given us some peace of mind. We don't feel alone."

58. Embrace Children.

While formalized procedures and policies benefit children and families in tangible ways, intangibles can be equally important. Companies that recognize the importance of children in their employees' lives and make even the smallest steps to embrace and support the family are rewarded with reduced turnover, increased productivity, and an increase in employee loyalty and commitment. Small steps can make a big difference.

• CELEBRATE BIRTHS AND ADOPTIONS.

Instead of looking upon employees' new parenting roles as disruptions and problems in the workplace, some employers actively and publicly welcome the new child. Allstate gives free infant care seats to new parents. Other companies give shares of stock or savings bonds. Apple Computer and G.T. Water Products give new parents $500. Fel-Pro gives $1,000 to new parents, as well as $100 to newlyweds and to employees' children who graduate from high school.

- SCHEDULE AN ANNUAL KIDS AT WORK DAY IN YOUR WORKPLACE.

The Ms Foundation for Women has started a national Take Our Daughters to Work Day, calling on individuals, schools, and organizations to take girls age nine to fifteen to various places of work, so they can see women in all kinds of jobs, from sound technicians to doctors. Similar days for boys should be held.

- INVITE CHILDREN TO COMPANY BANQUETS AND AWARD CEREMONIES.

Just as parents attend school awards, kids should be able to see their parents in moments of glory.

- SPONSOR A BABY VISITATION PROGRAM.

Enlist employee volunteers to visit new parents when babies are born to give them information about parenting resources, and follow up during infancy. Helps workers who've taken maternity/paternity leave feel they are still connected with the company and feel less isolated.

"As a parent, your greatest concern will always be your children," says Robert O'Keefe, vice president of industrial relations at Fel-Pro, one of the most family-friendly companies in the nation. "If an employer really wants to turn on a parent, it should do something for the children.

And I'm telling you, we get loyal people by doing that, people who will go to the wall for us."

—From *Companies That Care*

59. Create a Family Track (for Employees with Family Needs, Whether or Not They Have Children).

- REJECT THE MOMMY (OR DADDY) TRACK.

The suggestion that such workplace segregation—creating a so-called Mommy Track—would be good for parents and good for business has been made by Felice N. Schwartz. In her now-famous *Harvard Business Review* article, "Management Women and the New Facts of Life," in which she argues that corporations should recognize two different groups of women managers: those who prioritize career and those who need a flexible schedule to put children first. (She did not use the phrase Mommy Track; reporters did.)

Schwartz declares that women in management cost corporations more than men do. Her article argues that employers would do best by identifying whether a woman is "career primary," which means she can be worked long hours, promoted, relocated, and generally treated like a man, or "career and family-oriented," meaning she is valuable to the company for her willingness to accept lower pay and little advancement in return for a flexible schedule to accommodate family needs.

But such a plan would hurt mothers in the workplace, especially single mothers, further deepening the feminization of poverty and the economic hardships of two-career families. By singling out women to be tracked, such companies would be actively discouraging ambitious women from expecting any company arrangements for family time, as well as ignoring the family role of fathers. How will a man be able to claim his family needs him if his wife's whole career has been restructured so *she* can be available?

- CREATE A BROADER FAMILY TRACK.

An alternative to the demeaning Mommy Track is to create a Family Track with provisions for all employees who belong to families, including those families without children. Family-friendly workplaces will not become a reality, at least not in any equitable form, as long as parents and non-parents are seen in competition with each other for special needs. Instead, companies should emphasize a better balance between work and other human requirements.

According to a 1988 DuPont survey, 33 percent of DuPont's male employees said they would like to work part-time and be with their families more. DuPont, Corning, Merck, and many other big companies already have "family interest" policies—carefully worded to be nonsexist—that allow men to take a greater part in child-rearing.

Arlie Hochschild, author of *The Second Shift: Working Parents and the Revolution at Home*, writes that many people are starting to feel they ought to be able to pursue outside commitments *other* than family. Some would like to go back to school, maybe for a work-related degree, but maybe not. Others are committed to volunteer projects such as working with the homeless, or to a pursuit like making scenery for a local theater—something that calls on talents that aren't used on the job. Companies that allow time for such commitments will cut down on absenteeism because of illness or depression and increase productivity.

60. Work for Flexibility, Flexibility, Flexibility.

During the first half of this century, our parents and grand-parents fought for the forty-hour workweek; the goal was achieved for many workers in the 1950s and 1960s, though briefly. Now the average workweek is creeping beyond forty-eight hours per week for salaried employees and above sixty for self-employed people and professionals. Facing the reality of lengthening work hours, what the current generation of parents seems to value most is *flexibility* in the workplace.

- COMPANY: ESTABLISH FLEXIBILITY TRAINING SESSIONS FOR MANAGEMENT.

Teach supervisors and managers to look at employee productivity and abilities within jobs, rather than their willingness to take on more duties and follow the traditional career path.

The use of flexible scheduling might increase faster if employees weren't afraid to ask for it. Almost 70 percent of companies surveyed by the Conference Board said employees avoid using flextime policies because they believe bosses measure commitment by "face time"—hours spent at the office—rather than output, says *Work-Family Roundtable*, a Conference Board publication.

A growing number of companies, including Warner-

Lambert and Xerox, are offering flextime training. Managers are taught to work out compromises with employees, and enlist employees as business partners helping to solve a mutual problem.

CONVINCE YOUR COMPANY OF THE BENEFITS OF JOB-SHARING

Employee Retention: Policies that reduce stress on parents are less costly than severance pay or training new employees.

Job Performance: Pooling the skills of two employees (such as a veteran who knows the organization and a newcomer with up-to-date technological knowledge) enhances the capabilities of the position.

Work Scheduling and Continuity: Job-sharers can fill in for each other when sick or on vacation, or when the person in the position needs to be in two places at the same time (such as at a meeting and in the office). They can double up and overlap hours during peak work-load times.

Management Objectives: In budget crunches companies can pair employees for training, cross-training, and taking over for someone who is retiring. This can be an alternative to layoffs.

—Source: Maggi Payment, Director of the San Diego Center for Worktime Options, "Job Sharing: Two for the Price of One," San Diego *Daily Transcript*, February 19, 1990

- OFFER ALTERNATIVE SCHEDULING.

The rigid nine-to-five schedule is decidedly un-family-friendly and difficult to match with children's school hours. Personalized work hours are among the most common family-friendly options, and cost the company nothing. Most arrangements require the employee to agree to and stick with a set schedule that fits the parameters of the job and the needs of the family. The shortened workweek is one option, with employees working a four-day week. Such arrangements needn't be limited to office workers. Kingston Warren, a manufacturer of automotive weather-seal systems, has offered a compressed four-day schedule to production employees for over ten years.

- INCREASE EMPLOYEE CAPABILITIES.

Cross-training, or training employees in co-workers' duties, helps solve many of the employer's traditional fears about family leave. Workers and managers who know the basic duties of each other's jobs can fill in for each other as the need arises, be it for a few hours or a few months.

- BRING PART-TIME WORK INTO THE NINETIES.

Parents would embrace part-time work opportunities eagerly, except for one major drawback (besides money)—part-time work supposedly does not include benefits. But many of the companies listed in *Companies That Care* offer benefits to part-timers who work at least twenty hours a week. Many use part-time work as a phase-in process for parents who have been on maternity or adoption leave, allowing the parents and children to gradually adjust to other child-care arrangements.

To dismiss the impression that part-timers are not involved in their work, NCNB, one of the ten largest banking institutions in the United States, changed the name of its part-time work program to Select Time. The company takes the attitude that those working part time in order to spend more time with their children will someday be back on the fast track when their family's needs decrease, and continues to allow them to advance within the company. Joy Cone, a manufacturer of ice cream cones, commonly offers part-time options with benefits to production workers.

- PUSH FOR FLEXIBLE VACATION TIME.

In addition to offering more vacation time, some companies are realizing that employees benefit from being allowed to use time off in short increments, as little as one hour at a time. Citicorp has instituted such a plan, and employees take hourly increments of vacation time to coach their children's soccer teams, attend school performances, etc.

- REQUEST TIME OFF RATHER THAN
  (OR IN ADDITION TO) PAY RAISES
  OR OVERTIME PAY.

Employees might willingly forego annual salary increases in favor of increased time off, either as vacation time, sick leave, or simply personal time to be used as the employee wishes.

61. Explore the Homework Option.

Consider working for your company from home, or start a home-based business. The number of U.S. company employees who work at home during business hours rose 38 percent in 1991 to 5.5 million, according to Link Resources, a New York research and consulting firm.

- WORK PART TIME AT HOME.

Convince your employer that you could be even more productive if you worked some hours at home. Save time by not dressing for work, not commuting, not socializing with co-workers, answering senseless phone calls, etc. Prove that you can be more productive at home.

- WORK SMARTER AT HOME, BUT NOT NECESSARILY SHORTER.

Be forewarned that working at home can be even more time-consuming than working in an office, but you can have more control over your hours.

- ENLIST UNIONS IN PROTECTING HOME WORKERS.

Unions argue that work-at-home plans exploit employees, but could be more effective by ensuring that workers are protected. In Chicago, Illinois Bell, an Ameritech unit, is testing a work-at-home arrangement for twelve service representatives and says their productivity is 40 percent higher than average. Sandra Murray, president of one of the International Brotherhood of Electrical Workers locals involved says the union regards the program "as a test, to see if it will fit the needs of an evolving work force."

- PROTECT EMPLOYERS AS WELL.

Employers who are at the forefront of the telecommuting movement have developed some strategies to make sure the system works for them. Levi Strauss asks employees to set up separate, quiet work spaces in their homes. Pacific Bell requires workers to work specific regular hours and attend staff meetings in the office. UNUM Life Insurance has a written agreement covering liability and confidentiality issues. Such arrangements also offer telecommuters a greater sense of security and guidance.

62. Adopt a Cafeteria Approach to Benefits.

Flexible benefits packages give employees the option of meeting family needs as they change. Such packages are particularly beneficial to two-career families, who can juggle their varying needs between the two packages and come up with a wide ranging comprehensive family protection plan. Some companies offer elder-care subsidies as an option in the package.

63. Reexamine the Day-care Dilemma.

On-site day-care centers have been praised as the ideal solution to employees' child-care woes, and some leading companies have done an admirable job of providing this service. But on-site centers are prohibitive for many employers, primarily because of expense but also because of strict and sometimes irrational government regulation. However, there are many other ways to assist employees with day care, from the obvious to the imaginative.

GET A DAY-CARE DIALOGUE GOING WITH YOUR BOSS.

Many working parents feel too intimidated to explore day-care possibilities with their boss. To get the dialogue going, Barbara Otto, spokeswoman for Nine to Five, the National Association of Working Women recommends that employees:

- "Discuss with co-workers their problems finding or paying for reliable day care.
- "Survey the existing arrangements they have to make, including how to handle sick days, holidays, and summers.
- "Find out what other companies are doing about day care, including competitors.

> • "Seek out allies inside the firm, including any women's task force or employee groups, as well as sympathetic executives in senior posts.
> • "Present suggestions at a meeting with executives, and have a fall-back position if you need to compromise."
>
> —Source: "Recession Stunts Growth of Company Day Care," Sherwood Ross, Reuters, May 12, 1992

• OFFER RESOURCE AND REFERRAL SERVICES.

The most common child-care benefit is one that assists parents in choosing care for their children by offering education in how to choose day care and information on what is available in the community.

• SUBSIDIZE DAY CARE.

Direct aid in paying for child care is becoming a common benefit, with employers offering a flat subsidy to all parents or a sliding scale program that adjusts subsidies to need. Polaroid, for example, has offered subsidies since 1971.

• SUPPORT COMMUNITY DAY-CARE EFFORTS.

Several companies contribute funds to expand the quantity and quality of child-care services in their community. DuPont financially supports ongoing caregiver recruitment and training programs. NCNB offers low-interest loans to new or expanding centers in South Carolina. Several companies subsidize centers that offer priority access to the company's employees.

- MAKE DAY CARE MORE ACCESSIBLE TO EMPLOYEES.

Locating day-care centers near the work site reduces the strain on parents considerably by allowing them easier access to their children. BE&K, one of the twenty largest industrial construction contractors in the nation, created a movable, temporary day-care site near a construction site in Georgia; the center will be dismantled and moved to the next construction site when needed. Arthur Andersen, a large accounting firm, offers on-site child care on Saturdays during tax season.

Some companies offer transportation services for children, who come to work with their parents and then are taken by company van to their child-care centers or schools. Some companies provide pick-up and drop-off stations for buses.

NOT SO RISKY BUSINESS: A STEP IN THE RIGHT DIRECTION

In September 1992, 137 companies and organizations announced that they had committed $25.4 million toward programs in 25 states to care for employees' children and elderly relatives. The companies included International Business Machines Corporation, American Express Company and Xerox Corporation. The initiative was billed as the largest of its kind in American business history. Dr. Bradley Googins, director of Boston University's Center on Work and Family, called it "a bold step for American corporations." The American Business Collaboration for Quality Dependent Care would fund 300 programs in 44 communities nationwide. These ranged from the development and expansion of child-care facilities and school vacation programs to in-home programs for the elderly. Ten day-care centers were to be built.

Work-Family Directions, a Boston consulting group, is helping to set up the programs, to be run by outside contractors. Each corporation decides which communities on which it wants to focus, contributing to new facilities or programs, or helping expand existing care centers, both public and private. The new centers will be run by independent operators. Employees will pay for the care; some companies may subsidize the cost. Employees will have priority in placing their children in new centers; remaining spots will be open to the general public.

—Source: "Companies Announce Unprecedented Dependent Care Initiative," Lisa Genasci, Associated Press, September 10, 1992, and other reports.

- CREATE A COST-FREE DEPENDENT-CARE BENEFIT AT YOUR COMPANY.

A dependent-care benefit gives tax relief to workers who choose to earmark up to $5,000 of their annual salary for child care or supervisory care for other family members, saving workers from paying taxes on that income. By offering this benefit, companies can reduce their total payroll, thereby avoiding taxes they would have paid. Unfortunately, many companies don't know about the benefit. "This is one of those incredible win-win situations that you don't believe exists, but does," says Denise Lilley, chief executive of The Voucher Corporation. Lilley's Cypress, California–based company administers dependent-care programs for 576 firms nationwide. The program was authorized in 1985 by the federal government; it's a legal, effective way for families to avoid taxes on the money they spend for dependent care.

Here's how the dependent-care program works:

- Workers estimate how much they will spend on child care over the next calendar year. Up to a maximum of $5,000 can be set aside.
- That money is subtracted from the employee's salary and, consequently, is untaxed. The employer, meanwhile, legally avoids paying Social Security tax on the money.
- A worker making $40,000 who designates $5,000 for child care will find a tax savings of nearly $2,000. The company would not have to pay its 7.65 percent share of the Social Security tax on the $5,000, a savings of $382.

—Source: "Here's a win-win benefit your company could offer,"
Michael Kinsman, *San Diego Union-Tribune*, May 29, 1992

HOW RECESSION EFFECTS COMPANY DAY CARE

During the 1980s, employer support for day care increased fourfold from 1981 to 1985. Still, fewer than 1 percent of U.S. employers today contribute to child-care programs for their workers, and during the recession of the early 1990s, the trend toward employer day care slowed. However, but this may change as an economic recovery takes hold and employers learn how good an investment child care can be. In 1992, the Los Angeles Water and Power Department reported to a congressional committee that its day-care programs return $2.50 for each $1 invested, exclusive of land and the cost of building on-site centers; productivity gain is measurable: turnover among participating parents dipped 5 percent, absenteeism fell 20 percent and 53 percent of the employees said they could concentrate better at work.

—Source: "Recession Stunts Growth of Company Day Care," Sherwood Ross, Reuters, May 12, 1992

- SPONSOR DAY-CARE SCHOLARSHIPS.

Join with other companies to create a fund for child-care scholarships, or do this within your company.

- ALLOW WORKING PARENTS TO USE THEIR SICK LEAVE TO CARE FOR SICK CHILDREN.

Morrison and Foerster law firm in San Francisco allows employees to use their own sick leave to take care of a sick child or family member. Kathy Dykstra, personnel manager for Morrison and Foerster, says of her company's sick leave policy, "The main reason we did it was to encourage a relationship of trust. The standard program in which employees can only take sick leave for their own illness encourages people to lie."

Such a policy should be available for all employees, whether or not they have children, to use with any family members.

64. More Visiting Hours, Please.

- LET EMPLOYEES CHECK IN WITH THEIR KIDS.

The "three o'clock syndrome" is distracting employees and attracting the attention of employers. Some studies estimate that some 10 million kids are home alone after school, while their parents worry at work. Some employers are helping to relieve those worries by giving employees access to phones and a few minutes free time to call their kids and make sure they are home safe. Others are offering after-school care at in-house child-care centers.

- ALLOW EMPLOYEES TO BRING THEIR CHILDREN TO WORK.

Bill Brecht, owner of a San Diego BMW car dealership, faced the day-care dilemma when two of his employees were pregnant at the same time. He researched child-care licensing procedures and found that licenses are not needed if the parent is caring for the child. Therefore, he allowed both mothers to bring their new babies to work.

"I have to admit I was wary about allowing babies in the office," he wrote, "but I pushed my fears aside when I was faced with losing two employees. . . . This experiment has been a resounding success. It has sent a spark through the store, breathing new life into the place. Any concerns about interrupting the flow of work have been laid to rest and things are running as efficiently as ever. I think this child-care arrangement is an alternative that many employers often overlook. I encourage other business owners to look at it and try it. A little flexibility is all it takes and the rewards reaped by everyone are infinite."

- SPONSOR A DAY CAMP FOR EMPLOYEES' CHILDREN WHEN SCHOOL IS CLOSED IN SUMMER MONTHS.

General Dynamics in San Diego collaborates with the YMCA to hold a camp during summer and holiday school vacations. The camp is held in company-owned park adjacent to offices; parents can visit kids during lunch hour.

• PROVIDE *FLEXIBLE* LEAVE POLICIES.

After the birth of her daughter, Jessie, Elizabeth Costanza Rauch arranged to spend one full day a week at her office at NCR Scripps Ranch, and the rest of her twenty-hour work-week at home.

65. Assist the Sandwich Generation with *Their* Parents.

Many employees are members of the sandwich generation, with children in school or day care and older relatives in elder care. This creates extraordinary stress not only on the workers, but also on the workers' children. An estimated one-third of the work force bears caregiving responsibility for older relatives; about half of those relatives are located more than 100 miles away. Some businesses are realizing that their employees and their productivity are suffering from the anxiety and hours away from work required to care for the elderly. Employees fear they will be accused of caring more for their families than their jobs and see their role as caregivers to older relatives as carrying the same stigma single parents feel.

• HELP EMPLOYEES CARE FOR ELDERS.

Several businesses, including IBM, offer resource and referral services including telephone networks for counseling, information about services in the elder's community and screened referrals. IBM offered the first nationwide elder-care referral service; several other companies now do the same. Others tap into local referral services.

- INCLUDE ELDER CARE IN TAX DEDUCTIBLE BENEFITS.

Some companies are offering pre-tax programs similar to those used for day care to help cover the cost of elder care.

- PROVIDE SUBSIDIES FOR ELDER CARE.

Travelers in Hartford, Connecticut, gives employees direct subsidies of $400 to $1,200 a year for elder care. First Hawaiian, a Honolulu bank, offers an elder-care subsidy of as much as $200 a month, an aid in retaining workers in the city's tight labor market. Some companies offer elder-care subsidies as part of their flexible benefit packages.

- OFFER LONG-TERM INSURANCE.

Another optional benefit gaining in popularity is long-term-care insurance to help cover the cost of nursing home care; the insurance is usually available for both spouses and their parents.

- MAKE COMPANY DAY-CARE CENTERS INTERGENERATIONAL.

Stride Rite opened the first intergenerational company day-care center in the nation in 1990, after surveying employees and finding that 25 percent were caring for older relatives and another 13 percent expected to take on caregiving roles for the elderly in the next five years. The center has space for fifty-five children and twenty-four elders, with separate and common areas located in the company's office tower. The program is open to the elderly in the community as well as those related to employees and allows them to be a part of children's lives.

66. Create Family Ties Time.

Some companies adopt schools and load them down with computers and volunteer tutors. This is a good thing. But there are a couple of problems with this approach. One is that some schools are favored while others go begging; another is that corporate attention can wander and the school can suddenly lose all of its support.

A more democratic approach is to encourage a kind of supply side volunteerism. Let your employees spread out through the community and do what they want to do, and give them the time to do it. Instead of depending on the company to decide the appropriate causes, give employees some credit for making good choices.

Employee enthusiasm for volunteering will likely increase.

In that spirit, here's a proposal for a new company policy— or a new law—that won't cost anything (in the long run) but will release an army of day-care inspectors, help prevent child abuse, and almost immediately improve day care, elder care, and the schools.

- THE FAMILY TIES PROPOSAL.

Employers should give every parent two to four hours per month to visit their child at day care or, if the parent has hired a baby-sitter or nanny, at home. The parent could split this time up into short visits, or one long one. Preferably, the visits to day-care and elder-care settings would be unannounced visits.

In order not to discriminate against non-parents, all employees have the right to use two to four hours a month to visit their parents in elder care, or to do volunteer work in elder-care, child-care, or school settings.

Employers should have the right to request proof of the visit, and to ask for up to one week's notice. Ideally, Family Ties time would be considered paid time off. Companies with six or fewer employees might be exempted from the requirement. No employee should be required to volunteer.

Precedents exist: Many companies, in their employee contracts, allow workers mental-health days, paid days off for anniversaries and birthdays, and paid and unpaid pregnancy leave. Also, employers are required by law to allow workers to take time off for jury duty.

If such a policy were widespread, it could help save taxpayers millions of dollars in court costs by decreasing the number of child abuse cases, by slowing the growth of public child protective agencies, and by decreasing the immeasurable, long-term psychological costs born by our children who feel left behind.

VOICES FOR FAMILY TIES

"Sometimes I feel like the guest star at home. I want to be in my kids' life more, and that doesn't just mean being at home more, but being in the other part of their lives, too. I've visited my daughter's school a couple times already.

One time I played the guitar for the kids. To have those two worlds connect—that would be great. My daughter asked the teacher if she would like it if I volunteered regularly, and the teacher said, 'Of course!' "

—Mike Papanek, the manager of an international data systems company in Northern California

"My boss gives me that type of flexibility. I sleep better at night knowing that my son is well cared for. I did have one day care that was leaving my eighteen-month-old son unsupervised—exactly for how long I don't know. Luckily, I found out within six weeks of placement. I found out because I showed up earlier than scheduled. The day-care person and I never discussed unannounced visits. I just assume as a parent that it's my right to check up whenever I please."

—Kathryn A. Bearss

"As a mother of two young daughters who have been in day care since they were nine weeks old each, I applaud (the proposal). Not all parents, especially mothers, are working out of choice. Since these women are usually in 'peon' positions, they often are not given any flexibility in their schedules. It's all very well for career women to write articles about flex hours and taking their children to work, but 'job' women most likely have no such privileges. My older daughter will start school next year. It would be delightful to be able to do a couple of volunteer hours a month in her class and spend more time with her, away from her little sister and chores at home. Her daddy would also love to do it, but of course his company would penalize him for time off."

—Kathy Cross

"As a non-parent, I think [the Family Ties proposal] is an idea whose time has come. It may not look realistic right at this moment, but others are thinking this way, too."

—Marcia Myers, with San Diego's Child Abuse Interdisciplinary Education Project

"Parents do have to be encouraged to get involved in schools more than my generation did. The schools just are not as good."

—Marjorie Carver, who describes herself as a Revolutionary Grandmother

SUCCESS STORY: HOW ONE COMPANY ADOPTED FAMILY TIES

The huge Southland Corporation, noted for owning or franchising every 7-Eleven convenience store in the universe, has adopted the Family Ties proposal. On March

12, 1990, Southland sent a letter to its 200 corporate office employees within the San Diego division announcing what Paul Schmidt, Southland's regional human resource manager, now calls a Family Ties program. The program adopted was identical to the one described above, with two exceptions. First: no government involvement. Second: the program would be a "shared cost" program.

Under the Southland approach, for example, an employee (this works slightly differently for salaried and hourly employees) can take up to four hours a month off work to visit or volunteer in a day care, elder care, or school. The employee will donate one or two work hours, for which he will not be paid, and the company will pay for one or two extra hours.

"My main interest is in improving education," said Gary Anderson, Southland's San Diego division manager. (He has no children of his own.) "We've got to get people more involved in the schools." Southland hopes to make the Family Ties option part of its permanent corporate benefits package across the nation.

"It's been a quiet benefit," says Paul Schmidt, human resources manager for the San Diego division. "It's like dental insurance: Some people don't use it, but those who do tend to use it over and over."

One Southland employee used her Family Ties time to visit her infant's child-care center. "She spent a half-day at her child-care center," says Schmidt, "and she discovered that she wasn't happy with the quality of care her child was getting." So the woman switched to a smaller day-care center. "She used two half-days of Family Ties time to visit the new center and decided it was a good child-care center, and she was happy with it."

It's likely that employee returned to her job less anxious and more productive. Indeed, Schmidt says that Southland believed in the beginning that Family Ties would be an expensive benefit, "but to be honest, it's not terribly expensive, considering the payback. Administration is a piece of cake. The employees simply fill out a form and we keep it on file.

"We've considered making the benefit more appealing by including giving a straight four hours of company time, but limiting the number of times during the year that employees can use it," says Schmidt. "Or, we could allow them to take two hours of personal leave time and two hours of company time."

Employees aren't likely to rush to do something that most companies have traditionally discouraged. Schmidt says he is considering setting up informal support groups for parents. "Giving them a time and place to meet, just telling them it's OK to get together and trade notes about family issues. No company representative would be there. That would stifle it."

- FOR FAMILY TIES, START SMALL.

Don't wait for a big formal program to start giving employees time off for their children and families. Employees at Software Products International in Sorrento Valley, California, are allowed to take time off for school awards ceremonies and the like, with the understanding that they will make up the time, reports employee Cynthia Fillmore. "My daughter and I have obviously benefited greatly by the atmosphere I work in . . . I'm allowed to be a part of her school life. I know her teachers and her friends and they know me. Her home and school life are not isolated from one another. They are intertwined."

- OFFER EMPLOYEES A PAID OR NON-PAID HALF-DAY OFF AT THE BEGINNING OF THE SCHOOL YEAR.

Give employees a chance to schedule doctors' appointments and physicals for their kids to get immunizations, etc. This could prevent health problems and sick-leave use later on.

- PROVIDE A STRUCTURE THROUGH WHICH EMPLOYEES CAN VOLUNTEER.

In Houston, at the investment bank MMAR Group, staff members prepare and deliver meals to needy children every Wednesday afternoon. The bank initially donated money to Kid-Care, the agency sponsoring the meals for kids program, but followed up by providing human assistance as well.

A COUNTY OFFICE OF EDUCATION ADOPTS FAMILY TIES

On March 1, 1992, the Riverside County Office of Education adopted the Family Ties program for its own staff. "We're calling our program TOUCH, which stands for Time Out Unifying Community/Home program," says

Carolyn Wylie, assistant superintendent of educational services.

The Riverside program allows administrative staff— whether or not they're parents—to take up to four hours of paid time off every month, which they match with up to four hours of their own time.

"That means that we'll be able to take up to a full day each month," says Wylie.

In the beginning, TOUCH will be available to 151 members of the administrative staff. If it works, the program potentially could be extended to the department's 1,000 employees.

"The time is right for corporations and institutions to establish good parent, family, and community support systems," says Dale Holmes, superintendent of the Office of Education. "It's good business."

Indeed, by offering their own employees Family Ties time, educational institutions can set an example for the private sector. And if schools offer teachers time to volunteer, then teachers are more likely to be supportive of adult volunteers in their classrooms. Teachers often point out that they're among the most isolated of parents; they don't even have phones in their rooms to call their own children.

Some teachers and principals believe that, by shifting work schedules, it would be relatively easy to informally allow staff time to volunteer. But in most school systems, such change almost always requires elaborate negotiation between administrations and teachers' unions.

67. Offer Corporate Support to Public Schools.

A growing number of businesses are targeting corporate enrichment programs at elementary schools and preschools.

- CREATE A COMPANY SPONSORED PROGRAM TO ENCOURAGE EMPLOYEE INVOLVEMENT IN SCHOOLS.

Hewlett Packard sponsors a program called Choices, in which employee volunteers visit eighth-grade classes to deliver the message that the choices students make in high school will directly relate to the career choices available to them when they finish school.

The same group that created Choices also has a program called Parenting for Education, an eight-hour seminar presented to employees by employers as a benefit.

- SOLICIT STUDENTS TO HELP WITH BUSINESS PROBLEMS.

Students in the computer program in Ortonville, Minnesota, developed an office-administration system for the local hospital and revolutionized the school's bill-paying system with an efficient new computer program. Ortonville is a rural, one-school town, yet it has had a comprehensive computer program for fourteen years.

- UTILIZE EMPLOYEE TALENTS
TO IMPROVE EDUCATION.

Ten years ago, Eric Bandurski, a research associate at the Amoco Research Center, in Tulsa, decided that he wanted to improve science training in the schools. At first, he volunteered in the classroom. Then, in 1985, he and his associates developed a more formal science curriculum that is now used in thirty-one schools. Twice a month, he and his colleagues train volunteers to run basic science experiments that they teach to the fourth and fifth graders at Tulsa's Barnard elementary school.

- PLEDGE TO HIRE INNER-CITY HIGH
SCHOOL GRADUATES.

Under the Boston Compact, Boston businesses have pledged to hire 1,000 graduates a year from inner-city schools. The Compact Ventures program provides remedial education and mentors for high school students in an effort to stem dropout rates.

- ADOPT AN ARRAY OF STRATEGIES.

Other strategies that parents and businesses have developed to reach the greatest number of students: a United Technologies Corporation offers continuing education to math and science teachers and grants them stipends for a summer session to experience the real-life applications of their subjects. Time, Inc. created the Time to Read curriculum used by employee volunteers to teach twelve- to eighteen-year-olds in New York

City. The program is now being used by more than thirty other companies including Allstate, HBO, and Xerox. Through the Adopt a Class program sponsored by the New York City Board of Education, volunteers from NYNEX Enterprises run bi-monthly discussion groups for intermediate students on business ethics, job interview techniques, and developing a budget.

68. Reduce the Hours You Spend at Work.

Employees do have some control over the amount of time they spend at work. Some ways you can take control of your hours include:

- FINE WORKERS AND SUPERVISORS WHO DELAY MEETINGS PAST NORMAL WORKING HOURS.

- JOIN A CAR POOL AND GAIN A RIGHTEOUS EXCUSE FOR LEAVING WORK ON TIME.

- CHOOSE FEWER HOURS INSTEAD OF MORE PAY.

When it comes time for the annual discussion about work evaluations and raises, ask to be rewarded with fewer hours rather than more money.

- SWITCH TO A LESS DEMANDING
SPECIALTY WITHIN YOUR LINE OF WORK.

Attorneys, for example, can choose to avoid courtrooms when kids are young, thus decreasing stress immensely.

- PLAN B: STAY IN CONTACT WITH YOUR
KIDS WHEN WORK KEEPS YOU AWAY.

A single mother who worked days as a home health-care worker and went to school at nights to get her degree as a social worker (and make more money for her family) found a novel way to stay in contact with her kids, who go to their grandmother's house after school every day. Each evening, she records a cassette for her kids to listen to after school the next day. On the tape she repeats her daily admonishments, such as: do your homework or read a book. She also jokes and compliments her kids.

Fact: It costs less to allow parental leave than to replace employees permanently—compare 32 percent of annual salary with 150 percent for replacing a manager and 75 percent for a non-manager. Costs considered: disability pay, leave-related changes in productivity and time spent training replacements.

—Source: Study by the Families and Work Institute, New York, 1992

69. Family Leave: Follow the Spirit of the Law.

Until 1993, the United States remained the only industrialized country with no national family leave policy. But in 1993, President Bill Clinton signed a national family leave bill that requires businesses with more than fifty employees to permit up to twelve weeks unpaid leave annually. Leave can be taken to care for a newborn or adopted baby, an elderly parent, or a sick child or spouse. Some states now offer even more; California Governor Pete Wilson signed the Family Rights Act of 1991, which offers most California employees up to sixteen weeks to care for a sick family member, give birth, or adopt a child.

Family leave laws, at the federal or state levels, affect only the largest of companies—a minority of employers. For example, only 5.6 percent of California's businesses have fifty or more employees, but those businesses employ 68 percent of California's workers. Also, family leave provisions help families only at times of childbirth or family emergencies, which for most families take place infrequently. Family leave does not address the daily strains between work and family.

Nonetheless, the adoption of state and national family leave laws is an important step in the right direction.

- MODEL YOUR COMPANY'S FAMILY LEAVE POLICY ON THE BEST.

There are plenty of existing company policies to use as examples as you create one that fits your employees' and company's needs.

IBM has a remarkable three-year family leave policy; other companies limit leave to everything from six months to one year. Several have written policies that allow employees to use their sick leave for family emergencies, or offer paid time off for short-term illness of family members on a case-by-case basis. Pacific Presbyterian Medical Center in San Francisco offers an innovative leave-sharing program that allows employees to donate unused paid time off to fellow employees facing emergency absences.

- CREATE A POOL OF REPLACEMENTS FOR EMPLOYEES ON FAMILY LEAVE.

Employers worry about how the work will get done if employees are allowed to take time off for family needs and emergencies. The obvious solution is to use temp agencies, but employers usually must pay a fee. There are other, more creative solutions. One company tapped into the local schools' pool of substitute teachers. Others keep a list of retirees who are delighted to come back to work for short periods of time.

Employees who have quit their jobs to stay home with their children are sometimes eager to get a break from home isolation and return to work while another employee is on family leave, especially if the company offers help with day care.

- MAKE SURE ALL EMPLOYEES KNOW ABOUT THE COMPANY POLICY.

Barbara Fitzsimmons of the *San Diego Union-Tribune* reports that, though the California family leave law appears to be working well, with few complaints from employers, this may be because not many people even know it exists. Rose Fua, an attorney with Equal Rights Advocates of California, says that to date, businesses are not required to tell employees that they have this right, unless they ask. Among employers, there is an unrealistic fear that people will abuse the law and take too much time off. But even if employees know about the law, many cannot afford to take off so much unpaid time from work.

• ENCOURAGE PATERNITY LEAVE.

In 1989, according to the Bureau of Labor Statistics, 20 percent of medium and large companies offered paternity leave. But few companies encourage male workers to seek flexible schedules or family leave. Two of five companies that grant family leave admit that they frown on men who put in for it, according to Catalyst, a New York City research organization.

70. Last Resort: Take Your Family Rights to Court.

The significance of the federal family leave law as well as family leave bills passed by individual states transcends the issue of family leave per se. These laws may, in fact, redefine how employers treat families in a variety of ways.

FIGHT FAMILY DISCRIMINATION IN THE WORKPLACE

Get ready for the Decade of Family Rights—and a storm in the courts.

Until now, parents have not pressed their cause against family discrimination in the workplace with much legal force. What if a mother goes home for a couple days to take care of her sick child in an emergency and is fired? In the current legal climate, she would be hard-pressed to lodge a successful lawsuit. Or, what if two men, equally qualified, apply for the same job? One man is actively involved with his family (he writes on the job application that he's a Cub Scout pack leader); another man is single and asserts that he'll be married to the company. The family man is denied the job. Does he have legal recourse? Not today.

In the past, lawyers who might have pursued family discrimination suits would have been hard-pressed to find legal precedents. Scratching around, they might have relied on English common law, the basis for the American legal system, under which families were considered a man's chattel—his property. Under these old laws a man could sue for the "wrongful interference with family relationships."

Remnants of this old law are still used by today's lawyers in personal injury actions, which allow them to sue for "the loss of comfort, care, and society." In other words, if a spouse is injured in, say, a car accident, the other spouse may sue for the loss of friendship, companionship, domestic services, or sexual closeness. Enterprising lawyers might have tried to stretch that body of law into the workplace, on behalf of families. Yet, there is virtually no legal discussion of family discrimination.

One reason for the absence of family discrimination suits in the courts is the current anti-litigation climate. Americans, by and large, are sick of lawyers and lawsuits, and the past decade has seen mostly conservative appointments to the bench—judges not particularly interested in creating radical precedents. A second reason is the lack of legal specifics. "There's no affirmative right here," says Joan Bertin, associate director of the Women's Rights Project for the ACLU. "Federal law as it exists tells employers what they can't do, but not what they should do, when it comes to families." Ironically, a third reason for the drought is that liberal lawmakers have focused solely, in employment discrimination law, on gender and race.

Parents, of course, come in all races and both genders. By focusing only on women's rights in, say, cases involving pregnancy and the workplace, men have been excluded as a legal and political constituency.

In employment law, families are not perceived as an identifiable group.

However, in 1993, President Bill Clinton signed a national family leave bill. Some states, such as California, offer even more.

The significance of these bills transcends family leave. The bills may, in fact, unleash a flood of court cases that could redefine how employers treat families.

"We could clearly use this (California) law to protect employees who are terminated for taking care of a sick family member, if the company refuses family leave," says Linda Workman, an employment law attorney with Monaghan and Strauss, and co-chairwoman of the San Diego Lawyers Club Child Care Committee.

One of the caveats of the bill is that the employer may refuse family leave if it creates an "undue hardship" on the employer. That's a fairly loose phrase; over time, the courts will have to define what it means. In the process, the legal climate surrounding the family and the workplace could be transformed. The bill does establish an affirmative right. In effect, the bill creates the legal *idea* of family rights in the nation's most populous state.

Similar bills are being adopted in other states and considered by Congress.

Add this development to another change: the increasing proportion of judges who are women. That in itself might not mean much. As a practical matter, women judges who are being appointed, at least in California, are mostly doctrinaire conservatives. Still, half of new graduates from law school are now women. Add this fact to the growing job pressure that these young lawyers feel. Perhaps more than most professionals, lawyers are forced to choose between career and family.

Don't expect lawyers to start suing their own firms anytime soon. However, do expect some of them to be more than usually sympathetic to clients who suffer because of family discrimination. During the past three decades, the civil rights and feminist movements flexed their muscles most effectively in the courts. That may soon be true of the coming family movement.

71. Vote with Your Feet—
and Your Resume.

If possible, choose employment with a family-friendly company. Use the family-friendly company checklist above when looking for a new job. Ask employers about such policies during job interviews. Compare policies. Here are a few good companies, as suggested by the Families and Work Institute, *Companies That Care, Childhood's Future*, and other sources.

- ALLEY'S GENERAL STORE.

A small, rural general store in Massachusetts, Alley's responded to the pregnancies of three employees by allowing the new mothers to bring their babies to work with them. When the children grew too active to remain in the workplace, the employers paid for the employees' child-care costs and staggered work schedules so that only two of the children needed to be in day care at any given time.

- APPLE.

When Apple announced its new family policy in 1991, the company devoted an entire page of its in-house newsletter to fathers, sending the message that the company's family policies applied to men, not only to women. The article described the double standard toward fathers and mothers, that women are expected by the typical corporate culture to balance work and family, but not men. Apple announced that this would no longer be the acceptable norm within their company.

- AT&T.

During labor negotiations in 1988 and 1989, AT&T and the unions representing its employees assembled a comprehensive family-care package with a new twist—a family-care development fund of $10 million to be administered by the company and the unions over three years. The fund supports community-based initiatives to improve the quality and availability of child care in areas where AT&T facilities are located. The fund also supports grass-roots groups of employees that seek out new opportunities for child care in their communities.

- BANKERS INSURANCE

In Miami, Bankers Insurance not only offers an on-site day care but also an on-site, two-room public grade school. The Dade County school district pays teachers while Bankers is responsible for construction and upkeep. Bankers annual rate of employee turnover is 17.6 percent, but among those parents who enroll their children in the company day care or the satellite learning center, the turnover rate is only 4.2 percent.

- DAYTON HUDSON CORPORATION.

The corporation's Target and Mervyn's stores have a nation-wide Family-to-Family program, which works with local non-profit agencies to recruit, train, and accredit child-care providers. The program not only helps employees, but the wider community as well.

- DUNNING, FORMAN, KIRRANE & TERRY.

This small Massachusetts law firm offers in-house day care to its twenty-two employees, and, in an unusual move for a law firm, offers part-time and flexible hours to both attorneys and support staff. The attorneys (even partners) are only asked to work weekend and evening hours in emergency situations, rather than as a regular part of their jobs. Evaluations are based not on the number of hours billed but on the quality of the work.

- IBM.

One of the most family-friendly companies in the nation. In 1989, IBM began to offer a *midday flex* program at two company sites, offering one to two hours of flexibility to the usual lunch period to allow parents to run family errands. At some IBM locations, employees are offered such convenience services as dry cleaning, shoe repair, and take-home foods.

- LOTUS DEVELOPMENT CORPORATION.

The company offers a month of paid parenting leave to mothers, fathers, and adoptive parents, and even to some grandparents under certain circumstances.

- NCNB CORPORATION.

One of the ten largest banking institutions in the nation offers paid parental leave for fathers, an important benefit that allows parents to extend the time they can be at home with their children by using one parent's leave and then the other's.

- NOSC.

The Naval Ocean System Center, a branch of the Navy Research and Development Laboratory in San Diego, California, allows new mothers to work at home, has an on-site day-care center, allows parents to use sick leave to care for children, and holds open houses at the offices so children can see where their parents work.

- OHIO BELL.

In January 1990, Ohio Bell made a *gradual return to work* option. The company's Family Care Policy provides a twelve-month leave, allowing the employee to return on a part-time basis over a period of three months, working at least twenty-five hours per week. The leave and gradual return together are limited to one year.

- STRIDE RITE CORPORATION.

Stride Rite opened an intergenerational center in 1990. The 8,500-square-foot space meets the needs of children as well as elderly relatives of company employees, offering supervised curriculum encouraging regular daily contact between elders and children.

WORKPLACE RESOURCES

Bay Area Employer Child Care Coalition
The Coalition has compiled a list of thirty-eight child-care options available to employers. 410 Bush Street, San Francisco, CA, 94108.

Families and Work Institute
A nonprofit research and advisory organization; studies what companies are doing for families and how they can do more. Publishes the *Corporate Reference Guide to Work-Family Programs* and conducts the Fatherhood Project, supporting men in nurturing roles. 330 Seventh Avenue, 14th floor, New York, NY, 10001; (212) 268-4846.

Mothers' Home Business Network
Offers advice and support services on starting home-based businesses, provides forum for members to communicate with each other, publishes a quarterly newsletter, *Homeworking Mothers*, and several informational booklets. PO Box 423, East Meadow, NY, 11554; (516) 997-7394.

New Ways to Work
Offers guidelines for judging flextime requests and other work options. 149 Ninth Street, San Francisco, CA, 94103; (415) 552-1000.

Nine to Five
National Association of Working Women, 614 Superior Avenue, NW, Suite 852, Cleveland, OH, 44113-1306; (216) 621-9449.

Work-Family Directions
This Boston company offers SchoolSmart, a telephone consultation service offered by employers to employees that helps parents learn how to motivate their children, solve learning problems, and select schools. Corporations subscribing to the service include Eastman Kodak, Hewlett-Packard, and others. Also helping with the American Business Collaboration for Quality Dependent Care. 930 Commonwealth Avenue, Boston, MA, 02215-1274; (617) 278-4000.

The Home and School Institute
A Washington-based nonprofit organization that offers workshops on fostering motivation, problem-solving, and teamwork skills in children. Employers host workshops and give workers time off to attend; clients include IBM, Minnesota Mining and Manufacturing (3M). Also publishes the booklet *Home Learning Recipes*, to help parents work with children on homework, and *The Survival Guide for Busy Parents*. Trinity College, Washington, DC, 20017; (202) 466-3633.

"Work and Family," The Wall Street Journal
Sue Shellenbarger. Newspaper column covering trends, programs, and private and public sector policies.

Work and Family Life
Newsletter on balancing job and personal responsibilities, published by Bank Street College of Education, 610 W 112th Street, New York, NY, 10025, (212) 663-7200, ext. 286; Circulation Office WFL, 6211 West Howard Street, Chicago, IL, 60648; (312) 875-4400.

The Conference Board
A business research group operates the Work and Family Information Center and publishes the *Work-Family Roundtable*. 845 Third Avenue, New York, NY, 10022; (212) 759-0900.

Books
Companies That Care: The Most Family Friendly Companies in America—What They Offer, and How They Got That Way, Hal Morgan and Kerry Tucker. New York: Fireside/Simon & Schuster, 1991. 351 pp. $12.95.

The Second Shift: Working Parents and the Revolution at Home, Arlie Hochschild. New York: Viking, 1989. $18.95.

Working from Home: Everything You Need to Know about Living and Working under the Same Roof, Paul and Sarah Edwards. Los Angeles: J. P. Tarcher, 1985. 436 pp.

YOUR IDEAS FOR YOUR WORKPLACE

WHAT YOU CAN DO IN YOUR PLACE OF WORSHIP

No institutions are in a better position to make a difference for children than our places of worship. Churches, synagogues, and other places of worship are already focusing in creative ways on the needs of children and families, but much more can be done.

72. Support Children and Families.

As joblessness, child abuse, divorce, and marital stress ripple throughout the community, churches increasingly offer programs for the prevention of family problems.

This isn't new. For years, the Catholic church has done a good job at premarital counseling. But as family forms change, so do church programs.

Many now offer support groups for single parents and step-parents. One Presbyterian church, for example, offers a divorce-recovery workshop, while another soon will start a ten-week recovery program for children of divorce. "We also offer an after-school Bible study and crafts program for children," says the Reverend Richard Thompson, the church's associate pastor. "Kids have dinner here. For some of them, this is the only sit-down, family-style dinner they get."

- DECREASE ISOLATION.

Help children and adults by training lay people in basic counseling skills—especially listening skills. "In earlier decades, if a child's parents were going through a divorce, the child could open up his or her heart to a neighbor or an uncle," says Maurice Graham, associate pastor of Bon Air Baptist Church in Richmond, Virginia. "Today, that's a luxury. We need to train more people how to listen, how to be spiritual friends."

- OFFER JOB-SEARCH SERVICES.

One of the best ways to help kids is to find jobs for unemployed parents. The Job Seekers Network is sponsored by the Foothills United Methodist Church in La Mesa, California. The network's newsletter is edited by Kirk Gentry, an unemployed banker. Job seekers can advertise in the newsletter for free; it's sent out to the 1,500 members of the church and, says Gentry, "hopefully members will pass it on to friends outside the church."

- ESTABLISH A CAREGIVING NETWORK.

Robert A. Hickman describes his Unitarian church as "a multi-generational community that consists of individuals, couples, and families that share certain liberal religious values and a sense of purpose—one of community service." In 1983, he formed The Caregiving Network, a program through which volunteers within the church community offer short-term support services: listening to problems, counseling, visiting those isolated at home, driving others to medical appointments, being available for phone conversations.

POISED TO DO MORE

Are churches and other places of worship doing enough to build a community of support for families? Not according to a group of church leaders sitting around a table in the offices of the national Baptist Sunday School Board in Nashville, Tennessee.

"Most of us grew up in neighborhoods and towns where the church was part of the community, and support for families came naturally," says Maurice Graham, associate pastor of Bon Air Baptist Church in Richmond, Virginia. Graham, a former missionary, now counsels parents and children.

"Churches are already doing a lot to help families," he says. "But we've got to do more."

Graham and other participants in this recent discussion among Southern Baptist church leaders see three breakdowns that churches must try to correct.

The first is within the church's congregation.

Churches must offer more training of parenting skills and parent support groups. But first, says Graham, parents need to be able to be open about their feelings, about their parenting.

"It has taken me a long time to let down and open up and say I'm not strong all the time," said one of the women at the table, a Sunday school teacher.

"I'm a grandmother. My daughter-in-law is a single parent. My son divorced her, I didn't divorce her. In some churches, if you open up about issues like this, you put yourself on the line as a parent and as a spiritual person. You risk being judged twice."

"Too many churches suggest that there's a single right way to parent, to be a family, as if parenting can be taught by recipe," says Gerald Hickson, pediatrician and lay volunteer at Woodmont Baptist Church in Nashville.

Someone asks, rhetorically: "How would Jesus have conducted a family support group? Would he have used the cookbook method? Or would he have answered questions with questions?"

The second breakdown is structural: how churches view the time pressures of parents and church staff.

"Some churches expect parents to show up on Sunday night and participate in church activities. The minister judges us harshly when we don't show up," says one woman.

"Many of the non-parents don't know or have forgotten what it's like to be caught in the working-parent rat race, to be chronically sleep-deprived, to try to stay awake Sunday night."

The people around the table agreed that many churches are becoming less flexible with their own employees.

The third breakdown is between the church and the community.

Focusing almost exclusively on the members of their own congregations, many churches have become psychological islands within fragmented neighborhoods.

Hickson sees a need for more political action. "In my church, we fight over whether we should support legislation for better education and day care," he says. "As a pediatrician, I want to grab my brethren and show them the families I deal with, show them the desperate need for better day care."

Most important, churches must reach beyond their own walls to weave a support system for all families, whether or not they're considered religiously correct. If churches aren't capable of that kind of compassion, what institution is?

Many churches and other places of worship are beginning to do just that, and in the process challenging their own institutional isolation within the larger society.

73. Organize Activities That Help Families Connect.

- START A PARENT NETWORK.

At Ohr Kodesh Congregation in Chevy Chase, Maryland, parent networking is part of the synagogue's theological mission. "A key concept for our congregation is the Hebrew word *chesed*, translated as 'loving care,'" says Rabbi Lyle A. Fishman. "Visiting the sick, comforting the mourner; these are examples of *chesed*. These acts of loving care tie people together over time and the generations."

When a child is born to someone in the congregation, Rabbi Fishman (himself a father of small children) sends a list to the parents of other Ohr Kodesh families with children born during the same three-month period. Names, birthdates, addresses, and phone numbers are included on the parent network list. "Parents can pick up the phone and ask for help if a child is ill, or they can share a list of baby-sitters, or trade baby furniture—or simply connect with someone to relieve the sense of isolation that many parents feel."

• OFFER CHURCH-SPONSORED FAMILY
RETREATS.

For example, Coast Hills Community Church in Aliso Viejo, California, sponsors an annual ski trip for twenty to thirty families. Family mission trips are sponsored as well. In the past, the church has arranged to take children and their parents to an orphanage to do construction, paint, and distribute food and clothes.

• DESIGN SERVICES FOR FAMILIES
WITH YOUNG KIDS.

Ohr Kodesh's Rabbi Fishman offers *Tot Shabbat*, a monthly, twenty-five-minute religious service focused on children. The service includes abbreviated prayers, a blessing, and maybe a discussion about an upcoming holiday. The rabbi uses an illustrated prayer book and invites kids to participate. Afterward, during refreshments, parents naturally make and sustain friendships. "I find it ironic that people feel they must go to outside organizations to help them as parents," says one mother. "People often don't think about looking within their own congregations for help with parenting, but it's right here!"

• FORM FAMILY CLUSTERS.

Mobile families, uprooted from their extended families, often turn to a religious community for support. Churches can help families network by forming family cluster groups: Encouraging families to share a few stories on Sunday morning can be an excellent way to get things started. A church-based support group can offer a sense of "extended family" for five families with children ranging in age from six months to sixteen years of age. The group should meet at least once a month for potluck dinners, picnics in the park, singing, bowling, and camping. No formal discussion needs to be planned. The families inevitably gain a heightened awareness of each others' needs through simple contact. A supportive web is woven almost without anyone noticing.

"I can remember watching another father in our group (we call it a 'covenant group') playing soccer with my nine-year-old daughter," one father, involved in a church-sponsored family-cluster group, recalls. "Somehow I was touched to see another man taking an interest in my child. At the same time I was throwing a football around with the sons of another family."

A CIRCLE OF GRACE

Nancy Streeter says that she didn't fully realize the importance of her church in providing a network of supportive parents until she and her husband learned that their infant son had been born with a serious birth defect.

Three years ago—a few days before Christmas—she and her husband were told by physicians that their infant, Nathan, had cerebral palsy. For the next two weeks, her fellow parents from Rancho Bernardo Presbyterian in Poway, California, were at their doorstep with a hot meal. "I never knew how meaningful it was for someone to give me food, until I experienced a moment of devastating grief when I couldn't even conceive of what to make for dinner," Streeter says today. The nurturing did not end with the meals; since that time, the Streeters and their son Nathan have been deeply involved in what their church, Rancho Bernardo Community Presbyterian, calls a "grace circle," a group of parents of young children who meet monthly to discuss the issues and pressures of raising children. Upon occasion, they cook food or baby-sit for one another, especially when there is crisis—a surgery, a death, or sudden unemployment.

But day-to-day nurturing counts just as much as help during a crisis.

"About a year ago, after a three-day weekend, all of us in the circle had been with the kids all day," Streeter recalls. "We all felt that we could have killed our kids that day, that we couldn't take it anymore. We didn't judge each other, we just laughed in agreement. It almost makes me cry to talk about it. We call each other on the phone and say, 'How you doing?' I can't tell you how important it is to me to be able to give and receive that kind of support, and how important it is that Nathan is in a church where his physical differences aren't as important as the person he is becoming.

"A year ago, when surgery was performed on my son's legs, my fellow parents showed up again at my door, with food," recalls Nancy Streeter. "Without their enthusiasm and their caring for my son, my husband and I could not have given him the quality of life he has today. I remember so clearly how our church's child-care director cried with us when we first learned about Nathan's cerebral palsy, but she immediately reached out to hold Nathan, and said, 'You tell me what I need to know and I will do it because I love this baby.' Nathan has known only love in our church, and so have we."

74. Rediscover the Sabbath.

For both Jews and Christians, the Sabbath has traditionally been a day of rest and ritual, a break from the weekly routine, and a time to spend with family. Churches and synagogues can encourage their members to observe the Sabbath as a special day focused entirely on the family and the spirit, when work is stopped, the TV turned off, and the heart turned inward.

Steven Bayme, director of the Jewish Communal Affairs Department of the American Jewish Committee in New York and director of the Institute on the Jewish Family, sees the Sabbath as "sacred time." Beginning Friday at sundown, he leaves work and his hectic schedule behind and turns his full attention to his family. "My children look forward to the Sabbath as a time of joy," he says. "On Friday night, we have a dinner surrounded by Jewish rituals; this is an opportunity for extended conversation, with no pressure to meet any deadlines, a time when we have friends over."

Your family's Sabbath doesn't necessarily have to coincide with your church's Sabbath. In fact, the time spent doesn't need to be specifically religious, but it does need to be sacred. One woman, a Methodist, says, "It's so easy to get caught up in the rush, even on Sunday, when I'm so busy teaching Sunday school, volunteering with a literacy program, going to district and regional church meetings, and coming into the office to put in a few hours of work. You almost need a formal ritual to break that pattern." This woman has decided that Saturday is her personal Sabbath.

75. Blend the Generations.

One resource for family support that a church or synagogue should not neglect is seniors. Many church communities are experimenting with ways to intentionally blend the generations.

- OFFER INTERGENERATIONAL FAMILY SUPPORT GROUPS.

Schedule regular intergenerational discussion sessions where parents, grandparents, and kids share their lives with each other.

- COMBINE PROGRAMS FOR ADULTS AND KIDS.

One Presbyterian church started a program to link adult choir members, as mentors, with children's choir members. The coordinator of the program extended an invitation through the church newsletter and made announcements directly to the adult choir. The program was particularly popular among older adults whose grandchildren lived far away.

- INVOLVE SENIORS IN DAY CARE AND NURSERY SCHOOL.

The nursery school director at Ohr Kodesh Synagogue invites members of the congregation who are of grandparent age to come to the nursery school in effect as surrogate grandparents. These grandparents come on a regular basis and share time with the kids, some of whom rarely see their real grandparents.

- INCORPORATE FAMILY TRADITIONS IN CHURCH RITUALS.

A Methodist church celebrates Easter with an Easter Bread Reception. Members are encouraged to ask parents and grand-parents for recipes for a favorite Easter bread, then bake a batch and bring it to church on Easter Sunday. After the services the church holds a reception with coffee, juice, and baskets of homemade bread from the members.

SCRAMBLED AGES

Scrambled Ages is an experimental program designed to bring the generations together devised by the members of the Rancho Bernardo (California) Community Presbyterian Church. This is a once-a-week one-hour program meeting on Sunday mornings from eleven to twelve. Scrambled Ages uses drama, skits, music, dance, the arts, games, etc. following themes such as "The Whole

World in God's Hands" (an ecology theme), "Thank God for My Body" (dramatizing skills using different parts of the body), "Christmas for Others" (making gifts for children to give through church-related agencies). Children and seniors plan the programs together. Older adults share their talents in woodcarving, gardening, sewing, painting, and music.

76. Provide High-quality, Low-cost Day Care.

One of the most important services churches, Jewish community centers, and other religious institutions offer parents is day care, including care for infants and corresponding parenting classes. Ideally, the center should provide for children from families that are members of your religious institution but also for families that are not members. If possible, promote cooperative child care, which requires parent involvement and encourages parent connections.

- START A DROP-IN DAY-CARE CENTER STAFFED BY VOLUNTEERS.

The director of children's ministries for one church writes: "We have a Parents' Morning Out program. Parents drop off their kids on Thursday morning for three and a half hours, for six dollars. Once a month, we offer Parents' Evening Out. We provide a meal, entertainment, and a nap for the kids—and relief for the parents. It's increasingly important for us to care for families as well as infants and children. So often, parents can't find good child care, or they're fearful of the child care that's available. They need a break from their stress."

- OFFER FREE CHILD CARE DURING CHURCH SERVICES AND PROGRAMS.

Many churches offer baby-sitting or day care so parents can attend services. That care can be extended on into the morning, freeing parents for a quiet breakfast together.

77. Work to Strengthen Marriages.

Strengthening marriages is among the most important roles of the church or synagogue. Some churches offer Friday night marriage-maintenance classes; fathers' classes; parenting and faith classes; and when all else fails, divorce-recovery workshops and recovery programs for children of divorce. Classes offered in marriage and parenting should be offered to the wider community. "Usually half of the people who attend our classes are not members of the church," says one mother. "Our purpose is not evangelism, but many of these people have joined the church."

CHURCHES CAN IMPROVE MARRIAGES

"I'm impressed with the ability of churches to improve marriages. The Catholic Church is quite good on this issue. The Archdiocese of Chicago, for example, has very impressive programs for preparing people to be married and continue to be married. But Protestant churches over the past thirty years have moved in the other direction; they've decided that they have been too concerned about the family, and that they ought to be more concerned about Apartheid and other social, global, or environmental issues.

"It would seem to me that the best way to insure a population with ongoing interest in global issues is to strengthen the family. I also believe it's misguided to place those two areas of concern—global/social issues and family health—in competition with each other. Nonetheless, Protestant churches have drifted away from an emphasis on marriage and family. To cut to the chase, I think people should fight within their churches to create family-strengthening programs.

"This reemphasis would come from a very old tradition. During the Baptism ceremony in Protestant churches, parents stand with the baby and the congregation takes a pledge before one another and before God to act as an extended family for that child; they basically say: 'We are helpers and supporters for this mother and father for raising of this child.' As a child, I was remembered by the people in my church. They sent me cards on my birthday, watched out after me in often small but significant ways. Yet so much of that has been forgotten. Here we have the potential for a strong supportive community for the parents and child, a potential to relearn and build upon this old tradition. One of the secrets of the growing "mega-churches" is that they have caught on to the need that young parents have for help and community in a larger environment that is unfriendly and hostile to children and families.

"The return to an emphasis on helping families doesn't have to start with the minister or the rabbi, but with the people in the pew."

—David Blankenhorn, president, Institute for American Values

78. Form Children and Youth Groups.

• CREATE A THEATER GROUP FOR KIDS.

In Poway, California, Dick and Suzanne Thompson's daughter Julia attends a church children's program, the Summer Funner Theater, that Suzanne says is a powerful source of networking, a self-esteem builder for all children involved, and an inclusive model for the church in community.

"Children from ages four years through college meet from from 9 A.M. to 12 noon," she says. "Children are grouped into rough age categories in small groups led by junior and senior high school students. At the end of each week, the children perform a musical, after just five morning rehearsals together. Every single person has a line (up to 100 are allowed to attend each session). While the musical always has a religious theme, it is nondoctrinal, and anyone is welcome to attend. People from all denominations, and ones who do not attend a church, all enroll their children. They are never asked about their faith or denomination, and the program makes no apologies for the Biblical themes or the humorous ways they are woven into contemporary vignettes.

"On Thursdays, parents are invited to attend a talent show. Children are eager to volunteer, and they watch each other with respect. Parents work off tuition by serving snacks or working on scenery or costumes.

"Each summer Julia attends, I watch with amazement as the chaos is quietly formed into a cooperative venture where everyone is ready to do their part for the performance."

Such a program, says Suzanne, builds a sense of community among children, which they will be able to extend into adult life.

• CREATE A YOUTH COMMUNITY CHOIR.

"Where I grew up in Kansas, a local church started a choir for junior high and senior high school kids that invited anyone from the community to join," writes mom Lori Berger. "They grew and grew and performed at many different churches and functions. They did music the kids enjoyed, and it became the 'in' place to be. To my knowledge, they never preached or tried to recruit anyone for their church, but as a result of that group many, many kids were saved from a life of vice, and many were brought into the church. But the best thing about it was the sense of community and connectedness that all these kids felt coming from all over town, from all different religions and all different backgrounds."

- SPONSOR CHILDREN'S SPORTS TEAMS.

Church members can elect to support a local little league or soccer team, providing T-shirts, uniforms, and an enthusiastic cheering squad. This is a great way for members who don't have children to get involved with kids.

79. Provide Support Programs for Teens and Young Adults.

- SPONSOR PARENT-TEEN DIALOGUES.

Give parents and teenagers a structure through which to discuss money, curfews, sexuality, dating, drug abuse, and other stresses that can be difficult topics to broach.

- STAY IN TOUCH.

Following graduation from high school, young adults experience a difficult and often lonely transition into the adult world. One mother suggests that churches publish the young people's post-graduation plans in the Sunday bulletin, and that church members stay in contact with those who have moved away by writing letters or sending care packages. "This is one way," writes Kathy Thompson, "to keep a strand in the web connected to them without pressure."

- SCHEDULE GROUP ACTIVITIES FOR TEENS.

Provide an alternative to other activities by creating an array of social events at local ice-skating and roller-skating rinks, the bowling alley. Support hiking and camping youth groups.

- ENLIST TEENS IN CHURCH AND COMMUNITY PROJECTS.

Form work crews to clean up church grounds and paint buildings. Help them reach out to the larger community by organizing a cleanup crew for the neighborhood.

80. Reach Out to the Larger Community.

- MAKE THE CHURCH'S NEIGHBORHOOD SAFE.

In Detroit, the Reverend Lee Earl, pastor of the Twelfth Street Baptist Church, formed a company called Reach, Inc. to buy drug houses. With $300,000 in church assets, the company bought the houses and evacuated the tenants. Church members renovated the buildings (the program even created some paying jobs) and sold them to members of the congregation. Reverend Earl offered mortgages to buyers who were unable to get loans through banks because of poor credit ratings; once the owners had established a credit history by making their house payments to the church, Reach sold the mortgages to banks and used the money to buy more houses. In the nine years since Reach began, crime in the Twelfth Street community has been reduced by 37 percent.

• LINK UP WITH COMMUNITY SERVICES.

Churches can extend beyond their neighborhoods by teaming up with suburban and inner-city congregations to sponsor programs for abused and runaway children, the homeless, and other families in need. Some also form partnerships with nonsectarian programs that reach populations not normally served by the church.

For example, in San Diego county, a program called Tutor Plus links up people from the middle-class Solana Beach Presbyterian Church with homeless children in the inner-city Kids At Heart program for regular times of study and homework support. This program gives children the most valuable commodity—time with adults.

• GET INVOLVED WITH LOCAL SCHOOLS.

Organize a volunteer pool of church members ready and willing to help the schools with everything from tutoring to playground supervisions. Allow schools to use church and temple auditoriums and classrooms for special projects.

• HOST CLASSES AND PROGRAMS
FOR COMMUNITY SERVICES.

Some churches offer court-mandated parenting classes for parents of abused and neglected kids; programs are sometimes supervised by local hospitals. Church members can volunteer to follow up with parents in need of emotional support and role models.

> "The church can't wait for the community to come and say, 'We need your help.' We need to go out and ask how we can help families in stress. As Martin Luther King said, 'We can't be the taillights of society; we've got to be the headlights.' "
>
> —Reverend Dan Meyer-Abbott, Mission Hills United Methodist Church, San Diego, California

81. Be Family-friendly Employers.

• ACT AS A ROLE MODEL
FOR BUSINESSES.

As churches grow in size, their administrative officers often believe that the church should become more businesslike, which is often good news for the books, but bad news for church employees. The flexibility that smaller churches often informally offer employees with families fades. Places of worship, more than any other institution in society, should set the example as family-friendly workplaces. (See "What You Can Do in Your Workplace.")

- TAKE A SABBATICAL.

Patterson Community Church in Patterson, California, took a "sabbatical year," during which all meetings, except those that were essential, were canceled—the emphasis was on family life and personal growth. The goal was to slow down the hectic life that families were leading, starting with the often overwhelming agenda of the church itself. While a year may be too long for some churches, an occasional six-week stretch might be appropriate, especially if the minister emphasizes that the time away from church meetings and business be spent for family activities.

82. Become Political Activists for Children.

Churches and synagogues have a built-in block of voters who can help push legislators to pass family-friendly legislation. It may take some heated discussion to choose issues to support, but it's well worth the effort.

In Tucson, Arizona, the Pima County Interfaith Council is sponsoring a door-to-door grass-roots organizing campaign to make Tucson a child-friendly city. Paula Osterday, a middle-class, thirty-six-year-old mother who is one of the organizers of this effort says, "We're trying to develop a vision of how a whole city could be child-friendly. It's not enough for me to sit in my nice house with my burglar alarm; it's not just my kids, it's all kids. As a middle class woman, my eyes have been opened. To see a mother in a poor Hispanic neighborhood stand beside her fellow parents and confront an entrenched politician who has forgotten how to care—that gives you hope. The process is transcendent. I now believe that the right people will emerge. We're not alone."

PLACE OF WORSHIP RESOURCES

Active Parenting
A book and video program used by more than 2,000 groups nationwide. Frequently offered by synagogues and churches, also used in some schools. 4669 Roswell Road NE, Atlanta, GA, 30342.

Moms in Touch
Prayer groups, PO Box 1120, Poway, CA, 92074-1120; (619) 486-4065.

National Council of Jewish Women
Community service and advocacy programs including the Center for the Child and the Work/Family Project to raise community and corporate awareness of family needs and issues. 53 West 23rd Street, 6th Floor, New York, NY, 10010; (212) 645-4048.

Dial Hope
A manual for setting up telephone prayer lines. Pastor Richard B. Hayward, 2130 Ulric Street, San Diego, CA, 92111; (619) 277-0523.

Home By Choice
A national Christian organization for mothers who choose to be at home. Offers a bimonthly newsletter. PO Box 103, Vienna, VA, 22183; (703) 242-2063.

Sunrise Books, Tapes, and Videos
Educational resources that are not specifically Christian but contain strong principles and Christian values. (800) 456-7770.

Youth Specialties
Publisher for church youth resources. (800) 776-8008.

Focus on the Family
A very thorough magazine on state and federal laws affecting families; Christian. 801 Corporate Center Drive, Pomona, CA, 91768.

Books
The Family Covenant: Love and Forgiveness in the Christian Home, Dennis B. Guernsey. Elgin, IL: David C. Cook Publishers, 1984.

On Being Family: A Social Theology of the Family, Ray Anderson and Dennis B. Guernsey. Grand Rapids: Wm. B. Eerdmans, 1985. 168 pp.

Parenting Isn't for Cowards: Dealing Confidently with the Frustrations of Child-Rearing, Dr. James C. Dobson. Waco, TX: Word Books, 1987.

Serendipity Books. Waco: Creative Resources, Word, Inc., 1972. Mini courses in Christian Community, Christian Lifestyle, and Christian Encounter; good for working with intergenerational groups.

YOUR IDEAS FOR YOUR PLACE OF WORSHIP

_____
_____
_____
_____
_____
_____
_____
_____
_____
_____
_____
_____
_____
_____
_____
_____
_____
_____
_____
_____
_____
_____
_____
_____
_____
_____

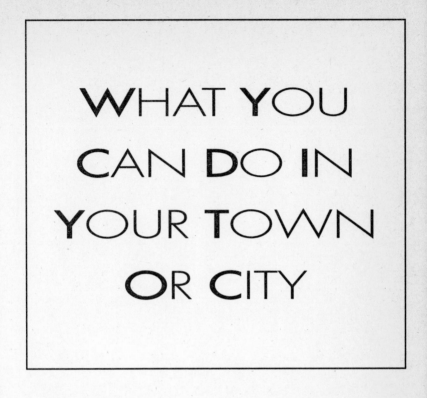

WHAT YOU
CAN DO IN
YOUR TOWN
OR CITY

In the next decade, the most economically healthy cities and towns will be those that market themselves as being family friendly. A family-friendly city is by definition more humane for everyone, whether or not they have children of their own. As one Seattle city councilman says, "The city must have a living memory. You cannot import your whole population each generation. If public policy does not affirm the importance of families, then the city very possibly does not have a future."

Cities should be judged on two levels. The first is in terms of infrastructure, i.e., the physical manifestations of the web— how, for instance, developers design new housing developments. The second is socially and psychologically, including the human resources policies of your downtown companies toward families with children. This level also includes the social and psychological connections among educational institutions, companies, places of worship, and neighborhoods.

We must challenge our towns and cities to adopt the official goal of becoming family-friendly.

Where do we start? By seeing our towns and cities through the eyes of children.

83. Conduct a KidsPlace Survey.

In the mid-1980s, a Seattle civic group started what has since been named the KidsPlace project—the first organized effort by a major American city to make the urban environment pro-child. The KidsPlace project began by taking groups of elementary school kids on field trips around the city. The kids were asked to draw pictures and write stories and poems about what they saw and then, at the end of each trip, meet for a few minutes with then Seattle Mayor Charles Royer. Seattle's idea has been copied around the country by parent and civic groups. The answers gathered by KidsPlace surveys in other cities (you'll read them throughout this chapter) suggest how to reverse anti-child urban damage and how urban life could someday be for all of us, whether or not we have kids. For example, according to a survey of 1,600 kids in the San Diego school district, kids find the San Diego skyline boxy and boring, and its streets scary. On the other hand, what kids like the most about downtown is that it's different from their neighborhood.

84. Welcome Children in Existing Town Centers and Downtowns.

In the Seattle KidsPlace survey, youngsters described the obvious: They didn't like the downtown waterfront "because there wasn't any place to touch the water." And new buildings with blank walls at street level "scared the kids."

Dr. Robert Aldrich and Seattle's KidsPlace project convinced some developers and architects that a pro-child urban design could increase retail profits in commercial districts. Among the eventual improvements: The waterfront architects, more likely to listen to kids than sociologists anyway, laughed and went back to the drawing board and designed new places for wading, for touching the water. Among the other recommendations:

- INCLUDE CHILDREN AND PARENTS
IN CITY-PLANNING DECISIONS.

In the planning process, interview parents and kids (if you have not already done this) about the *specific* human amenities that they could envision as part of the downtown neighborhoods.

Richard Bradley, president of the International Downtowns Association, says: "During the past fifteen years, all the focus was on office construction; we created a downtown environment of single use. Land values were driven so high that other uses, including urban housing, became next to impossible." Now that the building boom has slowed, we have a chance to make real cities. We can create cities that contain some civic conscience, cities that are actually fun to walk and live in, and relatively safe, multiethnic, multigenerational places with buildings that have human faces and leaders who have human hearts. "We've got to bring back the idea of the safe and supported public space," he says. "We've got to bring back the idea that cities are for people."

- DISCOURAGE STREET-LEVEL BLANK
WALLS.

Urban designers have known for years that such walls are intimidating to pedestrians, especially children.

- IN NEW HIGH-RISES, DEVOTE SPECIFIC AREAS OR WHOLE FLOORS TO CHILDREN.

Seattle considered short-term day-care centers, and shopping areas aimed at kids.

- VIEW FAMILIES AS A COMMERCIAL RESOURCE FOR DOWNTOWNS.

Families who feel welcome spend more money. If a city treats its children well, they'll treat the city well later on—commercially and socially.

- HOLD AN ANNUAL KIDS' DAY DOWNTOWN.

Schedule Kids' Day on a weekday, when businesses and city offices are open. Logistically you may need to have several Kids' Days scheduled during normal school hours, so teachers can supervise younger students. Junior high and high school kids could attend Kids' Day without their teachers and instead be assigned an adult buddy at the adult's workplace—banks, businesses, courts, police. Have special kids' prices for everything from bus rides to burgers at fast-food joints. Encourage parents and teachers to follow up on Kids' Day by having children write letters to businesses and government about their experiences with suggestions on how to make downtowns more child-friendly.

- CREATE A CHILDRENS' INFORMATION CENTER.

Many cities have information booths and centers for tourists and could easily add on a kid-sized booth dispensing information on downtown attractions, transportation, and special prices and services for kids.

- MAKE PUBLIC FACILITIES CHILD-FRIENDLY.

Did you ever watch a child try to use the telephone in a public phone booth? They can't even reach the touchtone buttons, let alone the coin slot. Allow children to use phones designed for the handicapped, which are usually at wheelchair level. Post bus and trolley schedules low enough for kids to read them. Include child-sized water fountains and child-sized seats and benches in plazas and parks.

THE TRANSREGIONAL LIFE-STYLE

The alarm clock goes off. It's still dark.

Dripping from the shower, Mom slaps sandwiches together. Dad stumbles through the house to the drip-grind coffee maker. Mom roars off with Mikey to a day care ten or fifteen miles away, then drives eighteen miles in the opposite direction to work. Dad jams Lenny and Missy into the Volvo and heads for the magnet school twelve miles to the south, where Missy spends her days. He drops Lenny at the school bus stop; Lenny will ride the bus forty-five minutes to another magnet school. Then Dad drives to another county, where he puts in a twelve-hour day.

Such a lifestyle doesn't leave much time to get to know our neighbors or our children's teachers, or feel any sense of attachment to a place.

Social scientists and urban experts once showed some interest in the implications of workers commuting long distance. But the interest has faded. Meanwhile, Dad commuting long distance turned into Dad, Mom, Mikey, Lenny, and Missy commuting long distances, leading these fragmented lives.

What are the effects of this strange explosion, this hurtling outward that families go through every weekday and even on the weekends? (Lenny and Missy no longer go to school with the neighborhood kids—possibly don't even know them. Mom or Dad drives them to play dates miles away.) Is the transregional life-style dangerous to our mental and physical health? Who is healthier, people who live the transregional lifestyle, or people who live a more localized existence, working and socializing close to home? Which of these two groups has the most heart attacks, the highest cancer rate, the highest rate of suicide, the most drug or alcohol use?

I called the American Planning Association's research department. The researcher was very helpful, but she couldn't find any useful reference to studies on the issue. Nor could William Fulton, editor of *California Planning* and Development Report. "That's not the kind of thing planners think about," said Fulton. "But it's astonishing all the things planners don't think about." We study how, say, ambient smoke affects our lungs; we can turn to scientific studies to help us make decisions about smoke in the workplace. City planners who route sewage think about health questions; surely they would think about how transregional living affects health. Maybe insurance companies ask this kind of question, but the people who plan cities apparently don't. (If you're out there, call.)

"I haven't seen any studies on that," says Bob Dunphy, senior researcher at the Urban Land Institute, an expert on commuting patterns. "In fact, a recent study done for the U.S. Department of Transportation shows that commuting distances have substantially increased—about 25 percent—over the past seven years."

So, if people are voting with their cars, they're voting for transregional living.

"People are always willing to trade a longer commute for a perceived improvement in their quality of life," says Fulton. "In California, they define that as seclusion, segregation, walling off the outside world, even though the safety may be illusion. People feel they have to make these choices for their children, but I'd like to know what the impact is of two generations of kids going everywhere via car pool, being totally dependent on adults."

The associated questions are subtle and fascinating. How, for example, does transregional living affect our sense of the public space, of democracy, of live theater, or of neighborhood life?

It would seem that most people live the transregional life-style because they feel they have no choice. But Fulton believes this way of living is actually based on choosing choice over convenience. "For example, you drive fifteen miles to take your kid to day care, rather than one in your neighborhood, because you choose the better day care." But do we really have a choice when good day care is so hard to find? Or when the school systems are timed to fit the needs of bus companies, not parents? Or when cities are designed for auto, not human, habitation? Maybe the real problem is that the right questions aren't being asked, by the planners or by the rest of us.

85. Make It Possible for Kids to Get Around Town.

- MAKE PUBLIC TRANSPORTATION ACCESSIBLE TO CHILDREN.

Offer special fares and bus passes for children. Post bus schedules where kids can read them.

- INCLUDE BICYCLE RACKS AT BUS STOPS AND TRANSPORTATION CENTERS.

Enable kids to ride their bikes to the nearest bus stop, lock up their bikes, then ride the bus or trolley to downtown or other attractions.

- INSURE THAT SIDEWALKS ARE BUILT TO CONNECT NEIGHBORHOODS.

"If kids planned Sacramento, we'd have more bus service and bike lanes," according to a Sacramento KidsPlace survey. "Kids would build wide, shaded sidewalks away from busy traffic, where they could walk, ride a bike, or sit on a bench. These sidewalks would go from neighborhood to neighborhood (so kids could visit their friends), go to shopping areas (so kids could run errands), go to transportation centers (so kids could lock their bikes and get on a bus or light rail train), and go to places of employment (because kids want to work)."

- INCREASE THE NUMBER OF CLEARLY MARKED CROSSWALKS IN AREAS CHILDREN FREQUENT.

Use older kids or adult volunteers to work as traffic guards at busy intersections near recreation centers, libraries, and parks, especially before and after planned activities, just like before and after school.

- ESTABLISH A CLEARLY MARKED BICYCLE LANE SYSTEM THROUGH THE CITY OR TOWN.

Designate bike trails in suburban and urban areas, including downtown, and mark them clearly with signs and painted lines on a road surface. Design a public information program to educate drivers about the bike-lane system. Encourage police officers to monitor traffic near lanes and ticket drivers who drive in them.

• ENABLE PRIVATE TRANSPORTATION
COMPANIES TO TRANSPORT KIDS.

Parents in Carlsbad, California, utilize a private transportation company called Kangaroo Carrier to shuttle their children to and from school and after-school activities. The company is fully licensed, meets the requirements of the Department of Motor Vehicles and California Highway Patrol. (Note: Enterprising teenagers could provide a similar service by walking kids to and from school and after-school activities.)

86. Take Back Parks and Playgrounds.

From Los Angeles to Manhattan, urban and suburban parks are falling prey to drug dealers, gang members, vandals. Children have fewer safe places to play. Unfortunately, many police departments are understaffed and underfunded and may not include park patrols on their list of priorities.

• CONTACT AN ADVISORY COMMITTEE
FOR YOUR LOCAL PARK AND RECREATION
ASSOCIATION.

Parents are often instrumental in the development of new parks and in the refurbishing of their local parks. It often starts when a couple of parents realize that the existing park equipment is unsuitable. Traditional park equipment is scaled for five- to twelve-year-olds and addresses mostly physical play.

Two- to four-year-olds need support for fantasy, social, and constructive play with open ended materials such as sand and water. Parents can voice their concern for the need for such equipment and play settings, along with their desire for tables and benches offering parents shaded, comfortable settings to supervise their children at play.

- **FORM A GRASS-ROOTS ACTION COMMITTEE.**

Organize a grass-roots action to take back the parks and playgrounds in your neighborhood, then join forces with similar groups in other neighborhoods to conduct citywide actions.

- **ENCOURAGE POLICE INVOLVEMENT IN YOUR COMMITTEE.**

Solicit assistance from the police in your initial efforts to take back the parks and playgrounds. Ask for a few officers to attend and patrol your activities, and make their presence known.

- **COMMUNITY CLEANUP DAY.**

Organize a community playground cleanup day. Have kids gather trash and pull weeds while adults repair and paint play equipment.

- **HOLD A CANDLELIGHT VIGIL IN YOUR PARK.**

Hold candlelight vigils in the parks or playgrounds in the evenings, when troublemakers are more likely to appear.

- SHIFT PUBLIC EVENTS TO THE PARKS.

Hold picnics, family days, school field trips, and as many group activities as you can think of in public parks or playgrounds.

- MAKE YOUR MARK ON THE PARK.

Have kids (particularly at-risk teenagers) design and paint a mural on the wall of the restrooms or other building. Petition the city to allow the community to rename the park to reflect the community's interests and heroes.

- SENIOR PATROL IN THE PARKS.

Suzanne Thompson, a mother in Poway, California, writes: "I just stumbled onto an interesting park. It's called Oakcrest Park, in Encinitas, California. It has a tot-lot, a restroom, basketball court, volley ball court, and a nice grassy hill with trees and tables. The unique aspect is that a slab was poured adjacent to the public restroom with RV hookups so a senior citizen couple can live there free of rent and utilities. This has cut down on illegitimate use of the park at night, has decreased vandalism of the bathroom, and has helped parents of young children feel more secure. I counted twelve moms and fifteen kids under the age of five using the tot-lot." (Some state and national parks have utilized such a policy for years.)

- ENCOURAGE YOUR CITY TO USE ANTI-GRAFFITI PAINT.

Encourage your town or city to paint park restrooms and other buildings with new graffiti-resistant paint. In September 1992

Dow Chemical Company announced the development of a transparent water-based coating that can be applied easily with spray, brush, or roller. The anti-graffiti paint, seven years in development, is apparently kind to the environment. The first such protective coatings could be on the market by the end of 1993.

- BUILD YOUR OWN PLAYGROUND.

Funding for new playgrounds is hard to come by in recessionary times, but architect Robert Leathers and other playground visionaries have found a workable solution. Leathers designs playgrounds according to a community's needs and imagination, purchases sturdy, indestructible, safe equipment, then organizes volunteers to build their community playground. The end product usually costs about one-third less than the usual price. "I love to see a whole family—a grandparent, parents, and a child—out there working," he says. "They've never had a chance to build something together like this."

- MAKE A SKATEBOARD PARK OR AREA FOR KIDS.

"Skateboarding is not a crime," reads a recent bumper sticker. But skateboarders are often treated as criminals and banned from neighborhood sidewalks and streets. Neighbors can hold a meeting with kids and decide on areas where the kids could skateboard without being hassled, as well as areas where they would not be allowed to go. Skateboarders can be allowed to use streets with little traffic during certain hours. Neighbors can lobby local businesses and schools to allow kids to use their parking lots after business hours. Skateboarders can organize and lobby their larger district or town to create a skateboard park. Neighborhoods and towns can sponsor skateboard contests to see which kids are best in the city. "They would be off the streets for three months practicing for it!" says Joan Bradley, mother of two teenage boys.

CONFRONT THE "NON-USE PHENOMENON" IN PUBLIC PARKS AND PLAYGROUNDS

The word recreation comes from the words that mean "to make over." We should make over our concepts of children's recreation. First step: Determine what recreational facilities kids are *not* using and why. In a survey of New York City's playgrounds, the New York *Times* found playgrounds in Brooklyn and the Bronx which had been without swings so long that parents said they could not remember when there had been any. Drugs aren't the only reason for the non-use of parks. In recent decades, park designers have produced thousands of boring, flat, green deserts, which children tend to avoid. (Instead, children tend to play on raw hillsides and in streets next to the parks. Part of the cause for such boring playgrounds and parks is municipal fear of legal liability. In San Diego, playground injuries result in the highest number of lawsuits directed against the city park and recreation department. "Most public playgrounds are absolutely lousy environments for everybody, ablebodied or not," according to Robin Moore, vice president of the International Association for the Child's Right to Play and author of *Childhood's Domain: Play and Place in Child Development*. The average public playground, Moore says, "is blacktop from end to end with a couple of pieces of old equipment. With luck, the swings still have seats. But the place is dangerous, boring, and not used." By contrast, some commercial playground and park developers are creating holistic parks, for the whole child, incorporating games, drawing areas, computers, tunnels made of cargo netting, where kids climb and scramble, and other well-padded exercise facilities.

87. Preserve Your City's Natural Spaces for Children.

Trees, flowers, and empty spaces add a natural and humane feeling to inner cities and suburbs and offer children the kind of experience with nature that parks cannot, yet often are destroyed by development. Protect the natural attributes of your city.

- ENCOURAGE YOUR CITY TO DO A CHILDREN'S ENVIRONMENTAL IMPACT STUDY.

In new developments make sure developers set aside open and natural space. A children's environmental impact report (which could also examine park and playground access and other design features) could also be done on existing neighborhoods, with the goal of refitting them with family-friendly features and protecting natural spaces.

- SAVE THE TREES.

Take note of plans to cut down trees to make way for buildings and streets. Protest loudly and visibly. Fifteen years ago, the city of San Diego decided to allow a developer to cut an endangered Torrey Pine; nearby residents surrounded the tree and faced down the saws. The tree still stands.

- ENLIST CHILDREN, PARENTS, SENIORS IN AN URBAN REFORESTATION PROGRAM.

One child, when asked in a KidsPlace survey how to improve downtown said, "Plant more trees and flowers." If you work in a downtown office building encourage the building owners to add trees and flowers to the outer entryways and courtyards. Potted palms in the lobby are not enough.

- CLEAN THE OUTDOORS.

Schedule periodic cleanup days in natural areas throughout the city. Involve schools, community service groups, etc. Pick up plastic off the beaches, paint over graffiti, clean up empty lots.

88. Create Community Hubs.

- ENCOURAGE YOUR CITY TO USE
  RECREATION CENTERS FOR AFTER-
  SCHOOL CARE.

Children who are too old for day care and too young to stay at home need a safe place to hang out, play, and do their homework until their parents get home. Neighborhood recreation centers are the ideal solution to the latchkey problem, but often do not have the staff or financial resources to provide supervision. Perhaps volunteers could fill the gap.

- SPONSOR A TEEN NIGHT AT THE
  COMMUNITY POOL OR RECREATION
  CENTER.

Teens like to stay out late and hang out with their friends, and need a place to go. Local pools and centers could stay open from 9 P.M. to midnight on Friday and Saturday nights, with parents volunteering one night a month as chaperones.

- CREATE PRE-TEEN AND TEEN CLUBS.

Teenagers are emphatic that what they want in their neighborhoods are places where they can get together without alcohol and drugs, but with minimal rules and maximum control by teens themselves.

- UTILIZE NEIGHBORHOOD SCHOOLS AS COMMUNITY CENTERS.

(See "What You Can Do in the Schools")

89. The Last Safe Place: Libraries As Family Centers.

In 1986, a California State Library study showed that users were as likely to say they were helped by a library in emotional ways as they were in getting information: 93 percent said it helped them to get motivated, feel good about themselves, calm down, or feel hopeful. Future libraries should offer the kind of atmosphere and services of the old town halls. They could become, in effect, community centers, meeting rooms for community and parent groups, education, media areas, concert facilities. Rather than simple book depositories, Strong suggests that libraries become quality of life centers, the physical and electronic mental fitness centers of their communities.

- INCLUDE LOCAL PERFORMANCES IN LIBRARY COLLECTIONS.

Neighborhood and central libraries can offer banks of videotaped or audiotaped samples of local work—high school bands, local theater productions.

- STOCK COPIES OF TEXTBOOKS USED BY LOCAL SCHOOLS.

Students could do their homework at the library without having to lug a lot of heavy books on their bikes or in their backpacks. And those who claim they can't do their homework because they forgot their book will have to find a new excuse.

- REACH OUT TO POTENTIAL LIBRARY USERS.

In Los Angeles county, library cards are issued at clinics serving pregnant women and babies. Moms and kids are encouraged to stop by their local libraries and get acquainted. New babies get a stuffed toy; older children learn how to check out books, or sit in on story-telling sessions. Families learn how to use the library.

- OFFER LATCHKEY KID PROGRAMS.

Greenville County Library in South Carolina has created a latchkey program that serves nearly 1,500 children who are asked to make a list of emergency telephone numbers for their parents' workplace, the sheriff's department, a neighbor, and the fire department. The most popular program is how to prepare meals, which shows children how to make snacks without using the potentially dangerous stove.

• CREATE A "LIBRARY GRANDPARENTS" PROGRAM.

Ask older adults to read books to children. In California, Grandparents and Books, a state-funded, community-based library program recruits seniors (whether or not they're grandparents) to read stories to children in public libraries. Community volunteers are given training in selecting and presenting children's books, in using puppets, flannel boards, and other special techniques. In 1989–91, 280 volunteers read to more than 43,000 children in California.

90. Encourage Local Businesses to Be Family-friendly.

• AWARD FAMILY-FRIENDLY DECALS TO BUSINESSES THAT ACCOMMODATE CHILDREN.

Encourage the city, the Better Business Bureau, or the Chamber of Commerce to create a family-friendly business program. Distribute decals and awards to restaurants with special menus and giveaways for kids, video parlors that give free rentals for improvements in grades, stores and businesses that sponsor Little League teams, and all businesses that treat children as valued customers.

- DISTRIBUTE AND DISPLAY "KIDS WELCOME HERE" SIGNS.

Businesses in cities from San Diego to Miami display signs reading "*Se Habla Español*," advertising the message that they welcome Spanish-speaking customers. Businesses from banks to boutiques could do the same for children, making it known that kids are valued customers. One Palm Springs, California, car wash gives one free car wash for each report-card A to driving-age students.

- ENCOURAGE BUSINESSES TO TREAT PARENTS AS PRIZED CUSTOMERS, AND CHILDREN AS FUTURE CONSUMERS AND EMPLOYEES.

Restaurants can offer children's menus and giveaways, stores can have kid-size seats where kids can rest while parents shop (great in clothing stores). A New York restaurant encourages mothers and their children who have recently moved to the city to drop in on Wednesdays at noon to meet each other. The restaurant publishes a newsletter for parents. One private postal service offers a child-sized desk and benches with coloring supplies where kids can play while parents take care of business.

- PUBLISH A FAMILY-FRIENDLY BUSINESS DIRECTORY.

Create a directory of businesses that genuinely contribute to children and family, and encourage all consumers to support those businesses. The directory can be financed through advertising, but would be more egalitarian (and probably more truthful) if businesses could be included only if they were recommended by customers.

- LOCATE COMMUNITY SERVICES IN MINI-MALLS AND SHOPPING CENTERS.

Many malls have meeting rooms used for everything from business conferences to bachelor parties. Such rooms can also be used as adult education classrooms, and headquarters for everything from Girl Scouts to kids' computer club meetings. Empty storefronts can be adapted as public health clinics, day-care centers, or used as neighborhood family centers.

91. Provide Opportunities for Children to Practice Community Skills.

- CREATE VOLUNTEER AND PAID JOBS FOR KIDS IN SCHOOLS, PARKS, RECREATION CENTERS, AND LIBRARIES.

Schools, parks, and libraries would be places where kids could have paid or volunteer jobs, helping younger children, building, cleaning, repairing, gardening, or running errands, suggests Sacramento's KidsPlace study.

- START A TEEN HOTLINE.

Teens Helping Other Teens is a San Diego teen hotline run by and for teens. Sponsored by Harmonium, an agency that focuses on youth counseling and social services, the hotline operates four evenings a week. Teen volunteers receive eight weeks training on active listening, crisis intervention, and referral procedures. Trained adults are always present. Operating on less than $2,000 a year, the hotline is funded by volunteer fund-raising.

- ABUSED KIDS CAN HELP OTHER ABUSED KIDS.

The Children Helping Children program in Madison, Wisconsin, brings together adult counselors, teen-age survivors of incest, and children age five to twelve who have been physically, sexually, or emotionally abused. By talking to younger kids, the teens (who work together as group leaders) get to see how fragile and vulnerable they were when their abuse occurred. The younger children can see that other kids have survived their abuse. Parents are required to simultaneously participate in the Parental Stress Center, learning to control anger and curb abuse.

"When people begin volunteering young, normally they volunteer throughout their lives," says Charlotte Lunsford, national chairman of volunteers for the Red Cross.

—Robert P. Hey, *Christian Science Monitor*, December 5, 1988

92. Reach Out to Teens and Latchkey Kids.

• ESTABLISH A PHONE-FRIEND LINE, OR "WARM LINE," FOR LATCHKEY KIDS.

Set up a telephone hotline that kids can call after school when they're home alone. It can be used as a sounding board for kids who can't reach their parents and want to talk about how their day went, or by kids who are scared, having trouble with homework, or who just need contact. Washington, D.C., has PhoneFriend, staffed by volunteers who take calls from kids after school. Similar lines exist all over the country, some sponsored by local governments, others by business, local TV stations, and universities.

For example, the University of Pittsburgh's Generations Together program matches older persons with latchkey kids; the adults make personal or phone contact with kids each day after school to make sure they are OK.

• OFFER CLASSES IN SAFETY FOR LATCHKEY KIDS.

In Montgomery County, Maryland, former Peace Corps volunteer Elizabeth Sarno teaches children aged eight to thirteen how to take care of themselves when they are home alone. The course covers basic first aid, safety skills, how to deal with strangers, basic kitchen skills, and how to deal with loneliness and boredom. Classes like this are being taught in libraries, schools, and recreation centers.

- DEVELOP AFTER-SCHOOL, WEEKEND, AND SUMMER PROGRAMS FOR OLDER KIDS.

The age group too old for regular day care or camps and too young to work or join volunteering programs needs something to do in the summer. For example, the Mission Valley YMCA in San Diego offers a teen camp for ages eleven to fourteen. Kids go to the beach and amusement parks, hold sporting events, work on community service projects. They are supervised but have a role in planning and carrying out their activities.

93. Develop Organized Programs for Kids Who Are Surrounded by Crime.

The Choice program in Baltimore employs (for a minimal wage) young adults willing to commit a year or more to work in troubled neighborhoods. The workers are paired with individual children and stick to their charges like glue, make sure they go to school, attend court appearances, and stay out of trouble. Children kicked out of school for unruly behavior are tutored in Choice offices rather than being allowed to run free. As columnist George Will writes, "Baltimore spends between $40,000 and $60,000 to incarcerate a troubled child for a year. Choice requires just $6,100 in public and private money to monitor a child."

• INVOLVE POLICE OFFICERS, OTHER
AUTHORITY FIGURES, IN PROGRAMS
FOR KIDS.

Police Departments could sponsor a paint-ball shoot, teaching kids about gun safety, and a place for target practice and contests. One parent writes: "How about paint-ball war games for these teenage boys that love action, adrenaline rushes, and fun with friends. My kids go out twice a week with friends to play. The shame is they play where the Fire Department employees work, and never see the firemen. It's too bad. Great relationships could be made if they were there."

94. Make Family Courts Child-friendly.

In many cities, cases dealing with child abuse, neglect, and dependency are heard in the same courthouses as adult criminal cases involving murderers, rapists, and robbers. The ambiance is far from friendly, and can be terrifying for an already traumatized child. In a move toward child-friendly courts, Los Angeles County, which has the largest dependency court system in the country, opened what may be the country's first child-sensitive courthouse, The Children's Court, in August 1992. The $75 million complex includes scaled-down courtrooms with child-sized furnishings, stuffed animals, and jars of lollipops; waiting rooms where children's movies play on video screens; outdoor basketball and volleyball courts and playgrounds; a children's library; and several playrooms.

ADVOCATE A PUBLIC MEDIATION SERVICE FOR ADULTS AND CHILDREN

Here's a goal for attorneys and judges in your city: Create a citywide mediation service for adults, focused particularly on family and neighborhood disputes.

This tool is gaining cachet among judges, faced with overcrowded court dockets. In the mediation process, people sit down with trained mediators—often volunteers working with private firms—and resolve their dispute without going to trial. The mediator leads the parties through three basic steps: Both sides state their case to the mediator, they discuss all aspects of the conflict, and then they brainstorm, with the mediator's help, to come up with possible solutions.

"The mediator doesn't impose the solution on the parties," says Robin Seigle, a mediator for Community Mediation of San Diego. "They have to come up with the solution themselves, and abide by it or resort to legal action."

Del Mar attorney Janet Allen says the existing adversarial system is ill-equipped to deal with a world of emotion and an array of potential solutions.

In one child custody dispute, Allen helped a divorced couple, who had not spoken to each other for years, focus on their child's needs. "I asked them to close their eyes and try to feel what the child felt." At the final session, the husband was unable to show up because of a medical emergency, but the wife told Allen, "It's OK. We don't really need you anymore. You've taught us how to communicate."

"Our goal should be to have mediation take place as early in the dispute and as far from the courts as possible," says Pat Benke, associate justice of the Fourth District Court of Appeals. One way of increasing access is on the way: During routine conferences, judges of the superior court soon will be handing attorneys lists of mediators to whom the lawyers can refer people.

Ideally, a citizen should be able to find a mediator even if he or she can't recall the word "mediation." Finding someone to help settle a dispute should be as easy as walking to the neighborhood school or the library.

What if local government were to station mediators in small offices at schools or libraries. These mediators would be available for disputes between adults or children. Mediation would be built into the structure of daily life, instead of being hidden in the yellow pages.

95. Demand Family-friendly Policies from Local Government.

- PUSH FOR CITY CHILDREN'S CZAR.

Lobby your mayor to appoint a children's advocate in the mayor's office to review the actions of all city departments for the impact they have on children.

- ORGANIZE A CITYWIDE WEB OF CHILD ADVOCATES.

Involve child advocacy agencies, and recruit powerful citizens from business, journalism, health agencies, government. Meet regularly, adopt an agenda, and advocate change on behalf of children.

- INSIST ON KNOWING WHERE LOCAL POLITICIANS STAND ON FAMILY ISSUES.

Moral issues such as abortion and capital punishment are more than adequately covered in election campaigns. Voters should insist on hearing officials' positions on less publicized but critically important child and family issues: funding for education, libraries, recreation centers, and parks; establishing child-care coalitions and supervisory agencies; commitment to programs for kids.

A MODEL CHILDREN'S AMENDMENT

Foreshadowing an emphasis on children in the 1992 presidential race, a nationwide grass-roots political movement on behalf of children may have been born in San Francisco, a city with proportionately fewer children than any other major U.S. city. On November 5, 1991, San Francisco became the nation's first city to guarantee funds for children in its charter. Voters passed Proposition J, the so-called Children's Amendment, which will allocate 2.5 percent of future property-tax revenues for services for children and families, as well as prevent cuts in children's services for ten years.

"After spending years of my life chasing after politicians and political groups pleading with them to add children to their agenda, I said to hell with them, we're going to go directly to the voters," says Margaret Brodkin, director of Coleman Advocates for Children and the mother of two, ages twenty-three and thirteen. "And lo and behold, when the politicians saw the public support we were building, they started asking to join us."

When Brodkin and her small band of supporters began their effort, success seemed unlikely. An optimist by nature, Brodkin based her faith on a flurry of national polls which show Americans willing to spend tax dollars on services for kids. But half of the twenty-three members of Coleman Advocates' board of directors did not share her faith.

They pointed to the state of Washington, where a children's initiative sponsored by the Washington Alliance for Children polled 2 to 1 in favor before the election, but lost in the polling booth by nearly 2 to 1. In Dade County, Florida, a proposal to establish a special children's taxing district lost after the initial polls were favorable. Nonetheless, the San Francisco fight seemed worth the effort; even if the initiative lost, Brodkin believed, the issues would at least be placed squarely before the voters.

The Children's Amendment, which calls for no new taxes, requires that for the next ten years a proportion of property taxes (1.25 percent for the first year and 2.5 percent in each of the remaining nine years) be earmarked for children, adding $13 million to prenatal care, job training for teenagers, child care, and health and social services. The amendment required no new bureaucracy, and none of the new money can be spent for buildings, capital equipment, salaries or other areas with no direct benefit to children.

"Initially, we couldn't find one member of the city's board of supervisors who would support the amendment," says Brodkin. "They all said it was bad government, that it would tie the hands of officials. That's the traditional reaction to dedicated funding and financial set-asides. City budgets are written behind closed doors. Kids can't win behind closed doors."

To get the proposition on the ballot, Brodkin launched a petition drive, gathering 68,000 signatures; 21,000 more than needed. Support came from diverse corners of the city, from police, gay and lesbian political clubs, the Catholic archdiocese, the Gray Panthers, the Teamsters and the Green Party. Children delivered the signatures to City Hall in little red wagons. In August, a *San Francisco Chronicle* poll of 600 registered voters showed 72 percent were in favor of the amendment. Politicians, taking notice, scrambled on board the bandwagon. Eventually, seven out of the eleven city supervisors supported it.

Even so, Brodkin was worried as election day approached. Though national media noted the Children's Amendment, San Francisco media virtually ignored it. "The *Examiner* did one story," says Brodkin. "These local yokels—we had no local television coverage until after the national network affiliates did pieces."

Other children's initiatives around the country have been killed by last-minute lobbying targeted at senior citizens. In San Francisco, opponents of Proposition J, including the Chamber of Commerce, charged that the amendment would divert money rather than add to the pot. The proposition, they warned, would pit children against AIDS patients, public workers, and especially seniors.

When the vote came in, Brodkin was ecstatic. The amendment to the city charter passed with 55 percent of the vote.

Other cities and states are following San Francisco's lead.

Since the San Francisco election, Brodkin has been amazed at the reaction from around the country. She says she didn't anticipate the demand for information from local political groups, universities, people inside government and outside of it, and a number of cities.

"The Children's Amendment has caught people's imagination," says Brodkin. "We've learned that it doesn't take a great number of people to change the world. All we need is a little courage, and to quit waiting for the politicians to lead."

- ORGANIZE CITYWIDE VOTER-REGISTRATION DRIVES, TARGETING PARENTING-AGED VOTERS.

Involve children in the process.

ON BEHALF OF KIDS: DOOR-TO-DOOR DEMOCRACY

After the 1992 Los Angeles riot, the media wondered why nearby San Diego remained relatively calm. Ministers and leaders from San Diego's less affluent neighborhoods suspect that the San Diego Organizing Project was part of the reason.

For several years, SDOP, a grass-roots, interfaith organization, has been chipping away at San Diego's politicians, forcing them to pay attention to the needs of urban families and neighborhoods.

SDOP's most notable success was to focus the city's attention on the issue of drugs, culminating in the July 1991 passage of the Neighborhood Pride and Protection Plan, probably the first comprehensive anti-drug, anti-gang strategy adopted by a major U.S. city. The plan commits the city to eventually spend $28.4 million annually for neighborhood and community policing, and for after-school programs, neighborhood homework centers, graffiti eradication, and a host of other community-building efforts.

Typical political organizations bring together citizens already recognized as leaders, often representing monied interests or single issues; these organizations then endorse a candidate, usually with strings attached.

SDOP takes a different approach. Using a complex training program, it creates community leaders out of people who would normally consider themselves politically insignificant. These leaders go door-to-door and listen.

Over the past few years, SDOP's troops have conducted 15,000 living-room and kitchen-table conversations with San Diegans. They've also interviewed hundreds of politicians and city officials. SDOP leaders describe a wide gap between what policymakers and the people in the neighborhoods south of Interstate 8 consider the city's pressing political priorities.

Policymakers focus largely on sewage, the airport, the downtown library—bricks and mortar. Neighborhood people canvassed by SDOP are concerned about these issues, too, but are much more interested in topics closer to home.

They want more police foot patrols, more after-school programs, cleaner neighborhoods, better street lighting, healthy commercial centers, enforced housing codes, stronger anti-graffiti standards, affordable child care.

They want more attention paid to the urban infrastructure; they want the city to come up with a job-training and development strategy, as well as better schools.

SDOP has translated its findings into a kind of people's platform. It can be fairly criticized as vague, with no suggestions about how the city can afford or achieve such goals. But that vagueness is part of the strategy.

"We aren't prepared right now to suggest concrete solutions," says SDOP director Scott Reed. "We want to push the candidates to tell us what they're going to do to attend to these issues."

Every Saturday during April and May 1992, hundreds of SDOP volunteers knocked on their neighbors' doors to introduce the people's platform—to feed it back to the citizens who helped create it.

Volunteers registered new voters and encouraged them to vote in the California primary.

In a few weeks, SDOP volunteers made 20,000 home visits to introduce the platform.

The organization gathered nearly 1,000 San Diegans in a public forum for mayoral candidates. (Typical candidates' nights sponsored by other civic organizations are lucky to muster a turnout of 100.)

At the forum, SDOP introduced the platform to the candidates.

"We called this an accountability night, not just a debate," said Greg Bolden, co-chairman of SDOP. "No mayoral candidate was endorsed, but if promises were made, we're going to hold the new mayor to her word."

96. Establish a Comprehensive City Child-care Plan.

In Pomona, California, some kind of child care is available from 6 A.M. to midnight, seven days a week including holidays for children age six weeks to fourteen years. Pomona's twelve different programs serve 900 children and include centers for infants, toddlers, and preschoolers (some with Montessori-based programs); a day-care center next door to a school where teenage mothers study for the high school equivalency exam; six Head Start centers; programs for abused kids; centers located near freeway off-ramps for commuters; one center open daily until midnight (including weekends and holidays); some centers with mini-infirmaries for sick kids (1988 figures).

- CREATE A CHILD-CARE COALITION.

The Bay Area Employer Child Care Coalition is a group of business leaders trying to persuade corporations to help employees who have children or other dependent family members. Initially they asked 200 top employers in the area to join a program called One Small Step, in which they each agreed to make at least one improvement in their child-care policies.

- RECRUIT AND HIRE A GRANT WRITER WITH A PROVEN TRACK RECORD.

Funding for innovative child-care programs and other services for kids is available, if you know where to find it and how to get it. For example, California Department of Education officials say Pomona has an excellent system of child care partly because its administrator, Bill Ewing, is a master at writing proposals that communicate his concepts and needs in a concise manner that appeals to bureaucratic logic.

- LOCATE DAY-CARE CENTERS IN OR NEAR HIGH SCHOOLS.

Have students work part-time or volunteer with younger kids, possibly earn class credit. Knowing younger kids are watching them and mimicking their behaviors could decrease antisocial behavior among teens.

- ENCOURAGE DEVELOPERS TO PROVIDE ON-SITE DAY-CARE CENTERS.

San Francisco charges hefty developer fees to pay for day care in downtown office buildings. In Sacramento, the city government attempts to employ a jawboning technique to convince developers, when they apply for building permits, that they can make money with child care. As a result of the city's efforts, ten out of Sacramento's twenty-five major developers have built or planned child-care facilities in new developments.

- LOBBY YOUR CITY TO CREATE AFTER-SCHOOL PROGRAMS, ESPECIALLY IN POOR AREAS.

In Los Angeles, Mayor Tom Bradley proposed the city invest $700 million on tutoring and child care for children in gang-infested areas. Programs would take place after school for the hours until parents get home from work and thus keep children from staying home alone in dangerous neighborhoods.

CREATE SMART HOUSING

One day in 1988, Orange County developer Kent Salveson was talking to a tenant in one of his low-income housing complexes. She was a single mother, had five children, and she worked two jobs, at Van de Kamp's bakery at night and El Pollo Loco during the day. Salveson jokingly asked her, "How do you do it with five kids and two jobs? I have one 3-year-old running me ragged."

The woman answered firmly: "I want my kids to have a better education than I did; I want them to participate in the American dream."

For Salveson, this was a life-changing moment. He remembered the long dinner discussions with his highly educated parents. He had been blessed, as a child, with a home environment that served as a kind of educational incubator. "Education happens mainly around the dining room table," says Salveson. "If it doesn't happen there, what chance does a kid have in school?"

For years, Salveson had built typical, one-dimensional warehouse-style low-income housing complexes. But inspired by the talk with his tenant—and with the help of Guilbert Hentschke, dean of the University of Southern California School of Education—Salveson came up with a plan for a new kind of low-income housing designed to give children educational guidance similar to that which he enjoyed around the dining room table. The program is called EEXCEL, an acronym for Educational Excellence for Children with Environmental Limitations. Today, Kent Salveson's smart housing is spreading through Southern California. His first smart-housing development, a forty-six-unit apartment house, opened in September 1992 in South Central Los Angeles.

"To this day we have not had graffiti in our building, a white, four-story building that offers itself as a writing tablet," he says. At least three more complexes will be built during the next few years in Los Angeles. Salveson is working with municipal officials to finalize plans for similar developments in Oceanside and San Marcos.

Salveson's focus is on services, not architecture. His basic stucco apartment complexes typically include a laundry, a children's play area (some of his complexes offer on-site child care) and a centralized study area, equipped with computers and staffed by tutors and counselors. "When the kids get home from school, they head straight for the study center," says Salveson. The counselors, usually students from USC, receive free room and board plus a monthly salary of $1,000, paid by tenant rents, which range from $210 to $850. When parents can't make it to a parent-teacher conference, the counselor goes. Schools supply copies of textbooks for the library, so no child ever has the excuse of forgetting or losing a textbook. EEXCEL children receive $15 for each A and $10 for each B. Parents of children with good grades get rent reductions. "We offer real market incentives," says Salveson, who describes himself as a politically conservative Republican.

EEXCEL hopes to offer free space for police patrol stations. One complex will contain a one-acre private park. Children won't have to confront gangs when they play. USC's medical and dental schools offer some rudimentary care to residents. In addition, Los Angeles County Health Services will contribute an on-site health clinic at one of the complexes.

Does EEXCEL's total-immersion approach work? So far, evidence that it does is anecdotal. "We're already seeing significant turnarounds in a number of students. Two principals have reported that our students, whose homework is monitored, come to school so well-prepared that it's creating social pressure on other students to do their homework," he says. USC and the Urban Institute, headquartered in Washington, plan a two-year study of

EEXCEL's effectiveness. Government agencies and banks take part by offering low-cost loans combined with the rent paid by tenants to barely cover the costs of the program. Still, EEXCEL turns a small profit.

"If I wasn't making a profit, I wouldn't be doing this," he says. "If we don't start developing in a socially responsible way, we'll be developing ourselves out of business as a country."

97. Market Your City as Pro-child and Pro-family.

A family-friendly city could gain a competitive edge by promising potential new employers easier employee recruitment, less turnover, and higher productivity because workers aren't worrying about their kids all the time.

The availability of child care will either support or sabotage economic development.

Smart developers realize that if two-paycheck families are the only ones that can afford to buy houses, two-paycheck families are going to be a lot more interested in buying a house or condo in a development with day care and other family services.

Persuading cities to market themselves as family-friendly will become less difficult as the service economy spreads—and as more parents work outside the home.

The smartest cities will soon begin to recognize the economic advantages of becoming family-friendly. Cities could begin to market themselves as pro-child and pro-family. Where there's demand, there's opportunity.

TOWN/CITY RESOURCES

Center for Environment Structure
2701 Shasta Road, Berkeley, CA, 94708; (510) 841-6166.

Children's Environment Quarterly
Yearly subscription: $30. The City University of New York, 33 West 42nd Street, New York, NY, 10036.

Consumer Product Safety Commission
Publishes safety guidelines for playground equipment. Consumer Product Safety Commission, Washington, DC, 20207.

Harmonium, Inc.
10717 Camino Ruiz, Suite 104, San Diego, CA, 92126; (619) 566-5733.

International Association for the Child's Right to Play
IPA/USA Sunny Davidson, 1702 Downhill Drive, Wichita Falls, TX, 76302; (817) 767-6969.

International Downtown Association
915 15th Street NW, Suite 900, Washington, DC, 20005-2375.

National Civic League
Publishes the *Civic Index*, a tool for measuring community's civic standards. 1445 Market Street, Suite 300, Denver, CO, 80202; John Parr, (303) 571-4343

PICO

A national institute assisting parents and communities to organize themselves for fighting urban problems and for positive
social change. 171 Santa Rosa Avenue, Oakland, CA, 94610;
(510) 655-2801

Articles

"Reaching Out: the Greenville County Library's Latchkey
Kids Program," Ron Chepesiuk, *Library Journal*, 1 March 1987,
46.

"The Future of Public Library Services," Linda Crismond,
Library Journal, 15 November 1986, 42.

Books

The Handbook for Latchkey Children and Their Parents, Lynette
and Thomas Long. New York: Arbor House, 1983. 316 pp.
Used by latchkey programs around the country.

Childhood's Domain: Play and Place in Child Development, Robin
Moore. Dover, NH: Croom Helm, 1986. 311 pp. $21.95 plus
$3.50 shipping.

Community and the Politics of Place, Daniel Kemmis. Norman:
University of Oklahoma Press, 1990. 150 pp.

A Pattern Language: Towns, Buildings, Construction, Christopher
Alexander, Sara Ishikawa, Murray Silverstein. New York: Ox-
ford University Press, 1977. 1171 pp. $50.00.

YOUR IDEAS FOR YOUR TOWN OR CITY

_____
_____
_____
_____
_____
_____
_____
_____
_____
_____
_____
_____
_____
_____
_____
_____
_____
_____
_____
_____
_____
_____
_____
_____
_____
_____
_____

WHAT YOU CAN DO IN YOUR STATE AND NATION

Much of this book has dealt with the local ecology of childhood, but much of that environment is shaped in a wider arena. At the state and national levels, two areas demand special attention. One is the media; the other is politics. Parents and other adults who care about children are poised to affect change in these areas.

98. Send a Message to the Media—Especially TV.

Peggy Charren, longtime director of Action for Children's Television (ACT) believes passionately that variety, not censorship, should be the goal of parents who want to improve media influences on children. "What parents don't understand is that TV has an obligation to serve the public. I didn't know that when I started out—that the broadcast spectrum belonged to *me*. Trying to ban programs, however, is an inappropriate way to fight TV, too. You don't need a First Amendment for speech that everyone likes. We're talking about increasing choice, not limiting it. If a network does away with "Garbage Pail Kids" (a controversial CBS cartoon show prevented from airing because of public protest), there's no reason that network wouldn't respond the same way to public pressure directed at afternoon children's specials that deal with AIDS and teenage pregnancy. Petition for *increasing options*."

• START A LETTER-WRITING CAMPAIGN.

Write to television and radio networks and cable companies, asking them to increase the variety of children's programming and decrease the violence. Insist that stations reduce the number of program-length commercials aimed at selling toys.

• CREATE A NATIONAL FAMILY
EMPOWERMENT CHANNEL.

Devote more time to family issues, beyond entertainment. If existing stations can't find the time, perhaps an insightful entrepreneur will. Ted Turner, are you available?

Express your disapproval quickly.
Instead of waiting to write a letter, pick up the phone and call your local newspaper or radio or television station and register your dismay immediately. Ask for the network and the advertiser's customer-service phone numbers and call them as well.

Consumer complaints can kill an offensive ad campaign. For example, as Ann Landers reported in her column in 1988, when the Union Bay clothing company ran ads depicting teenagers playing a lethal game of chicken by driving their cars over a cliff, both teens and adults called and wrote the company as soon as they saw the ads. Union Bay was test-marketing the campaign, designed to attract the sixteen to twenty-four-year-old audience. (The final scene showed a denim jacket and a pair of jeans floating in the water below the cliff. The caption read: "Union Bay—Fashion That Lasts.") Union Bay quickly learned the campaign had failed the test and pulled the ads.

SHAPING TV FOR KIDS

In the future, the television industry, particularly the networks, will be forced to work harder to attract young viewers. This is partly because of TV fragmentation (100 cable channels competing for the same viewers). Another factor is the likelihood that school hours will be longer (cutting into afternoon TV time) and more demanding. While we'll see more electronics in the classroom, the screen that will dominate won't be the TV screen but the computer screen.

Ralph Whitehead, professor of communications at the University of Massachusetts, Amherst, points to the growing upscale-downscale split in the TV audience. The American middle class is diverging into two main groups—one more educated and affluent than the middle class has ever been, the other drifting slowly toward less education and poverty. For upscale children, he says, "watching TV will be as declasse as smoking cigarettes." That sounds like hyperbole, but upscale children may well prefer to spend more of their time on computers or the coming interactive technologies, which will integrate computers and video. "If the twenty-one-inch, low-definition generic TV set continues to display a flat, two-dimensional, mass-produced show like 'The Smurfs,' then television will become the KMart of the new electronic marketplace."

The question television executives should be asking is: What kind of shows will attract the upscale young viewers, with disposable income, and help bring the downscale audience up to scale? The most important element in such programming is that it should be more *reality-based*. Many of us sense that our children are growing up in an imitation society, an electronic bubble in which most of life's references are from television. Paradoxically, TV could encourage kids and parents to turn off the TV and *do something*.

For example, baby boomers love "This Old House" or similar programs that show how to remodel or build houses. How about "This Old Treehouse"?

How about more kid shows about other hands-on experiences, such as fixing or customizing cars, art, fishing, hiking?

Or story lines that show kids interacting with adults in the neighborhood, learning from them, getting help from them? (Ward Cleaver may never have removed his tie, but you did have a sense of place in the Beaver's neighborhood.) Or parents talking to other parents and to neighbors? "For two decades Americans wondered if Walter Cronkite had legs; for nearly a decade we have wondered if the Cosbys have neighbors," says Whitehead. Except for the grandparents, is there a community of support for this family, or did they raise their kids alone? To be a good parent or good neighbor today can be an act of quiet heroism, but that kind of heroism is seldom seen on TV. Mainly we get exploding Ninja warriors.

The most powerful forces in the television industry are on the side of the failing status quo. Of course, many people in the TV industry do want change. They need all the encouragement and lobbying they can get from parents and other Americans who care about children.

99. Voters: Mobilize a National Grass-Roots Family Movement.

- EMPLOY THE ORGANIZING TECHNIQUES OF PAST SOCIAL MOVEMENTS.

Many tools used by the civil rights, feminist, environmental, self-help, and other social movements can be used for the growing family movement.

- USE THE MEDIA.

Write "letters to the editor," demanding more coverage of family issues. Call in to radio and TV talk shows featuring candidates and ask about family issues. Bombard the station with calls from neighbors and friends and make the candidates respond.

Fact: In California, 69 percent of voters said they would be more likely to vote for a candidate who supports increased spending for children's programs even if it means an increase in their own taxes

—Source: California Children's Hospital Association Poll, November 1991

- EDUCATE POLITICAL LEADERS.

Invite politicians to speak in your neighborhood, your schools, your churches. Tell them about the problems children and families face in your area. Ask them where they stand on education, family leave, day care, and other issues facing families and children. Force them to answer with specifics.

- SUPPORT ELECTED OFFICIALS WHO SUPPORT FAMILY-ORIENTED LEGISLATION.

Volunteer on electoral campaigns and vote for legislators who get involved in family issues.

- MICRO-ORGANIZE.

Consider your parenting class, Little League team, neighborhood school, and workplace as political action committees. Discuss your problems/concerns on a personal and political level.

- REGISTER PARENTS TO VOTE.

Set up registration booths at day-care centers, schools, parks, recreation centers, even maternity hospitals—wherever children and parents can be found. Let parents register to vote when they sign their kids up for school.

- ENABLE PARENTS TO VOTE.

Lobby for changes in election laws, especially lengthening the voting hours or changing election day to Saturday. Set up polling booths at the same places as above. Organize a volunteer baby-sitter pool to care for kids while parents vote. Let parents know they can vote by mail.

A NEW VOTING RIGHTS MOVEMENT

Parents are beginning to rise up and say to politicians: You can't be pro-family if you're anti-parent and anti-child. So says Jack Levine of Tallahassee, Florida, a former suburban high school English teacher organizing what may be the country's most potent political effort on behalf of children. His tools are reminiscent of sixties grass-roots politics, particularly the effort to register Southern black voters. The stakes today are no less urgent.

"Politicians feed us pabulum. It's the 'Let Them Eat Values' approach to politics," says Levine, director of the Florida Center for Children and Youth, a private not-for-profit citizens' organization that has launched the Florida Children's Campaign, a nonpartisan political organizing effort.

"They preach to us, 'Come back to core family values,' but what they're really telling us is we're supposed to work longer, earn less, have a higher stress level in the workplace, give up even more time with our children, endure worsening health care and education for our kids."

So parents have two choices: Lay down with their kids and accept victimization, or stand up and fight back.

Doing so, politically, will be a new experience for many of us.

In recent decades, parents have voted even less than the general population. For example, in urban Florida's voting precincts, only two out of five parenting-age citizens are registered, and only half of them voted. That means that only one in five Floridians of parenting age is involved in the electoral process. No wonder politicians think: "Where's the reward for paying attention to child care, children's health care, or education?" Roots of alienation.

The reasons for the disfranchisement of parents range from apathy to lack of education to fatigue, but the roots go deeper. For one thing, electoral laws are anti-parent and anti-child. Set by Congress, our electoral laws were originally established for a slower, small-town, neighborhood-based society. But then came sprawling urbanization, two-career marriages and the rise of single-parenting.

Today, in most states, the polls are open only on Tuesday from 7 A.M. to 7 P.M. These are the hours when most parents are struggling to get the kids to school or day care, churn through a lengthening workday, commute home, zap the dinner, read a quick story to the kids, and collapse into bed.

"Most parents can't vote during their lunch hour, because there is no lunch hour or because the polling booth is an hour away," says Levine.

Laws governing voting times may be analogous to the literacy tests and other Jim Crow laws that kept blacks away from the polls—until the voter registration drives of the sixties. However, Levine says convincing incumbent politicians to change the current voting laws is like telling drug dealers to go back to school and get a minimum-wage job.

"Politicians look at you and nod, but you can tell they're thinking: 'What? Are you out of your mind? You're saying the system doesn't work? The system works for me.'"

Nonetheless, with a little help, parents can get back into the political game. For example, Levine's campaign will soon provide child care for voters. Coordinated Child Care, a network of Florida child-care centers, has pledged to keep day-care facilities open an extra two hours on voting days so parents can be responsible citizens and still be responsible parents.

However, the heart of the campaign is the voter registration drive.

"We're recruiting and training our own deputy voter registrars—parents, grandparents, PTA volunteers, child-care center directors," says Levine. "Wherever parents are, we'll flip down the legs of a card table and give them the chance to register to vote."

The campaign has already established 400 voter registration sites, but that number will soon grow to more than 1,000; the Florida PTA has pledged to set up tables at all of their member schools.

The registration drive won't be exclusive to parents. A

lot of grandparents and seniors out there are enraged at what they see happening to the next generation, Levine points out. The campaign is also asking companies, on employment applications, to identify unregistered voters. Florida's largest financial institution, Barnett Bank, is already registering customers when they open new accounts. As part of the campaign, public schools are changing their enrollment forms to identify unregistered voters. And as election day approaches, schools will send "Vote for Me" notices home with kids.

"Florida has slashed the education budget so much that teachers and principals are marching at the front of the parade," says Levine.

During six months of 1992, the campaign's goal was to register 250,000 new voters in the state—certainly enough political power to swing elections.

This approach is almost poetic in its simplicity. Politicians may not be able to keep track of their overdrafts. But when it comes to parents and children's issues, they may soon learn how to count.

- CREATE A NATIONAL ARMY OF WINTER SOLDIERS.

The Grey Panthers and other groups for older Americans are already moving toward more involvement in children's issues. No demographic group offers more potential to shift the national climate than seniors—older Americans are not only powerful politically, but physiologically younger than ever before, able to provide the muscle and money at the grass-roots that many parents may, in fact, be too harried to offer. Psychologist

Ken Dychtwald wants to create an Elder Corps, where groups of people will assist the aging. He notes that one retirement community in Arizona has about 2,000 volunteers working at its hospital and suggests that an Elder Corps would succeed because older Americans "want to work to put their experience and goodwill to public good." But why should such an Elder Corps focus only on the problems of its own cohort, the elderly? Why not unleash the volunteers to work on the problems of children?

- SUPPORT A NATIONAL SERVICE CORPS.

President Bill Clinton proposes that young Americans could pay for a college education by serving several years in a civilian national service corps. Such a program would offer millions of youngsters a realistic hope of attending college; they could help staff the day cares and other grass-roots children's programs that traditional volunteers, alone, will be unable to fulfill. Some observers have also suggested that a youth corps start earlier, in junior high or high school, thereby instilling the ethic of community service early.

"Working parents, if you think about it, could be the biggest special-interest group in the entire country, and their voting power is absolutely enormous."

—Anita Shreve, author of *Remaking Motherhood*

- SUPPORT A VOLUNTEER ORGANIZATION
THAT HAS ADOPTED CHILDREN'S ISSUES
AS ITS FOCUS.

Many volunteer groups have adopted children's issues as their focus. Some examples: Kiwanis has made a multi-year commitment to an education and action campaign entitled "Children: Priority One"; the Association of Junior League International has made a multiyear commitment to children's health; community foundations around the country have banded together to work as a coalition to strengthen the ties between civic leaders and children's programs; the AARP has made intergenerational issues one of its top priorities; the Food Research & Action Center, which links food banks around the country, has launched "The Campaign to End Childhood Hunger," which offers information and note cards designed by children's illustrator Tomie de Paola; the Unitarians have a special children's campaign of study and action.

- JOIN A PARENT TEACHER ASSOCIATION
OR SOME OTHER STATE- OR NATIONAL-
LEVEL EDUCATION OR CHILDREN'S
ADVOCACY GROUP.

The national PTA has a long history of activism on behalf of children. It has made special efforts in recent years to reach out beyond its core membership, and it continues to fight hard for the welfare of children and for education through greater parental involvement and national legislation.

The national PTA is comprised of a national board of directors, state PTAs, and local school districts with individual members. Its goals include a comprehensive parent-involvement program in every elementary school; restructuring public schools to meet the changing needs of children and families; the elimination of environmental health hazards such as radon, lead, and pesticides from schools and day-care centers; the guarantee of comprehensive, quality health care to every infant and child; improving children's and family television programming and increasing the use of technology to improve and reform education. The national PTA also publishes *What's Happening in Washington*, a newsletter that updates members on the PTA's legislative concerns and national activities. Other organizations similar to the PTA are known as Parent Teacher Organizations.

In 1992, the Coalition for America's Children emerged as a nonpartisan alliance of more than 250 local, state, and national nonprofit groups working together to raise concern for children to the top of the public-policy agenda. Led by Bob Keeshan, aka Captain Kangaroo, the Coalition advanced the notion that all candidates for public office should have a children's platform and urged volunteer organizations to launch public-education campaigns holding candidates accountable to kids.

Together, Coalition groups produced thousands of "Questions for Candidates" brochures, postcards to candidates, print and broadcast advertisements, videos, bumper stickers, and buttons—all on the theme "Who's for Kids and Who's Just Kidding?" In the fall of 1992, the Coalition hosted the first presidential debate on children's issues, by hosting their own satellite town meeting with representatives of the candidates. Five thousand people participated via satellite linked to forty-eight cities. Nonprofit groups can join the Coalition and receive these prototype materials at cost, ready to print, with the option of putting their organization's name as the contact.

- JOIN ONE OF THE NEW PARENT ACTIVIST GROUPS, SUCH AS PARENT ACTION.

Conceived by Bernice Weissbourd, T. Berry Brazelton, M.D., and Susan DeConcini in 1989, Parent Action was originally established as an arm of the Family Resource Coalition. They recognized that while there were organized constituencies for every interest group, from the Agriculture Council of America to the American Association for Retired Persons, there was no major national grass-roots organization representing the very special interests of parents. The founders, therefore, decided to start "the AARP for parents."

Parent Action is establishing state networks (SPANs), comprised of individual members, chapters, and affiliated organizations and companies. Activities of local chapters may be as diverse as forming baby-sitting co-ops; providing information and referral services to parents for good child care; completing community report cards; canvassing for family issues on national, state, local, and community levels; working as partners with local businesses on work and family solutions; conducting community volunteer efforts; improving schools or child care; conducting immunization campaigns; or providing emotional support and information in times of transitions. Parent Action is also developing a variety of discounts on goods and services for members. These range from a discount book buying service to reduced prices in hotels.

HOW TO CREATE A PARENT ADVOCACY GROUP—THE BASICS

If you decide to reach beyond your immediate family to become an advocate for children, the avenues can be bewildering.

Where do you turn for information or help? What's out there?

Michael Davis, an attorney in suburban Owings Mills, Md., confronted these questions when he decided to create a parent advocacy group; he and his wife, Ann, were worried about the quality of the neighborhood schools their children, now preschoolers, will attend.

"I've always been interested in grass-roots politics, and I happen to be a parent," he says. "I decided to start at the neighborhood level, the precinct level. I got some neighbors together to talk, and I asked each of them to talk to their friends, and we began to grow."

That's basic to starting a local advocacy group, he says. "Unless you have the money to advertise, in order to solicit members, you grow by word of mouth, but that has to be consciously organized."

From his previous political involvement, Davis knew the usefulness of affiliating his group with a larger organization.

He considered uniting parents through community and home-owners associations in his county. "But these suburban associations are usually dormant until something negative happens; they become energized to fight single-issue battles, but that enthusiasm soon dies away."

Eventually, he and his group of neighbors and friends chose to affiliate with Parent Action, a national organization headquartered in Baltimore. Parent Action's goal is to do for parents what the American Association of Retired Persons (AARP) does for retirees.

Davis now puts in two to three hours a day on behalf of his thirty-five-member chapter. How does he find the time? "By giving up other political activities that weren't specific to family issues."

The experience of organizing Parent Action statewide in Maryland taught Joann Levy that parents, despite their usual exhaustion, can organize themselves politically. She recommends to parents:

• Recognize your anger or dissatisfaction with the current conditions of childhood and family life in your community.
• Identify other parents who have similar concerns.
• Gather these parents in a living room or after a school event to explore the issues that you all have in common.
• Identify the resources and organizations already available to respond to children and families. "Most organizations will give out the names of parents who are involved. Call and ask about their organizations. Look for the groups that emphasize parents," she says.
• Adopt long-range and short-range goals but, especially in the beginning, emphasize short-term objectives. "It's easier to define a long-term goal than a short-term goal, but achieving short-term objectives is crucial—because it's energizing." Some short-term goals should be simple and immediately attainable.

"For example, get an article published in the local paper about your group. Or decide to double your membership within two months, or to help the local PTA double its. A longer-term goal might be to raise money for a playground, and beyond that, getting legislation passed."

- Among the objectives pursued by Parent Action chapters: combating drug dealers; creating baby-sitting co-ops and supporting child-care centers; registering parents to vote; and working for political candidates.

100. Beyond the So-called Cultural War: an Emerging Political Agenda.

The 1992 presidential campaign produced an especially harsh debate about the future of families; during the Republican convention, a "cultural war" was declared by commentator and presidential candidate Pat Buchanan. But today's families aren't at all easy to classify, culturally or politically. Any political discussion of family values must recognize one clear political reality: There aren't enough traditional families—dad at work and mom and the kids at home—to form a political majority.

Even in pre-World War II America, the trend was toward more diverse types of families. In the fifties, when the trend was briefly broken, only about 55 percent of American families fit the traditional mold. Today, only one in five families looks like the Cleavers.

At-home moms "cross every political, religious, and economic boundary," says Gae Bomier, director of public relations for Mothers at Home, an organization of 15,000 at-home moms. "Personally, I think politicians should value the family before they start talking about family values." A family snapshot taken one year may show mom at home with the kids and dad at work. The next year, the snapshot may show mom and dad at work. The year after, they're practicing tag-team parenting, with mom working the day shift and dad working nights, so an adult can be with the kids.

This complex new American family requires a more sophisticated political discussion about flexibility in the workplace and neighborhood support systems and schools as family-support centers. In fact, a new alliance may yet emerge between conservative Republicans and liberal and moderate Democrats.

Some potential areas of agreement:

- OFFER A MORE GENEROUS FEDERAL TAX DEDUCTION FOR CHILDREN.

In 1948 the personal exemption for each dependent under eighteen was $600, 42 percent of the national per-capita income. Last year, the exemption was $2,050, only 11 percent of the per-capita income. If the exemption had been indexed for inflation and growth in real personal income, today it would be $7,800, according to the Urban Institute. An exemption of $4,000 would permit more parents to work part time, or stay home with the kids, and it would ease the financial pressure on single parents. (Michelle Abrams, a mother, commercial artist, and frequent school volunteer, suggests: "Give tax breaks, in the form of tax credits or deferments, to parents and others for volunteering in public schools.")

- SUBSIDIZE HOME DAY CARE.

Parents who stay home with their children lose both a second income and a tax break for child care. One mother's solution: "Subsidize home care. Give a tax credit for the mother staying home with the children. If even 50 percent of the taxes we are paying for 1991 could be credited back since I stayed home, I would not have to return to work."

- REFORM DIVORCE LAWS.

Discourage separations by creating a braking mechanism, a waiting period of nine months for a divorce to become final. Or, perhaps institute a waiting period before people get married.

- PASS FAMILY-LEAVE LEGISLATION, AT THE STATE AND NATIONAL LEVELS.

In August 1993, the new federal family leave law went into effect, but state and county family leave laws sometimes mandate more generous leave time. Twenty states as well as Washington, D.C., and Dade County, Florida, require some employers to offer unpaid family leave of some kind, according to Center for Policy Alternatives in Washington, D.C. If your state has not passed this type of legislation, make sure it does.

WHAT THE POLLS SAY

The vast majority of Americans (88 percent) believe strongly that preparing children for school—making sure they are healthy and able to learn—is a high priority for education in this country.

—Gallup Organization for Phi Delta Kappa, 1990

Men and women equally (71 percent) favor health care for children. Parents are more likely to support a candidate who advocates improving health care for children (76 percent). But most non-parents (68 percent) also are willing to do the same.

—*Kid's Clout*, Penn + Schoen for the National Association of Children's Hospitals and Related Institutions, 1990

By a margin of five to one, people want more rather than less government support for prenatal care for pregnant women who can't afford it.

—National Opinion Research Center, University of Chicago, General Social Survey, 1990

By a ratio of seven to one, people want stronger government action on providing housing for poor families with children.

—National Opinion Research Center, University of Chicago, General Social Survey, 1990

The American electorate believes government should play an activist role in developing programs for children. There is virtually no difference in attitudes about the role of government in children's programs among voters with children and voters without.

—*Mandate for Children*, Greenberg/Lake and the Tarrance Group for the Coalition for America's Children, 1993

Voters see children's needs as integral to their concerns about broad national issues. When asked to choose, voters would prefer to invest in children now (74 percent agree) rather than cut back on children's programs to overcome the recession and deficit.

—*Mandate for Children*, Greenberg/Lake and the Tarrance Group for the Coalition for America's Children, 1993

When those who don't vote in every election were asked whether they would be more likely to vote if they thought their vote could have a real impact on the health and welfare of American children, nearly *two-thirds* said they would be much more likely to vote.

—*Kid's Clout*, Penn + Schoen for the National Association of Children's Hospitals and Related Institutions, 1990

A strong majority (59 percent) of voters say it is very important that candidates for public office at all levels should have a series of proposals on children's issues and half (50 percent) say they would be more likely to vote for a candidate who supported increased spending·for children's programs, even if it meant an increase in their taxes.

—*Mandate for Children*, Greenberg/Lake and the Terrance Group for the Coalition for America's Children, 1993

SOME KEY IMPERATIVES FOR CHANGE, AS SEEN BY THE CHILDREN'S DEFENSE FUND

• PROGRAMS FOR ASSISTING CHILDREN SHOULD ALSO HELP STRENGTHEN THE ENTIRE FAMILY.

Family is central to every child's life, but when parents cannot give adequate care, especially young parents who may not have even basic parenting skills, society should provide the kind of support and assistance that will teach them to nurture their children and help strengthen their family.

• EVERY TEEN MOTHER AND FATHER WHO HAS NOT FINISHED HIGH SCHOOL SHOULD HAVE ACCESS TO A SPECIALIZED SCHOOL WHICH IS EQUIPPED TO COPE WITH THE PROBLEMS OF TEEN PARENTS AND THEIR CHILDREN.

Teenage parenthood is one of the main reasons teens drop out of school and fall into poverty. School programs should be designed to help teen parents develop the parenting, learning, and job skills they need while providing their children with developmentally appropriate early childhood education.

• **QUALITY EARLY CHILDHOOD EDUCATION SHOULD BE AVAILABLE TO ALL CHILDREN.**
Children need to experience successful physical, social, emotional, and cognitive development to be able to embrace educational and social opportunities successfully. Whether called *child care, early childhood development,* or *preschool,* all programs for young children should be developmentally appropriate and focus on their educational needs. Public school systems should recognize the importance of early childhood education to the educational mission and help to ensure that quality programs are both available and accessible to all children who need them.

• **SUCCESSFUL PROGRAMS MUST BE BROADLY REPLICATED, SO THAT THEY ARE BOTH MORE AVAILABLE AND MORE ACCESSIBLE TO ALL CHILDREN IN NEED AND THEIR FAMILIES.**
We know what works in education and child development, but few successful programs ever get past the pilot stage and seldom reach more than a small percentage of the children who need them.

• **BUSINESS SHOULD PLAY A LEADERSHIP ROLE IN IDENTIFYING STRATEGIES FOR IMPROVING CHILDREN'S EDUCATIONAL DEVELOPMENT AND IN DETERMINING WHAT RESOURCES ARE NEEDED TO ACHIEVE RESULTS.**

Although many of the changes in public policy and practice that are needed to improve child development and education will result in cost savings down the road, other essential improvements will initially require new investments. Business should lend its expertise to improving the management of existing resources and to achieving savings in other government programs that can be reallocated to the needs of children and schools. Where necessary, business should provide support for increasing the level of resources. State government should be the prime target of business involvement in policy, since most decisions on policy, practice, and funding in education and child development are made in state legislatures.

—Source: The Children's Defense Fund

101. Keep the Faith; Keep Weaving.

You are not responsible for the whole fabric. If you weave only one strand, it will connect, and connect, and connect . . .

STATE/NATION RESOURCES

Action for Children's Television
20 University Road, Cambridge, MA, 02138; (617) 876-6620.

Administration for Children, Youth and Families
Department of Health and Human Services, 200 Independence Avenue, SW Room 711G, Washington, DC, 20201.

Campaign to End Childhood Hunger
Being waged by hundreds of citizen groups in all fifty states with video and other public-education materials. Food Research & Action Center, 1875 Connecticut Avenue NW, #540, Washington, DC, 20009; (202) 986-2200.

Children's Defense Fund
122 C Street NW, Washington, DC, 20001; (202) 628-8787.

Children NOW!
Offers information and referrals to Californians who want to become politically involved on behalf of children. 1930 14th Street, Santa Monica, CA, 90404; (310) 399-7444.

Coalition for America's Children
Offers public-education materials to nonprofit groups and public agencies involved with children's issues. One Farragut Square NW, 12th Floor, Washington, DC, 20006; (202) 638-5770.

Families and Work Institute

A nonprofit research and advisory organization that studies what companies are doing for families and how they can do more. Publishes the *Corporate References Guide to Work-Family Programs* and conducts the Fatherhood Project supporting men in nurturing roles. 330 Seventh Avenue, 14th Floor, New York, NY, 10001; (212) 268-4846.

Family Resource Coalition

A national resource program for parent education and support groups. The organization offers training to help people build community. 200 South Michigan, Chicago, IL, 60604-2404; (312) 787-0977.

For the Children

Similar to Parent Action, this organization is a broad-based citizens' effort to create "an AARP for children." 3615 Superior Avenue, Room 31, Cleveland, OH, 44114; (216) 431-6070.

Formerly Employed Mothers at the Leading Edge (FEMALE)

A support and advocacy group for women taking time from paid employment to raise their children. Over forty chapters nationally; $20 membership fee includes a monthly newsletter and ongoing assistance in starting and managing local chapters. P.O. Box 31, Elmhurst, IL, 60126; (708) 941-3553.

In the Company of Kids

Offers a set of educational materials for those who wish to help create local partnerships to bolster parenting skills and empower communities on behalf of children. 80 West Center Street, Suite 108-109, Akron, OH, 44308-1033; (216) 762-3700.

Institute for American Values
The institute publishes *Family Affairs*, a valuable and distinguished newsletter for people who care about family issues. A subscription is available free upon request. 250 West 57th Street, Suite 2415, New York, NY, 10107; (212) 246-3942.

International Child Resources Institute
1810 Hopkins Street, Berkeley, CA, 94707; (510) 644-1000.

Kidsnet
A clearinghouse for children's broadcasting; publishes, with the Library of Congress, *TV with Books Completes the Picture*, with suggestions and activities pairing reading and TV watching. Consumer Information Center, Dept. 58, Pueblo, CO, 81009.

MOMS (Moms Offering Moms Support) Club
Over fifty groups nationwide, provides information on starting and managing support networks for in-home mothers. 814 Moffat Circle, Simi Valley, CA, 93065; (805) 526-2725.

MOPS (Mothers of Preschoolers) International
Over 470 groups nationwide with the purpose of connecting mothers with each other. May be church related. 4175 Harlan Street, Wheat Ridge, CO, 80033; (303) 420-6100.

Mothers at Home
Dedicated to the support of mothers who choose to stay home to raise their children; serves as a forum for the exchange of information; publishes *Welcome Home*, a monthly magazine. 8310-A Old Courthouse Road, Vienna, VA, 22180.

National Association of Child Advocates
Serves child-advocacy organizations in forty states; can link you
to groups active in your community or state. 1625 K Street NW,
Suite 510, Washington, DC, 20006; (202) 828-6950.

*National Association of Children's Hospitals and
Related Institutions, Inc.*
401 Wyth Street, Alexandria, VA, 22314; (703) 684-1355.

National Association of Mother's Centers
Provides nationwide information on starting a Mother's Center
through the Mother's Center Development Project. 336 Fulton
Avenue, Hempstead, NY, 11550; (800) 645-3828.

National Black Child Development Institute
Provides information on the status of African-American children as well as publications and programs; there are forty
affiliates of the Institute around the country. 1023 15th Street
NW, Suite 600, Washington, DC, 20005; (202) 387-1281.

National Civic League
Offers assistance in community building, with an emphasis on
creating family-friendly cities. 1445 Market Street, Suite 300,
Denver, CO, 80202; (303) 571-4404.

National Committee for Citizens in Education
Monitors and encourages involvement in schools. 10840 Little
Patuxent Parkway, Suite 301, Columbia, MD, 21044-3199;
(800) NETWORK.

National Legal Resource Center for Child Advocacy and Protection and Center on Children and the Law
American Bar Association, 1800 M Street, Washington, DC, 20036.

National PTA–National Congress of Parents and Teachers
Parents, teachers, students, principals, administrators, and others interested in uniting the forces of home, school, and community in behalf of kids. Works for legislation benefiting children and youth. 700 North Rush Street, Chicago, IL, 60611-2571; (312) 787-0977.

National Urban League
500 East 62nd Street, New York, NY, 10021.

Parent Action
A grass-roots advocacy organization with an emphasis on the needs of parents. Advocates services and programs that are family-friendly and provides a range of other support for parents. Two North Charles Street, Suite 960, Baltimore, MD, 21201; (410) PARENTS (727-3687).

Partners for Liveable Places
Publishes several pamphlets, including *Family Investment Strategies: Improving the Lives of Children and Communities*. 1429 21st Street NW, Washington, DC, 20036.

PICO
A national institute assisting parents and communities to organize and fight urban problems. 171 Santa Rosa Avenue, Oakland, CA, 94610; (510) 655-2801.

Project Public Life

Publishes a bimonthly newsletter, *Public Life and the Citizens Politics Study Circle Guide*, designed to help people of all ages learn the skills of citizen politics. Humphrey Institute, University of Minnesota, 310 19th Avenue S, Minneapolis, MN, 55455; (612) 625-0142.

Books and Reports

No Kidding Around! America's Young Activists Are Changing Our World and U Can Too, Wendy Schaetzel Lesko. Kensington, MD: Activism 2000 Project, Information Project USA, 1992. 263 pp.

Kids Count Data Book, Center for the Study of Social Policy, 1250 Eye Street NW, Suite 503, Washington DC, 20005, 1992. State-by-state information on the conditions of children.

YOUR IDEAS FOR WHAT YOU CAN DO IN YOUR STATE AND NATION

_____

_____

_____

_____

_____

_____

_____

_____

_____

_____

_____

_____

_____

_____

_____

_____

_____

_____

_____

_____

_____

_____

_____

_____

_____

_____

_____

_____

_____

Send your ideas
for reshaping the environment
of childhood to:

Richard Louv
P.O. Box 3942
San Diego, CA 92163
or
c/o Anchor Books
1540 Broadway
New York, NY 10036

Richard Louv is the author of *Childhood's Future* (Anchor), *FatherLove* (Pocket), and *America II* (Penguin). He is an award-winning columnist for the *San Diego Union-Tribune* and a columnist and contributing editor to *Parents* magazine. He has appeared on the "Today Show," "Donahue," National Public Radio's "Fresh Air," and the Bill Moyers PBS series "Listening to America." He speaks frequently around the country on the subjects of children and families, community-building, and urban design. Prior to becoming a writer, he was director of Project Concern's OPTION program, recruiting and placing medical professionals in areas of need in the United States and abroad. He and his wife, Kathy Frederick Louv, a nurse practitioner, are the parents of two children, Jason, class of 2000, and Matthew, class of 2006.

More from Richard Louv on children,
parents, community, and society…

Childhood's Future

by Richard Louv

In the book that started the movement,
Richard Louv defines and explains the
missing element that is so vital to our
children's future–the web created by
extended families and communities.

"A passionate call for rebuilding community and family life…It reminds us
that childhood's present does not have
to be childhood's future."
–*New York Times Book Review*

"*Childhood's Future*…demands our
attention and energy as it challenges the
way we as a nation are raising our kids."
–*Child* magazine

ANCHOR BOOKS